Englisch
Redewendungen

**Idioms und
Phrasal Verbs**

MIX
Papier aus verantwortungsvollen Quellen
FSC® C108080

© Compact Verlag GmbH
Baierbrunner Straße 27, 81379 München

Alle Rechte vorbehalten. Nachdruck, auch auszugsweise,
nur mit ausdrücklicher Genehmigung des Verlages gestattet.

Chefredaktion: Dr. Matthias Feldbaum
Redaktion: Helga Aichele
Produktion: Frank Speicher
Titelabbildung: fotolia.de / BVDC
Umschlaggestaltung: h3a GmbH, München

ISBN 978-3-8174-9093-6
381749093/3

www.compactverlag.de

Vorwort

Eine Fremdsprache zu beherrschen, heißt auch, die Idiomatik der Sprache im Griff zu haben. Besonders im Englischen werden im täglichen Sprachgebrauch viele Redewendungen und Sprichwörter verwendet, die sich nicht einfach durch eine wörtliche Übersetzung oder das Nachschlagen in einem Wörterbuch erklären lassen.

Das richtige und sichere Verwenden der *Idioms* bedeutet, sich elegant und lebendig in einer Sprache auszudrücken. Doch dass dies nicht immer ein leichtes Unterfangen ist, macht gerade die englische Idiomatik deutlich, die ihre ganz spezifischen, spracheigentümlichen Tücken birgt. Die sogenannten *Phrasal Verbs*, eine Kombination aus Verb und Präposition oder Adverb, haben oft stark abweichende Bedeutungen. Auch werden in der englischen Idiomatik z. T. ganz andere Bilder benutzt, als wir sie aus dem Deutschen kennen.

Das vorliegende Buch ist speziell dafür konzipiert, zu einem zuverlässigen und gewandten Umgang mit der englischen Idiomatik zu führen.
Die häufigsten englischen idiomatischen Wendungen werden auf lernerfreundliche Art dem Benutzer nahegebracht: alphabetische Anordnung, Kennzeichnung der Stilebene, griffige Übersetzungen, erklärende Umschreibungen und leicht verständliche Beispielsätze dienen dazu, sich den Stoff Schritt für Schritt anzueignen und leichter einzuprägen. Ein Register am Ende des Buches ermöglicht das gezielte und schnelle Auffinden bestimmter englischer *Idioms* über das entsprechende deutsche Stichwort.

„Englisch Redewendungen" ist der ideale Begleiter für alle, die ein einwandfreies und flüssiges idiomatisches Englisch sprechen möchten.

Abkürzungen

Am.	amerikanisch
Brit.	britisch
jdm.	jemandem
jdn.	jemanden
jds.	jemandes
jmd.	jemand
o.s.	oneself
s.b.	somebody
Sl.	Slang
s.o.	someone
s.th.	something

A

able:
~ to breathe (easily/ freely) again — aufatmen können
Now that the crisis is over, we are all able to breathe easily again.

~ to do something blindfold(ed)/~ to do something standing on one's head — etwas mit links erledigen
Brian is an amazing driver – he is able to win the race blindfolded.

~ to take a joke — einen Spaß verstehen (können)

~ to take something — etwas aushalten können

about:
be ~ eight years old — ungefähr acht Jahre alt sein

be ~ to do s.th. — drauf und dran sein, etwas zu tun

up and ~ — wieder auf den Beinen
~ time — höchste Zeit
It is about time John brought back the car!

What ~ ... ? — Was ist mit ...?

above:
~ all — vor allem
~ board — offen, ehrlich
~ suspicion — über jeden Verdacht erhaben
~ one's station — das Benehmen entspricht nicht der sozialen Position

get ~ oneself — eingebildet sein, sich überschätzen

Don't get above yourself, you are no better than the rest of us.

~ par	über dem Durchschnitt
not to be ~ doing s.th.	sich nicht zu fein sein, etwas zu tun
Absence makes the heart grow fonder. (Sprichw.)	Die Liebe wächst mit der Entfernung.

accent:
to have an ~ you could cut with a knife	einen ausgeprägten Akzent haben

accident:
~s will happen.	Auf so etwas muss man immer gefasst sein.
by ~	zufällig
meet with an ~	verunglücken

accord:
of one's own ~	aus eigenem Antrieb, von selbst, von sich aus
with one ~	einstimmig
~ing to all accounts	alle behaupten; laut Berichten/Aussagen
~ing to s.o. or s.th.	laut ...
~ing to one's lights	im Rahmen seiner Möglichkeiten

account
~ for	erklären
Did they account for the delay?	
of no ~	bedeutungslos
on ~ of	auf Grund
She left her husband on account of his infidelity.	
on no ~ of	keineswegs

a few little aches and pains — ein paar Wehwehchen

acid test — Feuerprobe

across the board — für jeden gleich
The government decided to raise the taxes across the board.

act:
~ **the giddy goat**	sich wie ein Trottel benehmen
~ **of God**	höhere Gewalt
~ **upon/on**	auf Grund von etwas handeln

We have told them what to do – now it's up to them to act on our advice.

~ **up** — Theater machen, sich aufspielen, sich danebenbenehmen

get in on the ~ — auf einen fahrenden Zug aufspringen

get one's ~ together — sich zusammenreißen

be in the ~ of — gerade dabei sein, etwas zu tun

He was caught in the act of stealing the car.

~ **one's age** — sich seinem Alter gemäß verhalten, nicht albern sein

Stop being so childish, Susan. Act your age!

action:
~s **speak louder than words.** — Taten zählen mehr als Worte.
to get a piece of the ~ — ein Stück vom Kuchen abbekommen
~ **stations** — sich bereit machen

Once it had become clear that the tornado was coming, it was action stations all around.

active service — (noch) im Dienst

in actual fact — tatsächlich

add up to s.th. — 1. eine mathematische Summe bilden, 2. bedeuten

1. The shopping adds up to almost a hundred pounds.
2. I don't see what all this adds up to. What do you mean?

to come adrift — verloren gehen

advantage:
to have the ~ of — den Vorteil haben
He had the advantage of a first-class education.
to take ~ of — 1. jdn. ausnutzen,
2. eine Gelegenheit nutzen

1. The car dealer took advantage of his customer's gullibility.
2. I look advantage of the fine weather to play tennis.

after:
~ a fashion — mehr oder weniger
~ all — schließlich, letztendlich, doch
The party did not seem very enjoyable at the beginning but in the end, everybody had a good time after all.
~ all is said and done — schließlich, unterm Strich
After all was said and done the holiday was a success.
~ hours — nach Büro- oder Ladenschluss
He would often remain in the office after hours to complete his work.
be ~ s.o./s.th — jdm./etwas hinterherjagen
The bankrobber knew the police would be after him.

again:
~ and ~ — immer wieder
as much ~ — noch einmal so viel
now and ~ — ab und zu
there ~ — andererseits
time and ~ — immer wieder

against:
~ s.o.'s better judgement — wider besseres Wissen
~ the clock — im Wettlauf mit der Zeit
~ the grain — gegen den Strich
~ (the/all) odds — gegen starken Widerstand, entgegen aller Erwartungen
as ~ him — im Vergleich zu ihm

age:
act one's ~ — nicht albern sein, sich seinem Alter gemäß benehmen
at an advanced ~ — im hohen Alter
be of ~ — volljährig sein
come of ~ — volljährig werden
for ~s — seit langer Zeit

agree:
~ with s.o. — die Meinung von jdm. teilen
not ~ with s.o. — jdm. nicht bekommen, krank machen

Travelling by boat does not agree with me, it always makes me feel sick.

ahead:
~ of time — vorher, vor der angekündigten Zeit, früher

If you get there ahead of time you'll just have to wait.

get ~ — Karriere machen
It takes a lot of ambition if you really want to get ahead.

air:
~ one's knowledge — sein Wissen unter Beweis stellen
~ one's views — seine Meinung verkünden
in the ~ — 1. ungewiss, 2. in der Luft liegen

*1. We go to Paris tomorrow, but after that our plans are in the air.
2. There are rumours in the air of a strike at the factory.*

clear the ~ — die Situation klären
give o.s. ~s — sich zieren, vornehm tun
~s and graces — Allüren

Aladdin's cave — eine Schatzkammer

alive:
~ and kicking — lebendig, aktiv
It's good to see uncle Bob is still alive and kicking.

~ to s.th.	sich einer Sache bewusst sein
~ with	wimmeln von, voll sein von

The river was alive with fish.

all:

~ agog	in freudiger Erwartung

Everybody was all agog for the play to start.

~ alone	ganz allein
~ along	die ganze Zeit
~ being well	wenn sonst nichts schief geht

All being well, we should catch the plane.

~ the best	Viel Glück!
~ right	in Ordnung
~ the same	dennoch, trotzdem
for ~ I care	meinetwegen
for ~ I know	so viel ich weiß, schon möglich
not at ~	überhaupt nicht
~ but	beinahe, fast
to be ~ ears	ganz Ohr sein
on ~ fours	auf allen vieren
~ in	1. fertig, erschöpft,
	2. alles zusammen

1. They're all in after their marathon run.
2. The holiday will cost $ 200 all in.

~ in a day's work	gehört zu den Aufgaben, typisch
~ in good time	alles zu seiner Zeit
~ in all	alles in allem
~ in one piece	sicher, unversehrt, heil
~ my eye (and Betty Martin) (Am./Sl.)	Quatsch/vollkommener Unsinn

That's all my eye and Betty Martin. Don't believe a word of it.

~ one	unwichtig, egal

It's all one to me whether you go or stay.

~ out	mit Volldampf

The workers are going all out to finish the job by the end of the week.

~ over	1. überall, 2. vorbei, 3. typisch für
1. There were celebrations all over town.	
2. They did not leave until the excitement was all over.	
3. John handed in his essay late, but that's John all over.	
~ the same	1. gleich, 2. trotzdem
1. It's all the same to me.	
2. All the same, I think you're wrong.	
~ set	absolut bereit
All set? Then we can leave.	
~ and sundry	alle, Hinz und Kunz
for ~ that	trotzdem
to be ~ things to ~ men	es allen Leuten recht machen wollen
when ~'s said and done	unterm Strich, letzten Endes
~ the rage	der letzte Schrei
It seems to be all the rage for young girls to dye their hair green.	
not ~ there (Sl.)	nicht ganz bei Trost
~ thumbs	zwei linke Hände, ungeschickt
~'s well that ends well. (Sprichw.)	Ende gut, alles gut!
~ year round	das ganze Jahr über/hindurch

allow:

~ for s.o. or s.th.	in Betracht ziehen, berücksichtigen
Did you allow for any delays?	
~ of no argument	keinen Einwand zulassen, keinen Widerspruch dulden
make allowance(s)	Nachsicht üben wegen, berücksichtigen
We must make allowance(s) for her inexperience.	

along:

~ with	zusammen mit, in Gesellschaft von
be ~ in a minute	gleich kommen
I'll be along in a minute.	
~ the lines of	in der Art von
go ~ with (Sl.)	zustimmen, mitmachen

an eye for an eye, a tooth for a tooth   Auge um Auge, Zahn um Zahn

to be an also-ran   unter „ferner liefen" rangieren

to take s.th. amiss   etwas übel nehmen

and:
~ all that   und so weiter
~ a half   mehr als üblich
~ howl! (Sl.)   und ob! aber wie!
He is a great driver! – And howl! He can beat anybody!
~ no mistake   aber sicher
~ one knows it   man weiß
~ the like   und Ähnliches
~ what not (Sl.)   und so weiter und so fort

angel:
~ of death   Todesengel
~ of light   Lichtengel
~ of mercy   rettender Engel

another cup of tea   eine ganz andere Sache

answer:
~ back   frech werden, widersprechen
My mother always scolded me if I answered back.
~ for   die Verantwortung übernehmen
~ a purpose   geeignet sein, einen Zweck erfüllen
~ the call of duty   seine Pflicht tun, eine Pflicht erfüllen
~ to s.o.   sich jemandem gegenüber rechtfertigen
~ (to)   1. übereinstimmen, entsprechen, 2. hören auf

1. A man answering (to) that description was seen leaving the bank.
2. He answers to the name of John Doe.

any:
~ day   wann immer möglich
to not have ~ of it   nichts davon wissen wollen
~ old (Sl.)   jeder x-beliebige
~ minute now   jeden Moment
The film will start any minute now.

appearances:
to all ~   offensichtlich, anscheinend
keep up ~   den Schein wahren
~ are deceptive. (Sprichw.)   Der Schein trügt.

apple:
be the ~ of s.o.'s eye   jdm. besonders wert/
    lieb sein
His baby daughter is the apple of his eye.
an ~ for the teacher (Sl.)   ein Versuch, sich beliebt
    zu machen
the ~ of discord   Zankapfel

argue the toss   sich mit einer Streitfrage
    auseinandersetzen

arm^1:
~ in ~   Arm in Arm
keep s.b. at ~'s length   jdn. auf Distanz halten
within ~'s reach   in Reichweite

arm^2:
~ o.s. against   sich gegen etwas wappnen
~ o.s. with s.th.   sich mit etwas bewaffnen
armed to the teeth (Sl.)   bis an die Zähne bewaffnet

around the clock   rund um die Uhr

as:
~ a duck takes to water   ohne Schwierigkeiten, natürlich
He took to playing the trumpet just as a duck takes to water.
~ for you   was dich betrifft

~ it were	sozusagen
~ yet	bis jetzt
I thought ~ much	Das hab' ich mir gedacht.
~ the case stands	wie die Dinge stehen
~ a rule	in der Regel
~ a last resort	als letzter Ausweg

My father was a peaceful man and only used beating as a last resort.

~ a matter of course	selbstverständlich, an der Tagesordnung

You are expected to make your own bed as a matter of course.

~ a matter of fact	im Übrigen

As a matter of fact, I saw him yesterday.

~ and when	wann und wie
~ bad ~ ever	genau so schlimm wie eh und je
~ blind ~ a bat	stockblind

I'm getting as blind as a bat, I must get some spectacles.

~ bold ~ brass	unverschämt
~ busy ~ a bee	eifrig, bienenfleißig

The children were as busy as bees, playing in the sand.

~ clear ~ mud (Sl.)	sehr unverständlich

I'm afraid I can't see the point at all, your argument is as clear as mud.

~ cool ~ a cucumber	die Ruhe selbst

She never loses her temper, she's as cool as a cucumber.

~ dead ~ a dodo (Sl.)	mausetot
~ easy ~ falling off a log (Sl.)	sehr einfach, kinderleicht
~ easy ~ pie (Sl.)	babyleicht
~ far ~ I'm concerned	was mich betrifft
~ fit ~ a fiddle (Sl.)	kerngesund

The doctor told me I'm as fit as a fiddle.

~ good ~ done	beinahe fertig/erledigt
~ good ~ gold (Sl.)	sehr brav

The baby was as good as gold.

~ happy ~ a lark	quietschfidel

~ hard ~ nails	knallhart, steinhart
~ light ~ a feather	federleicht
~ mad ~ a March hare	total verrückt
~ mad ~ hell (Sl.)	wütend
~ of old	nach alter Sitte
~ plain ~ the nose on one's face (Sl.)	ganz offensichtlich
~ plain ~ day	sonnenklar
~ quick ~ a wink	blitzschnell
~ quick ~ greased lightning (Sl.)	wie ein geölter Blitz
~ regular ~ clockwork	präzise wie ein Uhrwerk
~ right ~ rain	in guter Verfassung
~ sick ~ a dog	hundeelend, speiübel
~ smart ~ a fox	sehr schlau, ausgefuchst
~ snug ~ a bug in a rug (Sl.)	warm, geborgen, sicher

The mother tucked her daughter up in bed and said: "There you are, as snug as a bug in a rug".

~ sparks fly upward	mit absoluter Sicherheit
~ sure as ten dimes buy a dollar (Am.)	sicherlich
~ thick ~ thieves	unzertrennlich, wie Pech und Schwefel
~ thick ~ two short planks	dumm wie Bohnenstroh
~ to the manner born	für etwas wie geschaffen sein

She rides a horse as to the manner born.

~ tough ~ old boots	zäh wie Leder
~ well ~ the next man	genau so gut wie jeder andere
~ white ~ snow	schneeweiß
~ wise ~ an owl	sehr weise

ask:

~ for the moon	das Unmögliche verlangen, nach den Sternen greifen
~ for trouble	Schwierigkeiten heraufbeschwören
~ me another!	Frag mich etwas Leichteres!
It's yours for the ~ing!	Du brauchst es nur zu sagen!

to look askance at s.o. or s.th.	misstrauisch betrachten, schief ansehen

at:

~ all	überhaupt

~ **all costs**	um jeden Preis
~ **all times**	ständig, immer
I have said it again and again, you have to tell me the truth at all times.	
~ **any rate**	auf jeden Fall
~ **death's door**	dem Tode nah
~ **every turn**	überall (wo man hinschaut)
The playful kitten gets under my feet at every turn.	
~ **first**	am Anfang, zuerst
~ **hand**	griffbereit
be ~ **it again** (Sl.)	schon wieder dabei sein, etwas zu tun
be ~ **s.th.** (Sl.)	etwas anstellen
~ **length**	ausführlich
~ **some length**	ziemlich lange
be ~ **loggerheads**	im Streit sein, sich in den Haaren liegen
The two brothers were always at loggerheads, they could never agree.	
~ **long last**	endlich
~ **a loose end**	rastlos, ziellos, unruhig, ohne Arbeit
John was at a loose end and was glad to join me for an evening in the cinema.	
(all) ~ **sea**	durcheinander, im Dunkeln tappen
~ **odds with s.o.**	uneins, im Streit
Don't pay attention to him, he's at odds with everyone today.	
~ **one fell swoop**	auf einen Schlag, auf einmal
~ **one's wits' end**	mit seiner Weisheit am Ende
I'm at my wits' end. What shall I do?	
~ **short notice**	kurzfristig
It is not easy to get an appointment with the dentist at short notice.	
~ **the crack of dawn**	bei Tagesanbruch, sehr früh
It's no fun, getting up to go to work at the crack of dawn.	

~ cross purposes	mit unterschiedlichen Zielen
~ the double	im Nu, im Eilschritt
~ the drop of a hat	im Nu, beim geringsten Anlass
Any elected official will defend the programme at the drop of a hat.	
~ the eleventh hour	fünf vor zwölf
~ the end of one's tether	fix und fertig
Stop getting on your mum's nerves, Alistair. Can't you see she's at the end of her tether.	
~ will	nach Belieben
no strings attached	konditionslos, ohne Nachteile
We received permission to use the old building with no strings attached.	

avenge:
~ o.s. on s.b. for s.th.	sich für etwas an jdm. rächen
leave no avenue unexplored	alle Möglichkeiten ausschöpfen, alle möglichen Informationen einholen
to avoid s.o. like the plague	jdn. meiden wie die Pest

away:
~ with that!	Weg damit!
right ~	jetzt gleich, sofort
to have it ~ with s.o. (Sl.)	eine Nummer schieben
an awful lot	sehr viel

B

baby:
a ~ in arms	Säugling; schwach
a ~ in the woods (Am.)	Naivling
to be left holding the ~	die Verantwortung für etwas aufgebürdet bekommen; etwas allein ausbaden müssen

back:
~ and forth	hin und her
bend over ~wards	sich übergroße Mühe geben
~ down	seine Meinung aufgeben
a ~ number	eine alte Ausgabe (einer Zeitung o. ä.)
~ off (Sl.)	in Ruhe lassen
~-seat driver	Besserwisser (der die Folgen nicht zu tragen braucht)
get off s.o.'s ~	jdn. in Ruhe lassen
to get s.o.'s ~ up	jdn. reizen, jdn. aus dem Häuschen bringen
~ s.o. or s.th. up	bestätigen
~stairs	geheim, nicht offiziell

You should not listen to backstairs gossip.

go ~ upon one's word	sein Wort brechen
go ~ on s.o.	jdn. im Stich lassen
hang ~	zurück bleiben, sich im Hintergrund halten
with one's ~ to the wall	mit dem Rücken zur Wand
to put one's back into s.th.	sich in etwas reinknien

bad:
~ blood	Feindschaft, böses Blut

Be careful what you do, there has been bad blood between them for a long time.

~ form	schlechter Stil, unhöflich

I cannot believe he borrowed your car without telling you – that's terribly bad form.

a ~ lot	bösartig, unzuverlässig
want s.th. ~ly	etwas unbedingt haben wollen
to be in a ~ way	in einer schwierigen Lage sein

bag:
in the ~	unter Dach und Fach
~ and baggage	mit Kind und Kegel
a ~ of nerves	ein Nervenbündel
a ~ of bones	spindeldürr, Haut und Knochen
~s of (Sl.)	reichlich
the whole ~ of tricks	alle möglichen Tricks

a baker's dozen	dreizehn (von der alten Sitte, einem Kunden, der zwölf Dinge in einer Bäckerei kaufte, ein Stück extra zu geben)

balance:
to hold the ~	das Zünglein an der Waage bilden
on ~	alles in allem
strike the ~	Bilanz ziehen

ball:
be on the ~	auf Draht sein
set the ~ rolling	den Stein ins Rollen bringen
have a ~	einen Mordsspaß haben
The ~'s in your court.	Jetzt sind Sie dran!

The balloon went up.	Die Bombe platzte.

bang:
~ in the middle	mittendrin, genau in der Mitte
~ one's head against a brick wall	mit dem Kopf gegen die Wand rennen
to go off with a ~	großartig funktionieren

bare:
~ one's heart	sein Herz ausschütten
~ one's teeth	die Zähne zeigen/fletschen
the ~ bones of s.th.	die Grundzüge von etwas

bargain:
~ counter	Wühltisch im Kaufhaus

~ing counter (Brit.)	Trumpfkarte bei Verhandlungen
~ for	rechnen mit
We didn't bargain for so many people coming to the party.	
to be a ~	ein Schnäppchen sein
to drive a hard ~	zäh verhandeln
into the ~	hinzu, obendrein
make the best of a bad ~	das Beste draus machen
strike a ~	einen Kompromiss schließen

bark:
His ~ is worse than his bite.	Bellende Hunde beißen nicht.
~ up the wrong tree	auf dem Holzweg sein

bat:
not to ~ an eyelid	nicht mit der Wimper zucken
like a ~ out of hell (Brit./Sl.)	wie ein geölter Blitz
He was so frightened he ran out of the house like a bat out of hell.	
have ~s in the belfry (Sl.)	einen Vogel haben
off one's own ~	auf eigene Faust, aus eigener Initiative, von sich aus

a bawling match (Sl.)	eine lautstarke Auseinandersetzung

be:
the ~-all and end-all	das A und O
for the time ~ing	zunächst, im Moment
~ a must (Sl.)	etwas, das man tun muss; es gehört dazu
It's a must that you visit Buckingham Palace when you're in London.	
~ all ears	ganz Ohr sein
Do tell me your story. I'm all ears!	
~ bushed (Am./Sl.)	erschöpft sein
~ poles apart	da liegen Welten dazwischen
~ in a blue funk (Sl.)	in wilder Panik sein
He was in a blue funk about having lost the documents.	
~ on one's beam-end(s)	pleite sein
~ beside oneself with joy	vor Freude ganz aus dem Häuschen sein

~ that as it may	wie dem auch sei
~ the spitting image of s.o.	jdm. wie aus dem Gesicht geschnitten sein

He is the spitting image of his brother, it is hard to tell them apart.

beans:

to be full of ~	voller Tatendrang sein
to spill the ~	ausplaudern, verraten

bear[1]:

~ fruit	Früchte tragen
~ up	durchhalten, standhalten
s.th. ~s watching	etwas muss im Auge behalten werden

Our situation is critical and will bear watching.

~ in mind	etwas berücksichtigen

Bear what I have said in mind when you go for the interview.

not to ~ close inspection	einer genaueren Untersuchung nicht standhalten können
a cross to ~	eine Last zu tragen

bear[2]:

like a ~ with a sore head	schlechte Laune, bärbeißig
~ garden	eine Räuberhöhle

beat:

~ about the bush	um den heißen Brei herum reden

Stop beating about the bush and come to the point.

~ it (Am./Sl.)	abhauen, verschwinden

Mary turned up as well, but we told her to beat it.

~ a retreat	den Rückzug antreten

We wanted to drive home despite the storm, but after a few minutes, we beat a hasty retreat to our hosts' house.

~ s.o. down	herunterhandeln
~ the band	alle übertreffen oder überraschen

~ one's brains out   sich den Kopf zerbrechen
~ one's breast   öffentlich Reue zeigen

beauty:
~ **is in the eye of the beholder.**   Schönheit liegt im Auge des Betrachters.
~ **sleep**   Schönheitsschlaf

becoming to s.o.   jdm. gut stehen
You should always wear that dress, it is very becoming to you.

a bee in one's bonnet   eine fixe Idee, einen Tick haben

He has a bee in his bonnet about changing the world.

before:
~ **long**   bald, binnen kurzem
~ **you can say knife**   plötzlich, blitzschnell
~ **you know it**   bevor man sich versieht
carry all ~ one   sehr erfolgreich sein

beg:
Beggar's can't be choosers.   In der Not frisst der Teufel Fliegen.

I shall take whatever job is offered, beggars can't be choosers.
~ **the question**   eine Fage aufwerfen
~ **to differ**   anderer Meinung sein

beginner's luck   Anfängerglück

behave like a bull in a china shop   sich wie ein Elefant im Porzellanladen benehmen

behind:
~ **closed doors**   hinter verschlossenen Türen
~ **one's back**   hinter jds. Rücken
~ **the scenes**   hinter den Kulissen

saved by the bell   in letzter Sekunde gerettet

have under one's belt	in der Tasche haben
bend:	
~ over backwards to do s.th.	sich übermäßig anstrengen, etwas zu tun
He is bending over backwards to get the task done.	
be round the ~	nicht alle Tassen im Schrank haben, verrückt sein
He is completely round the bend.	
the benefit of the doubt	im Zweifel für den Angeklagten
best:	
at the ~ of times	bestenfalls
~ bib and tucker (Sl.)	die feinste Kleidung, die man besitzt, Festkleidung
We had to go and see the boss, so I put on my best bib and tucker for the occasion.	
be all for the ~	zum Besten von jdm. sein
in the ~ of all possible worlds	unter perfekten Bedingungen
the ~ of British luck	(meist iron.) viel Glück dabei!
the ~ that money can buy	das Feinste vom Feinen
get the ~ of s.th.	am besten wegkommen
to the ~ of my knowledge	nach bestem Wissen
put the ~ foot forward	so schnell wie möglich gehen
bet one's bottom dollar	absolut sicher sein, alles darauf setzen
I'll bet my bottom dollar he is going to be late again!	
better:	
~ late than never	besser spät als nie
to think ~ of s.th.	es sich anders überlegen
to go one ~ than s.o.	jdn. übertreffen, eins draufsetzen
between:	
in ~	mittendrin, dazwischen
~ ourselves	unter uns
read ~ the lines	zwischen den Zeilen lesen

beyond 24

~ **the devil and the deep blue sea** (Sl.)	zwischen Hölle und Fegefeuer, in der Klemme

He couldn't make up his mind as to what to decide. He was obviously between the devil and the deep blue sea.

~ **you, me and the gate-post** (Brit/Sl.)	unter uns gesagt

Between you, me and the gate-post, their marriage is not going well.

beyond:
the back of ~ (Sl.)	wo sich Fuchs und Hase gute Nacht sagen

No wonder house prices are cheap in this area, it is the back of beyond, nobody would want to live here.

That's ~ **me.**	Das ist mir zu hoch.
live ~ **one's means**	über seine Verhältnisse leben

If we continue to live beyond our means we'll never get rich.

~ **(all) bearing**	unerträglich
~ **all measure**	über die Maßen
~ **belief**	unvorstellbar
bid somebody good-bye	sich von jdm. verabschieden
bide one's time	geduldig auf etwas warten

big:
the ~ **battalions**	die Mächtigen (mit negativem Anklang)
a ~ **bug** (Sl.)	jmd. Bedeutsames
a ~ **cheese** (Sl.)	hohes Tier
a ~ **hit**	großer Erfolg, großer Renner

So far, he had not earned a lot of money, but his new play was a big hit.

the ~ **stick**	überlegene Gewalt
to get too ~ **for one's boots**	größenwahnsinnig werden
the bigger the better	je mehr, desto besser

bill and coo	miteinander turteln
bind s.b. hand and foot	jdm. Freiheiten nehmen

bird:

a ~ of passage	Wandervogel
the ~ has flown	der Vogel ist ausgeflogen
The early ~ catches the worm. (Sprichw.)	Morgenstund' hat Gold im Mund.
A ~ in the hand is worth two in the bush. (Sprichw.)	Ein Spatz in der Hand ist besser als eine Taube auf dem Dach.
~ s of a feather flock together. (Sprichw.)	Gleich und Gleich gesellt sich gern.
kill two ~s with one stone (Sl.)	zwei Fliegen mit einer Klappe schlagen

When you go to the chemist's for your prescription, you could bring me my medicine, that would be killing two birds with one stone.

the ~s and the bees	die Bienchen und Blümchen
in one's birthday suit	nackt, im Adams-/Evakostüm

bit:

~ by ~	Stück für Stück, nach und nach
a ~ much	ein starkes Stück

His request of both more pay and more days off work was a bit much.

a ~ of all right (Sl., altmodisch)	große Klasse
a ~ thick	übertrieben; begriffsstutzig

bitch:

~ about s.th.	über etwas lästern
a ~ of a day (Am.)	ein mieser Tag

bite:

~ back a remark	sich eine Bemerkung verkneifen
~ off more than one can chew	sich zu viel zumuten
~ the dust	ins Gras beißen; scheitern
~ the hand that feeds you	den Ast absägen, auf dem man sitzt

bits and bobs	verschiedener Kleinkram
bitten:	
Once ~, twice shy.	Ein gebranntes Kind scheut das Feuer.
What's ~ him?	Was ist mit ihm los?
a bitter pill	schwer zu akzeptieren, eine bittere Pille
black:	
~ and blue	grün und blau (geschlagen)
be in s.b.'s ~ books	bei jdm. schlecht angeschrieben sein
a ~ day for s.b.	ein schlechter Tag für jdn.
a ~ look	ein finsterer Blick
a ~ mood	schlechte Laune
~ out	umkippen, das Bewusstsein verlieren
~ sheep of the family	das schwarze Schaf der Familie
in ~ and white	schwarz auf weiß
blacken:	
~ s.b.'s name	jdn. anschwärzen
~ the picture	etwas schlimmer machen, als es ist
blame the other fellow	Verantwortung für etwas weiterschieben
Whenever something went wrong, he blamed the other fellow.	
a wet blanket	ein Spielverderber
at full blast	auf Hochtouren
blaze a trail	den Weg bahnen, Pionierarbeit leisten
bleed s.b. white	jdn. (finanziell) ausnehmen
blind:	
a ~ alley	eine Sackgasse

~ drunk	volltrunken
turn a ~ eye	ein Auge zudrücken
a ~ fury	rasende Wut
the ~ leading the ~	eine Situation, in der unfähige Leute andere unfähige Leute anweisen, etwas zu tun; ein Blinder führt einen Blinden

The attempted reorganisation is a classic case of the blind leading the blind, as nobody understands anything.

to have a ~ spot	einen Schwachpunkt haben
~ to the world	volltrunken

blink:
~ the fact	eine Tatsache ignorieren
in the ~ of an eye	urplötzlich, blitzschnell

blood:
~ is thicker than water.	Blut ist dicker als Wasser.

He may be a thief but he is also my son, and I must help him. Blood is thicker than water.

bad ~	böses Blut

There has been bad blood between Zoe and her sister for ages.

blue ~	blaublütig, adlig
in cold ~	kaltblütig

The judge said the murderer had acted in cold blood, and therefore deserved the hardest punishment provided for by law.

squeeze ~ out of a stone	jdm. etwas aus der Nase ziehen; verlorene Liebesmüh

Trying to get a straight answer out of him is like trying to squeeze blood out of a stone.

~ and gut	gewalttätige Szenen in Film oder Theater
blot one's copy book (Brit.)	sich unmöglich machen, seinen (guten) Ruf ruinieren

blow:

~ **the gaff** (Sl.)	nicht dichthalten
~ **hot and cold**	sein Fähnchen nach dem Wind drehen
~ **one's top** (Sl.)	vor Wut explodieren; vor Wut in die Luft gehen

If you irritate him much more he'll blow his top.

~ **off steam**	Dampf ablassen

Jack was so angry after the meeting, he just had to blow off steam.

have a ~-out	sich vollfressen
~ **up**	die Beherrschung verlieren
~ **s.th.**	etwas verpatzen
~ **s.th. sky-high**	etwas vollständig zerstören, ein Argument total widerlegen
~ **s.o. up** (Sl.)	anschnauzen
~ **the lid off s.th.**	etwas verraten/aufdecken

The boys were angry with David for blowing the lid off their plans to run away from home.

~ **one's own trumpet**	sich selber loben, angeben

She is not a modest person at all, she's always blowing her own trumpet.

~ **over**	vorübergehen, aufhören

We often have a row, but they soon blow over.

tell s.th. ~ by ~	in allen Einzelheiten erzählen/berichten
to get on the blower	sich an die Strippe hängen

blue:

a ~ movie	ein Pornofilm
feel ~	deprimiert sein, Trübsal blasen
the ~-eyed boy	jds. Liebling, Goldjunge
a ~ fit	sich sehr über etwas ärgern
~ **murder**	Zeter und Mordio

There'll be blue murder when she hears of this.

like a bolt from the ~	wie ein Blitz aus heiterem Himmel

His news came as a complete surprise, like a bolt from the blue.

once in a ~ moon — äußerst selten, alle Jubeljahre einmal

I have an aunt in Canada whom I see once in a blue moon.

blunder:
to ~ into s.th. — in etw. hineingeraten
to commit a ~ — einen Fehler machen

boat:
be in the same ~ — im selben Boot sitzen
have an oar in everyone's ~ — überall seine Finger im Spiel haben
push the ~ out — keine Mühen (oder Kosten) scheuen

body:
a ~ blow — ein herber Rückschlag
~ and soul — ganz und gar

the bogey man — der schwarze Mann

to boil down to ... — darauf hinauslaufen, dass ...
What it all boils down to is that he is going to leave her.

bold:
as ~ as brass — unverschämt, frech wie Oskar
a ~ front — vorgetäuschter Mut oder gute Stimmung

bolt:
~ s.th. down — etwas herunterschlingen
a ~ from the blue — ein Blitz aus heiterem Himmel

bone:
~ idle — stinkfaul
have a ~ to pick with s.b. — mit jdm. ein Hühnchen zu rupfen haben
make no ~s about s.th. — keinen Hehl aus etw. machen
I'm disappointed, I'll make no bones about it.

book 30

~ of contention — Zankapfel, Streitobjekt
The time he comes home in the evening has always been a bone of contention between me and my son.
to feel it in one's ~s — etwas im Gefühl haben

book:
in my ~ — so wie ich die Sache sehe, meiner Meinung nach

suit s.b.'s ~ — jdm. in den Kram passen
The arrangement will suit my book very well.
go by the ~ — sich genau an die Regeln halten
he is in s.b.'s good/bad ~s — jmd. ist gut/schlecht auf ihn zu sprechen
It's a closed ~ to me. — Das ist ein Buch mit sieben Siegeln für mich.
What a turn-up for the ~! — Was für eine Überraschung!

boon:
a ~ and a blessing — sehr willkommen
a ~ companion — ein guter Kumpel

boot:
My heart is in my ~s. — Das Herz ist mir in die Hose gerutscht.
The ~ is on the other foot. — Die Sache ist gerade umgekehrt.
~ s.o. out — jdn. hinausschmeißen

born:
~ to the purple — von königlicher oder aristokratischer Abstammung
~ with a silver spoon in one's mouth — mit einem silbernen Löffel im Mund geboren sein
She has never had to worry about money, she was born with a silver spoon in her mouth.
~ within the sound of the Bow bells — ein echter Cockney (Einwohner von London)
I was not ~ yesterday. — Ich bin nicht von gestern.

a bosom friend — ein Busenfreund

s.o. can not be bothered with s.th.	etwas interessiert jdn. nicht
bottle:	
to ~ out of s.th. (Sl.)	sich vor etwas drücken
a ~ party	eine Party, bei der die Gäste die Getränke beisteuern
one's bottom drawer	Aussteuer
one's bounden duty	jds. Pflicht und Schuldigkeit
bow:	
~ and scrape	katzbuckeln
~ to the inevitable	sich dem Unausweichlichen fügen
box:	
~ office	Kartenverkauf
on the ~	in der Glotze
to brace oneself	sich auf etwas gefasst machen
brass:	
It's ~-monkey weather!	Es ist saukalt!
the top ~	die militärische Führung
Clearly, the top brass is less than happy with the new policy.	
to get down to ~ tacks	zur Sache kommen
bread:	
~ and butter	Einkommen, Lebensunterhalt
I hate being a mechanic, but it's my bread and butter.	
~ and circuses	Brot und Spiele
break:	
~ away from	Abstand nehmen von
~ cover	aus der Deckung kommen
~ down (s.th.)	1. etwas niederreißen, 2. etwas überwinden, 3. zusammenbrechen
1. The police had to break down the door in order to get into the apartment.	

breast

2. *It took a long time to break down his inhibitions.*
3. *After the accident, she broke down completely.*

~ **new ground**	etwas völlig Neues machen, Neuland betreten

The firm broke new ground in computer technology.

~ **the ice**	die Stimmung auflockern, das Eis brechen
~ **out**	ausbrechen
~ **the spell**	einen Zauber brechen
~-**through**	ein (revolutionärer) Durchbruch
make a clean breast (of)	etwas offen eingestehen

breath:

a ~ **of fresh air**	neu, erfrischend

She has a wonderful personality, just like a breath of fresh air.

to save one's ~	sich seine Worte sparen
under one's ~	leise, geflüstert

He went away swearing under his breath.

breathe:

~ **one's last**	den letzten Atemzug tun
~ **a sigh of relief**	Seufzer der Erleichterung
~ **down s.b.'s neck**	jdm. im Nacken sitzen

I can't work with you breathing down my neck.

brick:

come down like a ton of ~s on s.o. (Sl.)	jdn. zur Schnecke machen

The manager came down like a ton of bricks on him for losing the money.

drop a ~ (Sl.)	einen Schnitzer machen
bridle one's tongue	seine Zunge im Zaum halten

bright and early	früh am Morgen
bring:	
~ **about**	verursachen, herbeiführen
~ **about a change**	eine Änderung mit sich bringen
~ **into play**	ins Spiel bringen
~ **o.s. to**	sich überwinden
She couldn't bring herself to apologise.	
~ **out**	zum Vorschein bringen
The crisis brought out the best in him.	
~ **s.b. down**	jdn. zur Strecke bringen
~ **s.b. down to earth**	jdn. auf den Boden der Tatsachen zurückholen
~ **s.b. in on s.th.**	jdn. hinzuziehen
~ **s.th. home to s.b.**	jdm. etwas klarmachen, erklären
~ **s.th. into the open**	etwas ans Tageslicht bringen
~ **s.b. to his senses**	jdn. zur Vernunft bringen
~ **s.th. to a close**	etwas beenden, zu Ende bringen
~ **s.th. to light**	etwas aufdecken, ans Tageslicht bringen
~ **s.th. up**	etwas erwähnen
~ **the house down**	Zuschauer zu begeistertem Applaus hinreißen
broach the subject	ein Thema zum ersten Mal ansprechen
broad:	
It's about as ~ as it's long.	Das ist gehupft wie gesprungen.
~**ly speaking**	allgemein gesprochen
to be broke (Sl.)	Pleite sein
a broken marriage	eine kaputte Ehe
a Bronx cheer (Am.)	ein verächtliches Zischen
brook no delay	keine Verzögerung zulassen
to brush s.th. up	etwas auffrischen

brute   34

brute force	rohe Gewalt
buck up! (Sl.)	Kopf hoch!
to kick the bucket (Sl.)	ins Gras beißen (Sl.)
to buckle down to s.th.	sich hinter etwas klemmen

build:
~ one's hopes on	seine Hoffnungen auf etwas setzen
~ castles in the air	Luftschlösser bauen

I like to sit in my chair just building castles in the air.

to bulk large	eine beherrschende Position einnehmen

His impending move to London bulked large, so he did not get a lot of things done.

bull:
like a ~ in a china shop	wie ein Elefant im Porzellanladen
go like a ~ at a gate	mit der Tür ins Haus fallen
bully for you (Sl.)	Applaus! Gratuliere!
to bum s.th. off s.o. (Sl.)	etwas von jmd. schnorren

bump:
~ s.b. off (Sl.)	jdn. um die Ecke bringen
~ into s.b.	jdm. in die Arme laufen

burn:
~ one's bridges behind one	alle Brücken hinter sich abbrechen

If you leave university now you'll be burning your bridges behind you.

~ one's boats	alle Brücken hinter sich abbrechen
~ the candle at both ends	sich Tag und Nacht keine Ruhe gönnen, sich übernehmen
~ the midnight oil (Sl.)	bis spät in die Nacht arbeiten

burst:
~ into laughter/tears	in Lachen/Tränen ausbrechen
~ into flames	in Flammen aufgehen
~ with pride	vor Stolz platzen

bury:
~ alive	lebendig begraben, von der Außenwelt abschneiden
~ the hatchet	das Kriegsbeil begraben
~ the past	einen neuen Anfang machen

business:
~ is ~. (Sprichw.)	Geschäft ist Geschäft.
the ~ in hand	das aktuelle Problem
That's none of your ~.	Das geht dich nichts an.
Mind your own ~.	Kümmere dich um deine eigenen Angelegenheiten.

but:
~ good	gründlich
~ me no ~s!	Keine Widerrede!

These are my orders and I want you to but me no buts about it now!

I cannot ~ (help him)	ich kann nicht anders als (ihm zu helfen)
the next ~ one	der Übernächste
No ifs and ~s!	Kein Wenn und Aber!

butcher:
to take a ~'s at s.th. (Sl.)	etwas betrachten, abschätzen
to butt into a conversation (Sl.)	sich ins Gespräch einmischen

butter:
~ s.b. up	jdm. Honig um den Bart schmieren
She looks as if ~ wouldn't melt in her mouth. (Sl.)	Sie sieht aus, als könne sie kein Wässerchen trüben.

have butterflies in one's stomach
Schmetterlinge im Bauch haben; ein flaues Gefühl haben

I am really nervous about the interview, I have butterflies in my stomach.

button one's lip (Sl.)   die Klappe halten

buy:
- **~ a pig in a poke** — die Katze im Sack kaufen
- **~ that** (Sl.) — etwas akzeptieren
- **~ s.th. for a song** — etwas ganz billig erstehen

John was thrilled. He had managed to buy a well-preserved copy of a valuable old book for a song.

- **~ s.b. off** — jdn. abfinden

I'm determined to have my rights. I'll not let them buy me off.

by:
- **~ accident** — zufällig
- **~ all accounts** — so weit bekannt ist
- **~ all means** — unbedingt
- **~ and ~** — allmählich, nach und nach
- **~ any chance** — vielleicht, möglicherweise
- **~ anybody's standards** — aus jeder Sicht, wie auch immer man es betrachtet
- **~ chance** — zufällig
- **~ common consent** — mit allgemeiner Zustimmung, einstimmig
- **~ courtesy of** — durch die freundliche Unterstützung von
- **~ definition** — per Definition, definitionsgemäß

Having obtained a university degree at some point in life does not make you an intellectual by definition.

- **~ design** — absichtlich
- **~ dint of s.th.** — in Folge von, durch
- **~ fair means or foul** — koste es, was es wolle
- **~ the ~** — übrigens, nebenbei bemerkt
- **~ the fire** — am Kamin, zu Hause
- **~ a hair's breadth** — knapp, um Haaresbreite

The athlete just missed breaking the record by a hair's breadth.

- **~ all means** — in jedem Fall
- **~ and large** — im Großen und Ganzen
- **~ hook or ~ cook** (Sl.) — auf Biegen und Brechen

~ no means	auf keinen Fall
~ the dozen	im Dutzend
He always buys his wine by the dozen.	
~ the dozens	zu Dutzenden
The fans flocked to the concert by the dozens.	
~ the scruff of the neck	am Kragen, am Schlafittchen
He grabbed me by the scruff of the neck and threatened to hit me.	
~ the skin of one's teeth (Sl.)	mit Ach und Krach
I just managed to catch the bus by the skin of my teeth.	
~ the sweat of one's brow	im Schweiße seines Angesichts
~ way of	1. (auf dem Weg) über, 2. als, 3. mittels
1. You get to London from Dover by way of Ashford.	
2. By way of greeting, he complained about modern railways.	
3. What do you think about relaxing by way of a trip to the continent this year?	
~ the way	im Übrigen, übrigens
~ word of mouth	mündlich
I've only heard by word of mouth that I've got the job, I'm waiting for written confirmation.	

C

cake:
like hot ~s — wie warme Semmeln, sehr schnell
His latest book is selling like hot cakes.
a piece of ~ — einfach, leicht, eine Kleinigkeit
He pretended that going into the lion's cage was a piece of cake.
that takes the ~ (Sl.) — das ist unglaublich/das Schärfste (iron.)

call:
~ at s.b.'s house — bei jdm. vorbeischauen
~ for s.b. — nach jdm. rufen, jdn. abholen
~ off s.th. — etwas abblasen
We were going to go to the disco, but decided to call it off.
~ on s.b. — jdn. besuchen
~ s.b. names — jdn. beschimpfen
~ a spade a spade — die Dinge beim Namen nennen
~ it a day — Feierabend machen
~ to mind — ins Gedächtnis rufen
~ the tune — den Ton angeben
to give s.o. a ~ — jdn. anrufen, sich bei jdm. melden

a callow youth — grüner Junge

can¹:
~ do! (Sl., altmodisch) — Kein Problem!
~ do worse than — es könnte schlimmer sein, als
~ a duck swim? — Aber klar!

can²:
carry the ~ (Sl.) — die Schuld auf sich nehmen, die Verantwortung übernehmen

candle:
be not worth the ~ — nicht der Mühe wert sein

burn the ~ at both ends	sich überarbeiten, überanstrengen
Poor Gary is completely worn out, he has been burning the candle at both ends lately.	
not fit to hold a ~ to s.o.	jdm. nicht das Wasser reichen können

can't:
he ~ see beyond the end of his nose	er sieht nicht über den Tellerrand hinaus
It's not good asking John what went on, he can't see beyond the end of his nose.	
one ~ see one's hand in front of one's face	die Hand nicht vor den Augen sehen können
I ~ stand it.	Ich halte es nicht aus. Ich kann es nicht ausstehen.

cap:
~ in hand	unterwürfig
put on one's thinking ~ (Sl.)	scharf nachdenken
There must be an answer to the problem, I must put on my thinking cap.	

to mark s.o.'s card (Sl.)	jdn. warnen; jdn. belehren

care:
~ killed the cat. (Sprichw.)	aufmunternd: Nimm es nicht so schwer!
I don't ~.	Das ist mir egal. Meinetwegen.
I couldn't ~ less.	Das ist mir gleichgültig.

carrott and (the) stick	Zuckerbrot und Peitsche

carry:
~ all before one	sehr erfolgreich sein
~ away	die Beherrschung verlieren
~ conviction	überzeugend sein
~ coals to Newcastle (Brit.)	Eulen nach Athen tragen
~ the day	den Sieg davontragen
~ the point	jdn. überzeugen
~ a torch for s.o.	für jdn. schmachten

~ on	1. sich aufführen, 2. weitermachen
1. Jane, stop carrying on like that, you ought to be ashamed of yourself.	
2. Carry on, you're doing just fine!	
~ one's point	andere von seiner Meinung überzeugen
~ s.b. shoulder-high	jdn. auf Händen tragen
~ s.th. too far	es zu weit treiben
~ weight	wichtig sein, Einfluss haben
There's no need to worry about John. What he says carries no weight.	
put the cart before the horse	das Pferd von hinten aufzäumen

case:

as the ~ may be	je nachdem
in any ~	wie dem auch sein mag, in jedem Fall
in ~	im Falle, dass; falls
just in ~	für alle Fälle; nur für den Fall, dass

cash:

be out of ~	nicht gut bei Kasse sein
~ a cheque	einen Scheck einlösen
~ down	Anzahlung
~ in on s.th.	aus etw. Kapital schlagen
for ~	gegen bar

cat:

Has the ~ got your tongue?	Hat es dir die Sprache verschlagen?
have a ~ nap	ein Nickerchen machen
let the ~ out of the bag	ein Geheimnis lüften, die Katze aus dem Sack lassen
put the ~ among the pigeons	Unruhe stiften, für Aufregung sorgen, Wirbel machen
rain ~s end dogs	wie aus Eimern schütten
wait for the ~ to jump	abwarten, wie der Hase läuft

catch:
~ a cold	sich erkälten
~ it	1. etwas verstehen, mitbekommen 2. Ärger kriegen

1. I didn't catch what he was saying.
2. If you are late again, you will catch it for sure!

~ a few rays (Sl.)	sich die Sonne auf den Bauch scheinen lassen.
~ a packet (Sl.)	sein Fett abkriegen
~ at straws	nach jedem Strohhalm greifen
~ me!	Das fällt mir nicht ein!
~ one's death of cold (Sl.)	sich den Tod holen
~ on (Sl.)	gut ankommen, populär werden
~ one's breath	verschnaufen; (vor Schreck) die Luft anhalten
~ sight of s.th.	etwas erblicken
~ s.o.'s eye	die Aufmerksamkeit auf sich lenken

The toy tractor caught the little boy's eye.

~ s.o. out	jdn. erwischen
~ s.o. red-handed	jdn. in flagranti erwischen
~ up with s.o.	jdn. einholen

cause:
~ a ripple	Wellen schlagen
~ a stir	Aufsehen erregen

certain:
make ~	sich vergewissern
That's for ~.	Das ist sicher.

A chain is only as strong as its weakest link. (Sprichw.)
Eine Kette ist nur so stark wie ihr schwächstes Glied.

as different as chalk and cheese
so verschieden sein wie Tag und Nacht

The brothers are as different as chalk and cheese.

chance:
~ acquaintance	Zufallsbekanntschaft
~ upon s.th/s.o.	etwas/jdn. zufällig finden
~ would be a fine thing	Schön wär's!
~ one's luck	sein Glück herausfordern
He never takes a ~.	Er geht nie ein Risiko ein.
stand a fair ~	eine gute Chance haben

change:
~ hands	den Besitzer wechseln, weitergegeben werden

That shop only ever changed hands once.

~ one's mind	es sich anders überlegen, die Meinung ändern
~ one's colour	erröten
~ course	die Richtung wechseln
~ and decay	natürlicher Verfall der Dinge
~ the face of s.th.	etwas grundlegend verändern
~ gear	die Taktik ändern, das Thema wechseln
~ horses in mid-stream	plötzlich einen anderen Kurs einschlagen
a ~ of heart	Sinneswandel
the ~ of life	Wechseljahre
~ one's tune	seine Ansichten ändern, andere Töne anschlagen

You'll soon change your tune when you hear what is in store for you.

~ one's ways	seinen Lebenswandel ändern
small ~	Wechselgeld

chapter:
~ of accidents	eine Reihe von Unfällen
give ~ and verse	genau oder sehr ausführlich zitieren

charge:
be in ~ of	der Chef sein, die Verantwortung haben
~ $ 5 for	$ 5 berechnen für
free of ~	kostenlos

~ s.th. to s.o. or s.th. *She charged her new car to her father.*	etwas auf Rechnung anderer kaufen
Charity begins at home. (Sprichw.)	Jeder ist sich selbst der Nächste.
chatter like a magpie	geschwätzig sein wie eine Elster
cheap at the price	der Preis ist angemessen
check: ~ **in** ~ **up** *The police are checking up on what we told them.*	(im Hotel) einchecken überprüfen
cheek: ~ **by jowl** **What a ~!**	eng zusammen, nebeneinander Was für eine Frechheit!
cheer: ~ **s.o. up** ~ **up!**	jdn. aufheitern Kopf hoch!
a chequered career	eine bewegte Laufbahn
chest: **get s.th. off one's ~** (Brit.) *Thank goodness I've told you. I've been wanting to get that off my chest for a long time.*	sich etwas von der Seele reden
chew: ~ **the cud** ~ **the fat** ~ **over s.th.** (Sl.)	wiederkäuen ein Schwätzchen halten etwas diskutieren, über etwas nachdenken
chicken: **~-feed** (Am./Sl.) *The cost will be chicken-feed in comparison to the gains.*	Peanuts, vernachlässigbar

~ out of s.th. (Sl.)	einen Rückzieher machen, abhauen

It's no good trying to chicken out now, you have agreed to the plan.

count one's ~ before they're hatched	den Tag vor dem Abend loben, sich zu früh freuen

child:
a ~ in such matters	unerfahren, naiv
~'s play	ein Kinderspiel
a chink in one's armour	jds. Schwachstelle, wunder Punkt

chip:
be a ~ off the old block (Sl.)	Der Apfel fällt nicht weit vom Stamm.
have a ~ on one's shoulder	einen Komplex haben
have had one's ~s (Sl.)	erledigt sein, ausgedient haben
chock-a-block	randvoll
chocolate box	ästhetisch angenehm, aber ohne Tiefgang; niedlich

Her pictures are quite nice, pleasant and unoffensive in a chocolate box sort of way.

choice:
have Hobson's ~	überhaupt keine Wahl haben
take one's ~	seine Wahl treffen

chop:
~ and change	rein in die Kartoffeln, raus aus den Kartoffeln
to get the ~	gefeuert werden
chuck it (Sl.)	etwas (hin)schmeißen
be back in circulation	wieder mitmischen
a city slicker (Sl.)	schlitzohriger Großstädter
civvy street (militärischer Sl.)	Zivilleben

clap:

~ eyes on	zu Gesicht bekommen
I haven't clapped eyes on him for several weeks.	
~-trap	Geschwätz
a clarion call for liberty	ein Ruf nach Freiheit
class distinctions	gesellschaftliche Unterschiede, Klassenunterschiede

clean:

be ~ out of s.th. (Am./Sl.)	gerade eben ausverkauft sein
~ forget	etwas vollkommen vergessen
make a ~ sweep	reinen Tisch machen
Cleanliness is next to godliness. (Sprichw.)	Ordnung ist das halbe Leben.

clear:

~ cut	scharf umrissen, eindeutig
with a ~ conscience	mit gutem Gewissen
~ as crystal	ganz offensichtlich
Jack's reason for going to London is as clear as crystal.	
~ the decks	klar Schiff machen
~ of	frei von
The river is clear of weeds and fun to swim in.	
~ off	weggehen, abhauen
~ one's character	jds. Unschuld beweisen
~ one's conscience	Buße tun, sein Gewissen erleichtern
~ one's throat	sich räuspern
~ the air	Missverständnisse aus dem Weg räumen
~ s.th. up	1. deutlich und klar machen, 2. aufräumen
1. I am trying to clear up the misunderstanding.	
2. You'll have to clear up your room before you invite your friends.	
~ up	schöner werden (Wetter)

clench

*The weather has cleared up.
we can go for a walk.*
to be in the ~ (Sl.) — von einem Verdacht befreit sein

The coast is ~. — Die Luft ist rein.

clench one's teeth — die Zähne zusammenbeißen

clever dick — Klugscheißer

click:
~ one's heels — die Hacken zusammenschlagen
~ one's tongue — mit der Zunge schnalzen

climate of opinion — die allgemeine Stimmung

climb the wall — die Wände hochgehen

clinch a deal — ein Geschäft abschließen

clip s.b.'s wings — jdm. die Flügel stutzen

cloak and dagger — geheimnisumwittert, mysteriös
He joined the intelligence services expecting a lot of cloak and dagger events, but was disappointed by the seriousness of the work.

clock:
It worked like ~work. — Es lief wie am Schnürchen.
work against the ~ — gegen die Uhr arbeiten

close:
a ~d book — ein Buch mit sieben Siegeln, unverständlich, ein Rätsel

Physics is a closed book to me.
behind ~d doors — hinter verschlossenen Türen
~ one's eyes to s.th. — die Augen vor etwas verschließen

be ~ at hand — in der Nähe sein
~ in on — umzingeln
the days ~ in — die Tage werden kürzer
~ on — dicht bei

at ~ quarters	dicht dran, nahe
~ **up shop** (Sl.)	Feierabend machen
It's six o'clock, time to close up shop for today.	
That was a ~ shave! (Sl.)	Das ging glimpflich aus.
That was a close shave! The van nearly ran you over.	

cloud:
~ **one's brain**	verwirren
a ~ on the horizon	dunkle Wolken am Horizont
in the ~s	in Gedanken
under a ~	mit angeschlagenem Ruf/Ansehen

live in clover	wie Gott in Frankreich leben

not have a clue	keine Ahnung haben
I haven't a clue where he is, ask his mother.	

turn one's coat	sein Fähnchen nach dem Winde drehen

The cobbler should stick to his last. (Sprichw.)	Schuster, bleib bei deinem Leisten.

cock:
~ **of the walk**	Hahn im Korb
~ **one's ear**	die Ohren spitzen
~**-and-bull story**	Lügengeschichte

coffee-table book	Bildband

cog in the machine	ein Rädchen im Getriebe

coin:
~ **money**	Geld scheffeln
I would not exactly say we are coining money, but we are doing okay so far.	
pay s.b. back in his own ~	es jdm. mit gleicher Münze heimzahlen
the other side of the ~	die Kehrseite der Medaille

cold:
in ~ blood	kaltblütig, absichtlich
~ comfort	(iron.) schwacher Trost
a ~ fish	eine kalte, unemotionale Person
a ~ fury	kontrollierte Wut
~ hands and a warm heart. (Sprichw.)	Wer kalte Hände hat, der hat ein warmes Herz.
give s.b. the ~ shoulder	jdm. die kalte Schulter zeigen
a ~ snap	Kälteeinbruch
the Cold War	der Kalte Krieg
throw ~ water on s.th.	die Begeisterung dämpfen

collar and tie	ordentlich angezogen
collect one's wits	seine fünf Sinne zusammennehmen

colour:
come through with flying ~s	einen glänzenden Sieg erringen
have a high ~	rot im Gesicht sein
off ~	nicht ganz fit
show one's true ~s	Farbe bekennen
~ up	rot werden

come:
~ about	sich ereignen
~ across	1. überqueren, 2. finden, zufällig treffen

1. He came across the road to greet me.
2. Tidying up my room, I came across a couple of old love letters.

~ again? (Sl.)	Wie bitte?
~ alive	munter werden
~ along!	Beeil dich!
~ amiss	ungeeignet sein
~ apart at the seams (Sl.)	die Selbstbeherrschung verlieren, ausrasten
~ clean (Sl.)	alles beichten
~ a cropper	stolpern, einen massiven Rückschlag erleiden
~ down on s.o. like a ton of bricks (Sl.)	jdm. über den Mund fahren
~ down with s.th.	an etwas erkranken

John is coming down with the flu, he must go to bed.
~ and go	gelegentlich, mal so, mal so
~ in handy (Sl.)	nützlich sein
~ hell or high water	egal, wie schwer es sein mag
~ into line with	übereinstimmen mit
~ into the open	offenbaren, mit etwas herausrücken

You must come into the open and say what you really think.
~ off it (Sl.)	Sag die Wahrheit, tu nicht so.
~ rain, ~ shine	unter allen Umständen
~ round	das Bewusstsein wiedererlangen
~ to a bad end	ein böses Ende nehmen
~ to blows	sich schlagen

The two brothers came to blows over the girl.
~ to grief	Pech/Unglück haben

He was learning to skate but came to grief at the corner.
~ to nothing	Es wird nichts daraus.
~ to one's senses	wieder zu sich kommen
~ to s.b.'s help	jdm. zu Hilfe kommen
~ to the point	zur Sache kommen

Come to the point, I can't wait all day.
~ to a head	sich zuspitzen (Situation)
~ to think of it	wenn ich es mir so überlege
~ unstuck	schiefgehen
~ up in the world	es zu etwas bringen

Since I started my new job I've really come up in the world.
~ up with s.th.	etwas vorschlagen, sich etwas einfallen lassen

It was Joseph who came up with the idea of moving house.
~ what may	komme was wolle

comic:
~ opera	eine Farce

common:
~ decency	Anstand

compliment	**50**

the ~ good	Gemeinwohl
~ ground	gemeinsame Basis
~ herd	die Masse, der Pöbel
~ knowledge	Allgemeinwissen
~ sense	gesunder Menschenverstand
have s.th. in ~ with	etwas gemeinsam haben mit

compliment:
return the ~	das Kompliment erwidern
fish for ~s	nach Komplimenten fischen, Komplimente erheischen wollen
~s of the season	Grüße zu Weihnachten und zum neuen Jahr

condition:
on ~ that ...	unter der Bedingung, dass ...
I'll come on condition that I receive a proper invitation.	
out of ~	in schlechter Verfassung

con trick	Schwindel, Beschiss

confirm:
~ one's worst fears	die schlimmsten Befürchtungen bestätigen
~ed bachelor	überzeugter Junggeselle

confound the prophets	sich entgegen aller Vorhersagen als erfolgreich erweisen
confusion reigns	es herrscht Chaos
conk out (Sl.)	ohnmächtig werden, einschlafen
be well-connected	gute Beziehungen haben
one's conscience pricks one	man fühlt sich schuldig
conspicuous by one's absence	durch Abwesenheit glänzen
contain oneself	sich beherrschen, den Ausdruck starker Emotionen unterdrücken

contradiction in terms	Widerspruch in sich
conversation piece	Ein ungewöhnliches Objekt, das oft zu Gesprächen Anlass gibt; Gesprächsentzünder

cook:
~ **the books** (Brit.)	Bücher fälschen
~ **s.o.'s goose**	jdn. ins Verderben stürzen

That's the way the cookie crumbles. (Am./Sl.)	Das ist der Lauf der Welt.

cool:
~**, calm and collected**	vollkommen beruhigt, gelassen
~ **customer** (Sl.)	ein souveräner Typ, ein gerissener Kerl
~ **it!** (Am./Sl.)/**Keep ~!** (Brit./Sl.)	Beruhige dich!
~ **off**	abkühlen
~ **down**	abkühlen, sich beruhigen
to let s.o. ~ **his heels**	jdn. warten lassen

cop it	in Schwierigkeiten kommen, bestraft werden
cops and robbers	Räuber und Gendarm
to cope with s.th.	mit etwas klar kommen
corner the market	den Markt beherrschen

The American companies cornered the market in modern art ages ago.

corridors of power	die Zirkel der Macht in Regierungen, Industrie etc.

cost:
at all ~**s**	um jeden Preis
to know to one's ~	aus eigener Erfahrung wissen
~ **a packet** (Am./Sl.)	extrem teuer sein
~ **s.b. dear**	jdn. teuer zu stehen kommen

His absent-mindedness cost him dear when he missed the exam date by mistake.

cough s.th. up. (Sl.)	mit etwas herausrücken
could:	
~ go s.th.?	Hättest du gerne ...?
I am parched – could you go a cup of tea?	
~ cheerfully murder s.b.	wirklich sauer auf jdn. sein
~ swear that	sich ganz sicher sein, dass ...; man hätte geschworen, dass, ...
couldn't:	
~ agree more!	Ganz deiner Meinung!
~ care less!	Das ist mir so etwas von egal!
count:	
~ against s.th.	gegen etwas sprechen
lose ~ of	sich verzählen, den Überblick verlieren
~ on s.b.	auf jdn. zählen
~ s.b. in	jdn. dazuzählen, jdn. beteiligen an
~ me out! (Sl.)	Ohne mich!
~ one's blessings	sich darüber im Klaren sein, wie gut es einem geht
~ the cost	die Vor-und Nachteile gegeneinander abwägen
~ the days	die Tage zählen
~ the pennies	genau rechnen, (häufig auch:) geizig sein
~ sheep	Schäfchen zählen
a country cousin	ein Landei
course:	
in due ~	zu gegebener Zeit
in the ~ of time	im Laufe der Zeit
of ~	natürlich
stay the ~	durchhalten
take it's~	seinen Lauf nehmen
~ of action	weitere Vorgehensweise
~ of history	der Ablauf der Ereignisse
The decision not to sign the treaty after all changed the course of history.	

~ of justice	rechtliche Regeln und Abläufe
to court death	mit seinem Leben spielen
send s.o. to Coventry	jdn. gesellschaftlich ächten/ schneiden

cover:
~ a lot of ground	1. weit herumkommen, 2. umfassend sein

1. We covered a lot of ground during our holiday in France.
2. His talk covered a lot of ground.

~ for s.o.	jdn. schützen
~ one's tracks	seine Spuren verwischen
from ~ to ~	von Anfang bis Ende (Buch)

crack:
~ a bottle	eine Flasche köpfen
~ a joke	einen Witz erzählen, einen Witz reißen
~ down on s.o.	jdm. gegenüber hart sein
to get ~ing (Sl.)	loslegen
He is ~ing up. (Sl.)	Er dreht durch.

crackerjack	Knaller, Bombe
crafty as a cartload of monkeys	sehr raffiniert
to cramp s.b.'s style	jdm. im Weg sein

I was overjoyed at seeing her, at the same time her parents' presence rather cramped my style.

a crash course	eine kompakte Unterweisung in kurzer Zeit, Crashkurs

create:
~ a bad impression	einen schlechten Eindruck machen
~ hell/murder	Ärger machen
creature comforts	leibliches Wohl

credibility gap
The credibility gap opened up by his report was widening all the time.

Glaubwürdigkeitslücke

to be up the creek

in Schwierigkeiten sein

creep:
~ and crawl
~ing paralysis

sich unterwürfig benehmen
schleichende Lähmung, Erstarrung

to give s.o. the ~s

jdn. nervös machen

Crime doesn't pay. (Sprichw.)

Verbrechen zahlt sich nicht aus.

crocodile tears

Krokodilstränen

cross:
~ a person's path
~ s.b.'s palm with silver

jdm. in die Quere kommen
jdm. Geld geben (für Gefälligkeiten)

He crossed the fortune teller's palm with silver.

~ a bridge when one comes to it

ein Problem lösen

I can't make up my mind on that point now, we'll cross that bridge when we come to it.

~ one's mind
~ one's fingers
~ the Great Divide
~ my heart and hope to die!

einfallen
Daumen drücken
sterben
Ich schwöre es!

to crown it all

der krönende Abschluss

crowning success

die beste Leistung, Glanzleistung

when the crunch comes

wenn es wirklich ernst wird

to have a crush on s.b.

verknallt sein

the crux of the matter

das wesentlichste Problem

cry:	
~ for the moon	das Unmögliche wollen, nach den Sternen greifen
~ havoc	verwüsten, rücksichtslos gegen jdn. vorgehen
~ one's heart out	sich die Augen ausweinen
~ o.s. to sleep	sich in den Schlaf weinen
~ing over spilt milk	wegen etwas weinen, das nicht zu ändern ist; sich ärgern
~ wolf	falschen Alarm auslösen
crystal clear	glasklar, offensichtlich
a cuckoo in the nest	ein Kuckucksei
off the cuff	improvisiert
a culture vulture	Kulturfanatiker(in)
cup:	
s.b.'s ~ of tea	jds. Fall/Ding sein
Frankly, cricket has never been my cup of tea.	
the ~ that cheers (but not inebriates)	Tee
The cure is worse than the disease. (Sprichw.)	das Mittel ist oft schlimmer als die Krankheit; die Mittel zur Lösung eines Problems sind schlimmer als das Problem selbst
The proponents of the return of capital punishment have clearly failed to grasp that the cure may well be worse than the disease.	
Curiosity killed the cat. (Sprichw.)	Frag nicht so viel! Zu große Neugier treibt den Vogel in die Schlinge
a curtain lecture	Gardinenpredigt
The customer is always right. (Sprichw.)	Der Kunde ist König.

cut:
~ **a fine figure** — gut aussehen, elegant sein
~ **and dried** — 1. nicht besonders aufregend, trocken, 2. geplant, vorbereitet

1. His speech was very cut and dried, there was nothing new in it.
2. His plans for leaving were all cut end dried.

~ **and thrust** — schneller Austausch von Argumenten

A lawyer needs to be quick-witted to survive the cut and thrust of the courtroom.

~ **back on s.th.** — einschränken, sparen
When the economy is weak the government must cut back on its spending.

~ **in on s.o.** — jdn. unterbrechen
~ **it rather fine** — es gerade noch schaffen
~ **off one's nose to spite one's face** (Sprichw.) — sich ins eigene Fleisch schneiden
But you love going to the theatre! If you don't go just because you are angry, it'll be cutting off your nose to spite your face.

~ **one's cables** — seine Verbindungen beenden
~ **s.o. dead** — jdn. links liegen lassen, jdn. schneiden

be ~ **out for s.th.** — das Zeug zu etwas haben, für etwas wie geschaffen sein

~ **s.o/s.th. off short** — unterbrechen
~ **s.o. to the quick** — jdn. zutiefst verletzen
~ **no ice** (Sl.) — keine Wirkung haben, keinen Einfluss haben

It ~**s both ways.** — Es hat seine Vor- und Nachteile.
a ~ **above s.o.** (Sl.) — etwas Besseres
a short ~ — eine Abkürzung
It is 3 miles to school by road, but there is a short cut through the park.

D

be a dab hand at s.th. — in etwas besonders tüchtig sein

dagger:
look ~s at s.o. (Sl.) — jdn. mit Blicken töten
at ~s drawn — auf Kriegsfuß stehen, in einem Zustand der offenen Feindschaft

damage:
the ~ is done — das ist nicht mehr zu ändern
What's the ~? — Was kostet der Spaß?

damn:
~ all — absolut nichts; so wenig, dass es der Erwähnung nicht lohnt

He got damn all for his last job, so no wonder he's bitter about the company!

~ and blast! — Verflucht noch eins!
not to give a ~ — sich den Teufel um etwas scheren

I'll be ~ed if I'll ... — Ich denke nicht im Traum daran, ... zu tun

a damp squib — ein Reinfall

dance:
~ attendance — jdn. den Hof machen
~ to s.b.'s tune — nach der Pfeife von jdm. tanzen

Darby end Joan — ein liebevolles verheiratetes (meist nicht mehr ganz junges) Paar

Say what you like about the Dellameres, I always feel they are a perfect Darby and Joan.

dark:
in the ~ — im Ungewissen
I am completely in the dark concerning his plans.
a ~ horse — ein unbeschriebenes Blatt
I don't know much about John, he's a bit of a dark horse.
a leap in the ~ — ein Sprung ins kalte Wasser
Starting a new job in a foreign country is always a leap in the dark.
keep s.th. ~ — etwas geheim halten

(not) to darken s.b.'s door again — jds. Haus (nie) wieder betreten

dash:
~ s.o.'s hopes — Hoffnungen enttäuschen/ zerschlagen
Failing the exam dashed all his hopes of getting a good job.
~ it all! (Sl.) — Verflucht! Verflixt!
~ to pieces — in Stücke schlagen
~ s.th. off — schnell schreiben, schnell erledigen
I'm in a hurry but must just dash off a quick note to my parents.
make a ~ for s.th. — sich stürzen auf, losstürmen

date:
be up to ~ — modern sein, auf dem neuesten Stand sein
~ back to — 1. auf eine Zeit zurückgehen, 2. herrühren
1. This cupboard dates back to the 17th century.
2. His limp dates back to his accident.

Davy Jones's locker — die See als Grab
After all his time at sea he ended up in Davy Jones's locker after all.

dawn:
~ on s.o. — jdm. klar werden

When will it dawn on him that he is talking a lot of nonsense?
the ~ chorus — das Singen der Vögel am Morgen

day:
~ of ~s — ein spezieller Tag
at the end of the ~ — schließlich
every other ~ — jeden zweiten Tag
fall on evil ~s — eine Pechsträhne haben

have a ~ off — einen freien Tag haben
Let's call it a ~! — Schluss für heute! Feierabend!
I'm feeling very tired, let's call it a day and go home.
make one's ~ — jdn. glücklich machen
My ~ is done. — Meine Zeit ist vorbei.
one of these ~s — bald, in den nächsten Tagen
see better ~s — bessere Zeiten sehen (fast immer in der Vergangenheit)

The motorcycle had obviously seen better days.
This is not my ~. — Das ist heute nicht mein Tag.
the other ~ — neulich, vor kurzem
this ~ week — heute in einer Woche
this ~ last week — heute vor einer Woche
to the ~ — auf den Tag genau
~ after ~ — täglich, Tag für Tag
~ in and ~ out — den lieben langen Tag, dauernd

daylight robbery — überhöhte Preise

dead:
a ~ loss — ein hoffnungsloser Fall
~ and alive — leblos, desinteressiert
~ and gone — seit langem tot
as ~ as a doornail (Brit.) — mausetot
in the ~ of the night — mitten in der Nacht
The burglers came in the dead of the night.
~ and buried — tot und begraben, aus und vorbei
That kind of idea is dead and buried.

deaf

a ~ certainty	eine absolut sichere Sache
~ easy	kinderleicht
~ on one's feet	erschöpft
~ tired/beat	todmüde
~ men (Sl.)	leere Flaschen
~ from the neck up	dumm, desinteressiert
~ letter	ein unzustellbarer Brief
~pan	ausdruckslos, ohne sichtbare Reaktion
be ~ to the world	tief und fest schlafen

You must give him a shake to wake him, he's dead to the world.

~ to s.th.	von etwas nicht betroffen
a ~ weight	eine schwere Bürde
~ to the wide	physisch erschöpft
~ wood	nicht mehr in Gebrauch, veraltet, nutzlos
over my ~ body	nur aber meine Leiche

If that dog comes into the house again, it will be over my dead body.

deaf:

~ and dumb	taubstumm
turn a ~ ear to s.th.	sich einer Sache gegenüber taub stellen

My mother turned a deaf ear to my pleas for a new dress.

be ~ as a post	stocktaub sein

It's not good shouting at grandfather, he's as deaf as a post.

deal:

It's a ~! (Am./Sl.)	Abgemacht!
~ a blow	einen Schlag versetzen
a great ~ of	eine ganze Menge von
~ in s.th.	mit etwas handeln
~ with	sich befassen mit, etwas erledigen

The Managing Director always deals with his post himself.

It's your ~.	Du bist dran (die Karten zu geben).
no big ~	keine große Sache, unwichtig

dear:
~ knows	niemand weiß
~ me	Oh je!
~ to s.b.'s heart	von jdm. sehr geliebt oder geschätzt

death:
one's ~ agony	Todeskampf
~ bed	Sterbebett
~ comes to us all (Sprichw.)	Einmal muss jeder gehen.
at ~'s door	den Tod vor Augen

The priest was called in as the patient was obviously at death's door.

bore s.o. to ~	jdn. tödlich langweilen
~ warrant	(schriftliches) Todesurteil
to look like ~ warmed up	wie eine wandelnde Leiche aussehen
~ on s.o./s.th. (Am./Sl.)	1. sehr effektiv gegen jdn./etwas, 2. gut/geschickt

1. This new cleaning fluid is just death on all stains.
2. He's just death on the tennis court.

a decent sort — ein anständiger Kerl

decide in favour of s.o/s.th. — sich für jdn./eine Sache entscheiden

decline:
~ and fall	Aufstieg und Niedergang
~ing years	hohes Alter

deep:
~ in thought	in Gedanken versunken
be in ~ waters	das Wasser bis zum Hals stehen haben
to go off the ~ end	sich aufregen

defeat one's purpose — ein beabsichtigtes Ergebnis stören

deliver the goods	tun, was von einem erwartet wird
delusions of grandeur	Größenwahn
demean oneself *Much as John annoyed me, I was determined not to demean myself by replying in kind.*	sich erniedrigen
den:	
a ~ **of iniquity**	ein Sündenpfuhl
a ~ **of thieves**	eine Räuberhöhle
get out of one's depth *The student was out of his depth in discussions on the Middle Ages.*	unsicher werden, ins Schwimmen kommen
dereliction of duty	Pflichtvergessenheit
have designs on s.o.	Absichten in Bezug auf jdn. haben
Desperate diseases require desperate remedies. (Sprichw.)	Der Zweck heiligt die Mittel.
devil:	
The ~ **makes work for idle hands.** (Sprichw.)	Müßiggang ist aller Laster Anfang.
be between the ~ and the deep blue sea	in der Klemme sitzen, zwischen Hölle und Fegefeuer
The ~ **one knows is better than the ~ one doesn't know.** (Sprichw.)	Besser ein bekanntes als ein unbekanntes Übel.
The ~ **looks after his own.**	Diejenigen, die es am wenigsten verdienen, haben das meiste Glück.
a ~ **with women**	ein Schürzenjäger
devoid of s.th.	ohne etwas

devotion to duty	Pflichtbewusstsein
dice are loaded against s.o.	jds. Chancen sind gering
did he fall or was he pushed? (iron.)	War er selbst schuld an seinem Unglück oder hat jmd. nachgeholfen?

die:
Never say ~! Nur nicht verzweifeln!
Nur nicht nachgeben!

to be dying for s.th. sich nach etwas sehnen, auf etwas brennen

~ hard trotz Widerstand bestehen bleiben

~ off 1. dahinsterben, 2. verschwinden, nachlassen

1. The trees in the wood are dying off.
2. The pain is dying off.

~ away sich legen/beruhigen
The wind is gradually dying away.

dig:
~ a pit jdm. eine Grube graben
~ in 1. (sich) eingraben, 2. sich einstellen auf (Sl.), 3. essen, 4. eine Sache anpacken

1. The wind was so cold the hikers had to dig in for the night halfway up the mountain.
2. We have a lot of points to discuss, better dig in for a long meeting.
3. The hungry man helped himself to a plate of food and dug in.
4. If you're worried about the project's outcome just go ahead and dig in!

~ s.o./s.th. (Am./Sl.) jdn./etwas mögen
I don't dig that kind of thing at all.

~ s.th. up 1. herauskramen, 2. aufstöbern, 3. finden

*1. Now where did you dig up
that piece of gossip?
2. I dug up a recipe for quiche
for a friend of mine.
3. Your boyfriend is very good-
looking. Where did you dig him up?*

a ding-dong (Sl.)	eine hitzige oder gewalttätige Auseinandersetzung
dip into one's pocket	in die Tasche greifen
dirt:	
throw ~ at s.b.	jdn. mit Schmutz bewerfen

*The election campaign was unfair.
A lot of dirt was thrown at the
candidate.*

treat s.b. like ~   jdn. wie Dreck behandeln

*My uncle is very unfair to my aunt.
He treats her like dirt.*

dirty:
to play a ~ trick on s.o.	jdn. reinlegen
a ~ word	ein Fluch oder eine Obszönität
~ works at the crossroads	unangenehme Arbeit, auch: Betrug
one's disappearing act	sich vor etwas drücken, aus dem Staub machen

*Now that I have time to take the
dog for a walk, that animal has
done the disappearing act again!*

Discretion is the better part of valour. (Sprichw.)	Vorsicht ist besser als Nachsicht.
a dismal failure	eine totale Enttäuschung
a displaced person	ein Flüchtling
keep s.b. at a distance	jdn. auf Distanz halten

*A pretty woman will always
have difficulty keeping men
at a distance.*

do:

~ a flip-flop on s.th. (Am.) — die Meinung ändern
The opposition accused the minister of doing a flip-flop too often.

~ away with — aus dem Weg räumen, beseitigen, töten
The murderer didn't know how to do away with the body.

to be ~ne for — erledigt sein
~ in (Sl.) — töten, um die Ecke bringen
~ s.th. (Sl.) — etwas verkaufen
~ s.th. up — etwas renovieren, in Ordnung bringen
~ well with s.b. — gut mit jdm. auskommen
Other people don't like the boss but I do quite well with him.

nothing ~ing — nichts zu machen
I could ~ with — ich könnte ... gut brauchen
That will ~. — Das geht. Das genügt.
That will do, John. You've had enough ice-cream for today.

That's easier said than done. — Das ist leichter gesagt als getan.
~ one's (level) best — sein Bestes geben
~ one's own thing (Sl.) — tun was man mag/will
I hate doing things with the crowd, I like to do my own thing.

~ one's bit (Sl.) — seinen Teil erledigen, seine Pflicht tun
~ s.th. the hard way — etwas ungeschickt anstellen
Don't try to hit that nail in with your shoe, that's doing it the hard way.

~ the dishes — abspülen
~ s.th. up — etwas reparieren
don't let s.o./s.th. get you down — Lass dich von niemandem/nichts kleinkriegen

Don't look a gift horse in the mouth. (Sprichw.) — Einem geschenkten Gaul schaut man nicht ins Maul.
~s and donts — Regeln, Richtlinien

dodge the issues — die Auseinandersetzung mit einem Problem vermeiden

dog:
the ~ days	die heißen Tage im Sommer
~-eared	Eselsohren, geknickte Ecken in Buch- oder Heftseiten o. ä.
~ eat ~	rücksichtsloser Konkurrenzkampf
Every ~ has its day.	Ein blindes Huhn findet auch einmal ein Korn.
go to the ~s (Sl.)	vor die Hunde gehen
a ~s dinner	in Unordnung
lead a ~'s life	ein Hundeleben führen
Let sleeping ~s lie.	Schlafende Hunde soll man nicht wecken.

a Don Juan — ein Herzensbrecher

donkey's years — lange Zeit

dot:
~ and carry	sich mühsam oder unsicher bewegen
~ the i's (and cross the t's)	sehr sorgfältig sein
on the ~	auf die Sekunde genau

double:
a ~ agent	ein Doppelagent
~ quick	so schnell wie möglich

doubt:
beyond a ~/without a ~ — zweifellos
Without a doubt, that's the best cake I have ever tasted.
in ~ — unsicher
If in doubt, follow your instincts.
shadow of a ~ — leichte Ungewissheit
The judge said he did not have a shadow of a doubt about the prisoner's guilt.

down:
~ and out	fertig sein
~ at (the) heel(s)	schäbig, heruntergekommen
~ in the dumps (Sl.)	traurig, deprimiert

When you're feeling down in the dumps, the best thing to do is treat yourself to something.
~ on one's luck — vom Pech verfolgt sein
go ~ the drain — in die Binsen gehen, für die Katz' sein

~ to earth — mit beiden Beinen auf dem Boden
to be ~ to s.o. (Sl.) — für jdn. zuständig sein
have a ~ on s.b. — jdn. auf dem Kieker haben
He's had a down on me ever since I won the prize.
~ memory lane — nostalgische Erinnerungen
a ~ payment — eine Anzahlung
~ tools — mit einer Arbeit aufhören, häufig: zu Beginn eines Streiks

drag:
~ one's feet — sich dahinschleppen, langsam machen

If you drag your feet you'll not get the contract.
~ s.th. out — in die Länge ziehen
~ on — (sich) in die Länge ziehen
The talk was boring and dragged on for hours.

down the drain — im Eimer

draw:
~ in one's horns (Sl.) — sich krumm legen müssen, sparen
~ a blank — eine Niete ziehen, nicht weiterkommen
~ one's last breath — seinen letzten Atemzug tun
~ s.b.'s attention to — jds. Aufmerksamkeit lenken auf
~ s.b. into s.th. — jdn. in eine Sache hineinziehen
~ the line at — die Grenze ziehen bei
~ s.th. to a close — etwas zu Ende bringen, beschließen

back to the ~ing board — nochmal von vorne
The days are ~ing in. — Die Tage werden kürzer.
~ it mild — sein Benehmen oder seine Aussagen mäßigen

~ a moral	eine Lehre aus etwas ziehen
~ s.b.'s teeth	jdm. die Mittel nehmen, mit denen er Schaden anrichten könnte

dread the moment   ein Ereignis mit Schrecken erwarten

dress:
~ing-down	eine Standpauke
~ed to kill (Sl.)	aufgetakelt wie eine Fregatte, sehr fein angezogen, herausgeputzt
~ the part	sich passend für einen Anlass kleiden
~ rehearsal	Generalprobe

in dribs and drabs   tropfenweise, häppchenweise

drink:
~ the cup of sorrow	großes Leid ertragen
~ like a fish	wie ein Loch saufen

drive:
~ a hard bargain	harte Bedingungen stellen
~ a wedge between	einen Keil treiben zwischen
~ into a corner	in die Ecke treiben
~ to despair	zur Verzweiflung bringen
~ s.o. nuts (Am./Sl.)	jdn. wahnsinnig machen

The sound of his voice is driving me nuts.

~ s.o. crazy/mad/potty (Brit./Sl.)	jdn. auf die Palme bringen
~ at s.th.	auf etwas hinauswollen

You know what I'm driving at.

~ s.th. home to s.o.	jdm. etwas klar machen
~ s.o. up the wall (Sl.)	jdn. verrückt machen

One day, all my troubles will drive me up the wall.

drop:
~ by ~	tropfenweise
~ by	vorbeischauen
~ in	unerwartet vorbeikommen
~ it! (Sl.)	Lass das!

a ~ in the ocean	ein Tropfen auf dem heißen Stein
~ a brick (Sl.)	ins Fettnäpfchen treten
~ names	in penetranter Weise mit sozialen Kontakten angeben
~ dead! (Sl.)	Scher dich zum Teufel!
~ off (to sleep)	einnicken, einschlafen
~ s.o.	jdn. fallen lassen
~ s.o. a line	jdm. schreiben
~ one's aitches (Sl.)	das „H" beim Sprechen unterdrücken (Zeichen einer niedrigen sozialen Herkunft)

drown one's sorrows (Sl.)   die Probleme im Alkohol ertränken

John is trying to drown his sorrows with a bottle of whisky.

a drug on the market   ein schwer verkäuflicher Artikel

drum s.th. into s.b.   jdm. etwas einhämmern

as drunk as a lord (Sl.)   stockbesoffen, sternhagelvoll

dry:
~ up! (Sl.)	Halts Maul!
a ~ run	ein Probedurchlauf, Test

duck:
take to s.th. like a ~ to water	in seinem Element sein
like a dying ~ in a thunderstorm (Brit./Sl.)	wie der Ochse vor dem Berg, keine Ahnung haben

due:
~ to	aufgrund
give the devil his ~	dem Kaiser geben, was des Kaisers ist
in ~ time	zur rechten Zeit

stand there like a stuffed dummy (Sl.)   wie Ölgötzen dastehen

to dump s.o.	jdn. loswerden
dust:	
~ **of ages**	die zerstörerischen Effekte der vergehenden Zeit
bite the ~ (Sl.)	ins Gras beißen
throw ~ **in s.o.'s eyes**	jdm. Sand in die Augen streuen
Dutch:	
~ **courage** (Sl.)	angetrunkener Mut
He had a couple of drinks at the bar to give him Dutch courage to face his wife.	
to go ~	eine Rechnung teilen
a ~ **treat**	ein geselliges Ereignis, bei dem jeder Teilnehmer seine eigenen Kosten trägt
duty:	
~**-bound to do s.th.**	verpflichtet
~ **call**	Pflichtbesuch
dyed-in-the-wool	durch und durch, mit tiefsitzenden und unwandelbaren Überzeugungen

E

each:
~ and every — jeder einzelne
~ according to his taste — jeder wie er mag

an eager beaver — Streber, Enthusiast

ear:
be all ~s — ganz Ohr sein
be up to one's ~s in work — bis über beide Ohren in Arbeit stecken
bend s.o.'s ~ (Sl.) — jdn. vollquatschen
fall on deaf ~s — tauben Ohren predigen
give one's ~s for s.th. — den rechten Arm für etwas geben
go in at one ~ and out at the other — zum einen Ohr hinein, zum anderen wieder hinaus
(play) by ~ — 1. nach Gehör spielen, 2. improvisieren

1. She plays the piano entirely by ear.
2. I haven't decided yet what to tell him, I'll play it by ear.

a flea in the ~ (Sl.) — (unangenehme) Wahrheiten
A salesman came to the door but I sent him away with a flea in his ear.

turn a deaf ~ — nicht auf etwas hören
He turned a deaf ear to all advice.

keep an ~ to the ground — Augen und Ohren offen halten
pin back s.o.'s ~s — jdn. übers Ohr hauen
pin back one's ~s — aufmerksam zuhören
Just pin back your ears and listen to what I've got to tell you.

early:
The ~ bird catches the worm. (Sprichw.) — Wer zuerst kommt, mahlt zuerst. Morgenstund hat Gold im Mund.
~ days — der Beginn von etwas
be ~ days yet — es ist noch zu früh, etwas dazu zu sagen

She seems rather overwhelmed with her new responsibility. – Oh come on, it is early days yet!

earn:
~ an honest penny	Geld mit ehrlicher Arbeit verdienen
~ one's living	sich seinen Lebensunterhalt verdienen

ease:
~ s.b.'s mind	jdn. beruhigen
at ~	zwanglos, bequem
~ off s.th.	1. sich befreien von, 2. erleichtern

1. He eased off his shoes gently as his feet were sore.
2. They eased off his task.

~ s.b. of his wallet	jdn. um die Brieftasche erleichtern
feel ill at ~	sich unbehaglich/nicht wohl in seiner Haut fühlen

easier said than done — leichter gesagt als getan

East or West, home is best. (Sprichw.) — Zu Hause ist es doch am schönsten.

easy:
~ come, ~ go. (Sprichw.)	Wie gewonnen, so zerronnen.
~ does it! (Sl.)	Lass dir Zeit! Vorsicht!
~ on the eye	gefällig, schön anzusehen
~ game	leichte Beute
~ in one's mind	entspannt, beruhigt

Your mother will not be easy in her mind until you have called her!

~ money	schnell verdientes Geld
on ~ terms	zu günstigen Bedingungen
Take it ~!	Immer mit der Ruhe!
~ to come by	leicht zu finden

A good friend is not easy to come by.

in ~ circumstances	finanziell gesichert

eat:

~ **away**	1. nagen (an), langsam entfernen, 2. ärgern, Sorge machen

1. The sea has eaten away much of the shore.
2. Fear of not passing the exam was eating away at her.

~ **humble pie** (Sl.)	sich demütigen
~ **like a bird/sparrow** (Sl.)	essen wie ein Spatz, nur kleine Portionen essen
~ **one's words**	seine Worte zurücknehmen
~ **out of s.o.'s hands**	jdm. aus der Hand fressen
~ **out**	essen gehen
~ **like a horse** (Sl.)	essen wie ein Scheunendrescher

No wonder he's fat, he eats like a horse.

~ **s.b. alive for breakfast**	jdn. leicht bezwingen können
~ **s.b. out of house and home**	jdm. die Haare vom Kopf fressen
~ **oneself sick**	essen, bis einem schlecht wird
~ **one's head off**	viel essen
~ **one's heart out**	sehr traurig sein

John ate his heart out when he had to leave home.

~ **until it comes out of one's ears**	essen, bis es einem aus den Ohren wieder rauskommt

edge:

be on ~	nervös sein, gereizt sein
have an ~ on one's appetite	hungrig sein
set one's teeth on ~	jdn. nervös machen
take the ~ off s.th.	einer Sache die Wirkung nehmen

eff and blind (Sl.)   fluchen

egg:

as sure as ~s is ~s (Sl.)	so sicher wie das Amen in der Kirche; ganz sicher; man kann sich drauf verlassen

~ s.o. on	jdn. ermutigen
The boy only threw the stone because the others egged him on.	
have one over eight (Sl.)	einen über den Durst trinken
either way	je nachdem
elbow:	
~ one's way	sich hindurchdrängen, sich durchboxen
~ out	vertreiben, verdrängen
have at one's ~	bei der Hand haben
an elder statesman	jmd., der ein Amt lange innegehabt hat und nach wie vor konsultiert wird
at the eleventh hour	fünf vor zwölf, in letzter Minute, kurz bevor es zu spät ist
end:	
~ one's days	seinen Lebensabend verbringen
~ to ~	aneinander gelegt oder gestellt
the ~ of the rainbow	der mystische Ort, an dem alle Wünsche in Erfüllung gehen
come to an ~	enden
get hold of the wrong ~ of the stick	etwas in den falschen Hals bekommen
make ~s meet	mit etwas auskommen
My hair stands on ~.	Die Haare stehen mir zu Berge.
put an ~ to s.th.	einer Sache ein Ende bereiten/machen
~ in	münden
The path ends in a road.	
~ up in	enden
You'll end up in jail.	
All's well that ~s well. (Sprichw.)	Ende gut, alles gut.
to no ~	zwecklos
the enemy at the gates	die bedrohliche Präsenz des Gegners

engage:
be ~d in — beschäftigt sein mit
~ in politics — sich in der Politik engagieren
be ~d — verlobt sein
~ in small talk — Belangloses reden

The English dearly love a lord. (Sprichw.) — Die Engländer schätzen sozialen Status.

enough:
~ is ~! — Genug! Schluss damit!
~ is as good as a feast. (Sprichw.) — Allzuviel ist ungesund.
~ and to spare — mehr als genug, reichlich
~ of a fool to do s.th. — dumm genug, etwas zu tun
~ to go round — genug für alle, reichlich

enter:
~ one's mind/head — in den Sinn kommen
~ into s.th. — etwas anfangen, sich auf etwas einlassen
~ the fray — sich ins Getümmel stürzen

entertain the idea — sich mit etwas beschäftigen

one's entrances end exits — wie jmd. kommt und geht

To err is human (to forgive devine). (Sprichw.) — Irren ist menschlich.

error:
the ~ of s.b.'s ways — jds. Fehlverhalten
Having realized the errors of his ways, he went back to apologize.
an ~ of judgement — Fehleinschätzung

escape attention — übersehen werden

eternal triangle — Dreiecksverhältnis

even:
~ and anon — ziemlich regelmäßig
get ~ with s.o. — es jdm. heimzahlen

ever:

~ more	mit der Zeit zunehmend
~ so	sehr, viel

every:

~ bit as bad	in jeder Hinsicht so schlecht
~ cloud has a silver lining. (Sprichw.)	Nach Regen folgt Sonnenschein. Wo Schatten ist, ist auch Licht.
~ dog has his day. (Sprichw.)	Auch ein blindes Huhn findet einmal ein Korn. Jeder hat mal Glück/eine Chance.
~ now and then	hin und wieder, dann und wann
~ other day	jeden zweiten Tag
~ single one	jeder Einzelne
~ man has his price. (Sprichw.)	Jeder Mann ist käuflich.

everything:

~ but the kitchen sink (Brit./Sl.)	absolut alles
~ from soup to nuts (Am./Sl.)	absolut alles
~ the heart could desire	was man sich nur wünschen könnte
~ under the sun	alles

evil eye	der böse Blick
The exception proves the rule. (Sprichw.)	Ausnahmen bestätigen die Regel.
the expectation of life	Lebenserwartung
expense is no object	Geld spielt keine Rolle
extremes meet	unterschiedliche Positionen prallen aufeinander

In the big cities of today, extremes of wealth and poverty meet at every corner.

eye:

the ~ of the storm	das Auge des Sturms; das Zentrum einer gefährlichen Situation

an ~ for an ~	Auge um Auge
keep an ~ on s.th.	etwas im Auge behalten
make s.b. open his ~s	jdm. die Augen öffnen
my ~!	Unsinn!
never take one's ~s off s.th.	die Augen nicht abwenden
private ~	Privatschnüffler
see ~ to ~	übereinstimmen
with an ~ to	mit Rücksicht auf

eyebrow:

be up to one's ~s in work/debt	bis über beide Ohren in Arbeit/Schulden stecken.
raise one's ~s	die Stirne runzeln

F

face:
~ to ~ — von Angesicht zu Angesicht, Auge in Auge
~ the music (Sl.) — Zorn über sich ergehen lassen
The boy broke the window and had to face the music when his father came home.
be ~d with — mit etwas konfrontiert werden/sein

~ up to a failure — einer Niederlage ins Gesicht sehen
~ down — mit dem Gesicht nach unten

fly in the ~ of s.th. — sich einer Sache widersetzen
have the ~ to do s.th. — die Stirn haben, etwas zu tun
in the ~ of death — im Angesicht des Todes
on the ~ of it — auf den ersten Blick, anscheinend

place a ~ — jdn. einordnen
pull a ~ at s.o. — Grimassen schneiden
put on a brave ~ — sich nichts anmerken lassen
save one's ~ — sein Gesicht wahren
show one's ~ — sich sehen lassen
I hate family gatherings, but I must at least show my face.
take s.th. at ~ value — etwas für bare Münze nehmen
keep a straight ~ — ernst bleiben, nicht lachen
It was very difficult to keep a straight face as the clown performed his tricks.

fact:
as a matter of ~ — in der Tat, tatsächlich
know s.th. for a ~ — etwas genau wissen
~ or fiction — Tatsache oder Erfindung
the ~ of the matter — der entscheidende Aspekt
the ~ remains — es trifft nach wie vor zu
~s and figures — belegte Tatsachen oder Ergebnisse

let the ~s speak for themselves	die Tatsachen sprechen für sich, die Ergebnisse bedürfen keiner weiteren Erläuterung
Faint heart never won fair lady. (Sprichw.)	Frisch gewagt ist halb gewonnen.

fair:
~-weather friend	ein Freund, der sich in schlechten Tagen zurückzieht
~ do's	gerechte Behandlung oder Beurteilung
~ enough! (Sl.)	Einverstanden!
~'s ~	man muss gerecht sein
~ play	anständiges Verhalten
the ~ sex	das schöne Geschlecht
~ to middling	es geht so, ganz in Ordnung
The party was not really good, only fair to middling.	
~ and square	offen und ehrlich, unzweideutig
with one's own ~ hands	mit den eigenen Händen
Did you cook dinner yourself? – With my own fair hands!	

fairy:
a ~ godmother	gute Fee
~ tale	Märchen, Lügengeschichte

fall:
~ all over s.o. (Sl.)	um jdn. viel Aufhebens machen
My friend falls all over my daughter whenever she comes to visit.	
~ back on s.o./s.th.	jdn. um Hilfe bitten, auf etwas zurückgreifen
~ down on the job	etwas nicht richtig machen, mit einer Arbeit nicht zurechtkommen
~ flat on one's face (Sl.)	auf die Nase fallen, ohne Erfolg sein
~ for s.o. (Sl.)	sich verlieben
a ~ guy	Sündenbock

~ on deaf ears	auf taube Ohren stoßen
~ on one's feet	auf die Füße fallen (wie eine Katze)
~ over backwards to do s.th.	sich beinahe überschlagen, etwas zu tun
~ into place	in Ordnung kommen, klar werden

When he told me his story, all the facts I had known before fell into place.

~ out with s.o.	sich mit jdm. zanken/überwerfen
~ short of s.th.	schlechter als erwartet
~ through	nichts werden, ins Wasser fallen

Our plans for a holiday in Spain fell through, we had no money.

false:
~ alarm	Fehlalarm
~ modesty	falsche Bescheidenheit
make a ~ move	einen Fehler machen

fame and fortune	Ruhm und Reichtum
Familiarity breeds contempt. (Sprichw.)	Zu große Vertrautheit erzeugt Verachtung.

family:
~ likeness	Familienähnlichkeit
~ man	Familienvater
~ planning	Geburtenkontrolle
~ tree	Stammbaum

fancy:
~ one's chances at s.th.	sich bei etwas gute Chancen ausrechnen
~ s.o. (Sl.)	jdn. attraktiv finden

far:
~ afield	weit weg
~ and away	bei Weitem

He is far and away the most distinguished actor of his generation.

~ away	geistesabwesend
~ be it from me to interfere	es liegt mir fern, mich einzumischen
~-fetched	an den Haaren herbeigezogen, weit hergeholt
~ from it!	überhaupt nicht!
~ gone	weit fortgeschritten
~ and near	weit und breit
~ removed from s.th.	sehr anders als
a ~ cry from s.th.	weit davon entfernt sein
as ~ as that goes	was das angeht
not to trust s.o. as ~ as one can throw him	jdm. nicht über den Weg trauen
after a fashion	mehr schlecht als recht, in gewisser Weise

fast:

~ asleep	in tiefem Schlaf
~ bind, ~ find. (Sprichw.)	Wohl aufgehoben ist gut gefunden.
a ~ buck	schnell verdientes Geld
~ and furious	aufgeregt, unruhig
a ~ worker	jmd., der schnell Kontakt zum anderen Geschlecht aufnimmt

fat:

a ~ lot of good	nutzlos
a ~ price	ein hoher Preis
the ~ years and the lean years	fette und magere Jahre
the ~ is in the fire	der Teufel ist los

father:

a ~ figure	Vaterfigur
~ and mother of a row	eine besonders hitzige Auseinandersetzung

fault:

The ~ is in ourselves, not in our stars. (Sprichw.)	Der Mensch schafft sich sein Schicksal selbst.
to a ~	übertrieben

favour:
in ~ of — zugunsten von
stand high in s.o.'s ~ — bei jdm. in besonderer Gunst stehen, gut angeschrieben sein

Would you do me a ~? — Können Sie mir einen Gefallen tun?

feast:
a ~ for the eyes — eine Augenweide
a ~ of talent — ein Überfluss an Begabung

feather:
a ~ in one's cap — eine Ehre, eine Belohnung
John earned a feather in his cap by winning the race.
~ one's nest — seine Schäfchen ins Trockene bringen

to be fed up with s.o./s.th. (Sl.) — etwas/jdn. dick haben, genug von etwas/jdm. haben

Feed a cold and starve a fever. (Sprichw.) — Bei einer Erkältung soll man viel, bei Fieber wenig essen.

feel:
~ free to do s.th. — das Gefühl haben, man darf etwas tun
Please feel free to borrow the book, I have read it.
~ out of place — sich fehl am Platz fühlen
~ like doing s.th. — Lust haben, etwas zu tun
~ for s.o. — es jdm. nachfühlen können
~ one's oats — in Hochstimmung sein
~ one's way — sich seinen Weg suchen
Sensing the opposition to their plans, they were feeling their way towards a solution.
~ s.th. in one's bones — etwas im Gefühl haben
~ the draught — unangenehme Veränderungen spüren (häufig: finanziell)
~ the pinch — Mangel spüren
~ up to s.th. — sich einer Sache gewachsen fühlen

fellow feeling	Unterstützung, Sympathie
The female of the species is more deadly than the male. (Sprichw.)	Frauen sind gefährlicher als Männer.
fence:	
come off the ~	sich für eine Seite entscheiden
sit on the ~	sich nicht entscheiden wollen
the festive season	die Weihnachtstage
few:	
~ and far between	selten, rar, sehr wenig
a ~ home truths	eine klare und direkt geäußerte Kritik
fiddle:	
a face as long as a ~	ein enttäuschtes Gesicht
play second ~	die zweite Geige spielen
~ around with s.th.	an etwas herumspielen
~ while Rome burns	sich in einer kritischen Situation unpassend benehmen
a field day	ein Tag voll erfreulicher Tätigkeit
fight:	
~ the good ~	entschlossen für etwas eintreten
~ like Kilkenny cats	so lange kämpfen, bis beide Seiten zerstört sind
~ like a tiger	wild kämpfen
~ a losing battle	sich um eine aussichtslose Sache bemühen
~ tooth and nail	unter Einsatz aller Mittel kämpfen
~ing fit	einsatzbereit, gesund
~ing talk	Herausforderung
a figment of the imagination	Hirngespinst
figure:	
~ out (Am./Sl.)	schätzen, erraten
a ~ of fun	Witzfigur

filthy 84

filthy lucre	schnöder Mammon

find:
~ a better hole	sich verbessern
~ one's feet	zurechtkommen
After a year in the job I'm beginning to find my feet.	
~ one's vocation	seine Berufung finden, die geeignete Aufgabe für sich finden
~ s.th. wanting	etwas als nicht ausreichend beurteilen
~ one's way	ankommen, finden
~ing is keeping. (Sprichw.)	Wer etwas findet, darf es auch behalten.

fine:
a ~ body of men	eine gute Truppe
~ and dandy	wunderbar, prima
Everything would be fine and dandy if only he could get the car started in time.	
~ feathers make ~ birds. (Sprichw.)	Kleider machen Leute
a ~ kettle of fish	ein schönes Schlamassel
a ~ thing	eine gute Sache
a ~ time (iron.)	zu spät, zum falschen Zeitpunkt
Six o'clock in the morning is a fine time for ringing somebody, you know!	
~ words butter no parsnips. (Sprichw.)	Nette Worte alleine helfen nicht weiter!
one's ~r feelings	die bessere Seite der menschlichen Natur
the ~r points of something	Details
the ~st hour	der wichtigste Augenblick im Leben

finger:
have a ~ in the pie (Sl.)	die Hand im Spiel haben
His ~s are all thumbs. / He's all ~s and thumbs.	Er hat zwei linke Hände.
He won't raise a ~.	Er wird keinen Finger krumm machen.

put one's ~ on it	seinen Finger auf die Wunde legen
twist s.b. round one's little ~	jdn. um den kleinen Finger wickeln

finish:
the ~ed product	Endergebnis
~ing touches	die letzten Korrekturen

fire:
get ~d	entlassen werden
get on like a house on ~	dicke Freunde sein
~ away!	Schieß los!
have got ~ coming out of one's ears	etwas nicht mehr hören können
play with ~	mit dem Feuer spielen

firm:
with a ~ hand	mit eiserner Hand
a ~ offer	ein sicheres Angebot

first:
~ and foremost	zunächst einmal, vor allem anderen
~ and last	wenn man alles berücksichtigt
~ thing in the morning	als erstes am Morgen, als allererstes
~ thing one knows	ehe man es sich versieht
~ cousin to s.th.	sehr ähnlich
the ~ fine rapture	die erste Freude an etwas Neuem, die nicht lange andauert
~ things ~	die wichtigsten Dinge zuerst
the ~ impression	der erste Eindruck
at ~ sight	auf den ersten Blick
~ come ~ served. (Sprichw.)	Wer zuerst kommt, mahlt zuerst.
The first day a guest, the third day a pest.	Am ersten Tag ein Gast, am dritten Tag eine Last.
from ~ to last	die ganze Zeit
From first to last he never treated his wife fairly.	

fish:
a fine kettle of ~ (Sl.)	ein schöner Schlamassel

~ for s.th.	nach etwas angeln
a ~ out of water	in ungewohnter Umgebung
have other ~ to fry	Wichtigeres zu tun haben
That's a bit ~y!	Das ist nicht ganz geheuer/legal.

a fisherman's story — Seemannsgarn

fit:

~ for human consumption	essbar
~ like a glove	genau passend
a ~ of laughter	intensives Gelächter
~ and proper	ordentlich
give s.b. a ~	jdm. einen Schock versetzen
be ~ as a fiddle	gesund sein wie ein Fisch im Wasser
in ~s and starts	schubweise
~ the bill	angemessen, passend
It's not ~ for her.	Es schickt sich nicht für sie.
throw a ~ (Sl.)	einen Anfall kriegen

fix:

~ s.o. up with s.th.	jdm. etwas besorgen
a ~ed idea	eine fixe Idee, Zwangsvorstellung

be flabbergasted (Sl.) — platt sein

flash:

a ~ in the pan	ein Strohfeuer
a ~ Harry	ein Lackaffe

flat:

to be singing ~	falsch singen
~ out (Sl.)	klar und deutlich

They told me flat out that they were reporting me to the police.

a ~ voice	ausdruckslose Stimme
that's ~	damit kein Zweifel entsteht

flay s.b. alive — jdn. ernsthaft bestrafen

fleet of foot — leichtfüßig; in der Lage, sich schnell zu bewegen

Being rather fleet of foot, I managed to get off the road just in time.

flesh:
~ and blood	Fleisch und Blut
neither ~, fowl nor good red herring	weder Fisch noch Fleisch
put on ~	dick werden
make s.o.'s ~ creep	jdm. eine Gänsehaut einjagen
~ s.th. out	auswalzen, anschaulich machen, mit Details versehen

The plan is good but now you must flesh it out.

flex one's muscles	die Muskeln spielen lassen
have a fling (Sl.)	das Leben genießen (sich gehen lassen)
flip one's lid (Am./Sl.)	plötzlich wütend werden
flog a dead horse (Brit./Sl.)	etwas für nichts und wieder nichts tun
flood the market	den Markt überfluten
flora and fauna	Flora und Fauna
a Florence Nightingale	eine engagierte Krankenschwester
flourish like the green bay tree	blühen und gedeihen

flower:
~ power	Sammelbegriff für die Ideologie der Hippiebewegung
~ children	Blumenkinder, Hippies

fly:
~ the coop	abhauen
~ high	ehrgeizig sein
~ into a rage	in Wut geraten

~ off the handle	die Beherrschung verlieren, aus der Haut fahren
a ~ in the ointment (Sl.)	ein Haar in der Suppe
~-by-night	unzuverlässig(er) Mensch
a ~ing start	ein guter Anfang
a ~ing visit	ein sehr kurzer Besuch
get off to a ~ing	glänzend wegkommen, (fig.) einen glänzenden Start haben
The bird has flown. (Sl.)	Der Vogel ist ausgeflogen.
There are no flies on him.	jmd. ist nicht dumm
fob s.o. off with s.th.	jdm. etwas andrehen

I asked for butter and will not be fobbed off with margarine.

follow:

~ in s.b.'s footsteps	in jds. Fußstapfen treten
~ one's nose (Sl.)	immer der Nase nach, geradeaus gehen
~ one's own bent	tun, was man will
~ one's suit	es jdm. gleichtun
~ s.b.'s example	jdn. nachahmen
~ s.b.'s lead	jds. Vorbild oder Beispiel folgen
~ suit	genau das gleiche tun, wie der Vorgänger

fond:

a ~ farewell	Abschied
in the ~ hope	in der ungerechtfertigten Hoffnung, dass

food:

~ to s.b.	was jdn. erfreut

Jack's difficulties were food to his competitors.

~ to the gods	sehr gut
~ for thought	etwas stimmt nachdenklich

fool:

a ~'s errand	eine sinnlose Sache
A ~ and his money are soon parted. (Sprichw.)	etwa: Ein Narr wird immer pleite sein.

live in a ~'s paradise	in trügerischer Sicherheit leben
make a ~ of o.s.	sich zum Narren machen
No ~ like an old ~. Sprichw.)	Alter schützt vor Torheit nicht.

foot:

be (back) on one's feet	(wieder) auf den Beinen sein
have one ~ in the grave	mit einem Fuß im Grab stehen
~ the bill	die Rechnung bezahlen
have feet of clay	eine verborgene Schwäche haben, auch nur ein Mensch sein

He may be a dictator, but his feet are of clay.

put one's ~ down	entschlossen handeln, einschreiten

When the girl wanted to stay late at a party, her father put his foot down.

put one's ~ in it	ins Fettnäpfchen treten
footloose and fancy-free	ungebunden

for:

~ ages	seit ewigen Zeiten
~ one	zum Beispiel
~ all I care	Es ist mir egal.

They can all lose their jobs, for all I care.

~ all I know	so viel ich weiß
~ all the difference it makes	Wenn man bedenkt, was für einen geringen Unterschied es macht
~ all one's efforts	trotz aller Bemühungen
~ all the world to see	so dass es jeder sehen kann
~ chicken feed (Am./Sl.)	für 'nen Appel und ein Ei, für fast gar nichts, für ein paar Pfennige
~ dear life	entschlossen
~ ever	für immer
~ fear of s.th.	aus Angst vor
~ good	für immer
~ hours on end	stundenlang
~ sure	gewiss

forbidden

~ the fun of it (Sl.)	nur aus Spaß
~ the time being	zunächst

forbidden:
~ fruit is sweetest. (Sprichw.)	Verbotene Früchte schmecken am besten.
~ ground	ein Areal, das man nicht betreten darf

force:
a ~ to be reckoned with	ein Faktor, den man in Betracht ziehen muss
~ s.b.'s hand	jdn. dazu zwingen, etwas zu tun
by ~ of arms	mit militärischen Mitteln
~ of habit	die Macht der Gewohnheit

a foregone conclusion	ein vorhersehbares Ende
forever and a day	für immer und ewig
Forewarned is forearmed. (Sprichw.)	Gefahr erkannt, Gefahr gebannt.

forget:
~ more about s.th. than s.b. else ever knew	einen deutlichen Wissensvorsprung in einer Sache haben

forgive:
~ and forget	vergeben und vergessen
~ s.b. his trespasses	jdm. seine Schuld vergeben

fork money out (Sl.)	(etwas unwillig) bezahlen
a forlorn hope	eine sehr schwache Hoffnung
Fortune favours fools. (Sl.)	Mancher hat mehr Glück als Verstand.
forty winks	ein Nickerchen

foul:
~ one's nest	das eigene Nest beschmutzen

a founding father	Gründervater
four:	
the ~ corners of the world	abgelegene Regionen
a ~-leaved clover	Glücksklee
~-letter words	Flüche
the fourth estate	die Presse
free:	
a ~ fight	eine Massenschlägerei
a ~ loader	Schnorrer
~ speech	Recht auf freie Meinungsäußerung
make ~ with s.th.	mit etwas umgehen, als gehöre es einem
make ~ with s.b.	sich jdm. gegenüber viel herausnehmen
~ and easily	lässig
~-handed	großzügig
a French letter	Kondom
a fresh start	Neuanfang
fret and fume	Ungeduld oder Angespanntheit zeigen

He spent ages in the bathroom while the rest of the group fretted and fumed.

A friend in need is a friend indeed. (Sprichw.)	Freunde in der Not gehen tausend auf ein Lot.
frills and furbelows	Firlefanz, überflüssige Dekoration
from:	
~ afar	aus großer Entfernung
~ beginning to end	von Anfang bis Ende
~ the cradle to the grave	von der Wiege bis zur Bahre
~ here to Eternity	für immer
~ log cabin to White House	vom Tellerwäscher zum Millionär
~ pillar to post	von Ort zu Ort

~ bad to worse	vom Regen in die Traufe
~ rags to riches	von Armut zum Reichtum
~ start to finish	von Anfang bis Ende
straight ~ the horse's mouth	direkt von der Quelle
~ the money point of view	unter Berücksichtigung der finanziellen Aspekte
~ time immemorial	seit allen Zeiten
~ the outset	von Anfang an
~ top to bottom	durch die Bank
~ the word go	so bald es möglich war

They have been trying to get into this business from the word go.

front:

have the ~ to do s.th.	die Stirn haben, etwas zu tun
put on a bold ~	einer Sache tapfer ins Gesicht sehen; tun, als ob man keine Angst hat

When you are afraid of a dog, it's best to just put on a bold front.

the fruits of one's labour	die Früchte von jds. Arbeit
out of the frying-pan and into the fire	vom Regen in die Traufe

full:

~ of hot air	voller Unsinn, (viel) unnützes Zeug (reden)
~ of beans	glücklich, übermütig
~ frontal	Nacktdarstellung
at ~ length	in voller Länge
~ pelt	mit Höchstgeschwindigkeit
~ steam ahead	mit aller Kraft
at ~ throttle	voller Energie
~ well	sehr wohl (adv.)

He knew full well that he was wrong.

have fun and games (Sl.)	herumblödeln, Unsinn machen
the fur begins to fly	die Auseinandersetzung geht erst richtig los

*It was only when I began to talk
back to him that the fur began to fly,
but I could not stand it any longer!*

furred, four-footed and feathered friends   Tierwelt

fuss:
~ and bother   unnötige Aufregung
make no ~ about s.th.   nicht viel Aufhebens machen
~ about   Aufhebens machen um

G

the gaiety of nations — allgemeine Erheiterung

gain:
~ ground — Fortschritte machen, an Boden gewinnen
~ on s.b/s.th. — sich jdm./etwas nähern, jdn. einholen

In the race, the American athlete kept gaining on his English rival.

gales of laughter — lautes Gelächter

gall and wormwood — eine Sache, an die man sich ungern erinnert

Seeing the pictures of another artist was gall and wormwood to Henry.

game:
be ~ for s.th. — bei etwas mitmachen
make ~ of s.b. — auf Kosten von jdm. Spaß haben, jdn. zum Besten halten

The ~'s up. — Das Spiel ist aus.
have the ~ in one's hands — die Sache fest im Griff haben
play the ~ — sich an die Spielregeln halten
Cheating is not fair. You must learn to play the game.

garden gnome — Gartenzwerg

gas up (Am./Sl.) — (auf)tanken

gather:
~ momentum — an Tempo gewinnen
~ ye rosebuds while ye may — man soll etwas genießen, so lange es möglich ist

run the gauntlet — Spießruten laufen

generation gap	Mangel an Verständnis zwischen Alt und Jung
generous to a fault	übermäßig großzügig, verschwenderisch
a gentleman's agreement	eine formlose, aber bindende Vereinbarung
the genuine article	authentisch

get:

~ **above o.s.**	sich überschätzen
You are getting above yourself, you'll never manage that.	
~ **ahead**	vorankommen, Karriere machen
~ **along with s.o.**	mit jdm. auskommen
They got along well from the moment they met.	
~ **along without s.o./s.th.**	ohne jdn./etwas auskommen
~ **an airing**	offen zum Ausdruck gebracht werden
~ **away**	1. entwischen, entkommen, 2. wegkommen, in Urlaub gehen
1. The police gave chase but the thief got away.	
2. I have worked so hard lately, I must get away for a few days.	
~ **away with you!**	Ach, hör doch auf!
~ **behind with**	in Rückstand geraten mit
I can't take time off to go to the cinema. I'm getting behind with my work.	
~ **the bird**	rüde oder rücksichtslos abgewiesen werden
~ **carried away**	sich mitreißen lassen
~ **down to business**	zur Sache kommen
~ **edgeways**	seitwärts, von der Seite
~ **in touch with**	Kontakt aufnehmen mit, anrufen
~ **it over and done with**	etwas ein und für alle Mal hinter sich bringen
~ **one's teeth into s.th.**	sich in etwas verbeißen
~ **out of hand**	außer Kontrolle geraten

We must discuss the situation carefully before it gets out of hand.
~ **out of my way!**	Geh mir aus dem Weg!
~ **rid of s.th.**	etwas loswerden
~ **s.th. off one's chest**	sich etwas von der Seele reden

Once she had got the whole story off her chest she felt better.
~ **to grips with s.b.**	sich mit jdm. auseinandersetzen
~ **to know s.th.**	etwas in Erfahrung bringen
~ **to the bottom of s.th.**	einer Sache auf den Grund gehen

The police have never really got to the bottom of that crime.
~ **wind of s.th.**	von einer Sache Wind bekommen

If my father gets wind of the plan, he'll forbid it.
I don't know what got into me.	Ich weiß nicht, was in mich gefahren ist.
It ~s about.	Es spricht sich herum.
Let them ~ on with it.	Lass sie nur so weitermachen.
~ **a break**	Glück haben

The applicant hoped he would get a break and win the competition.
~ **the chop**	entlassen werden
~ **a dusty answer**	eine enttäuschende oder ablehnende Antwort bekommen
~ **a hand**	Applaus bekommen

The singer got a good hand at the end of the concert.
~ **a bad name**	seinen Ruf ruinieren
~ **a move on** (Sl.)	von etwas angemacht werden
~ **a load off one's mind** (Sl.)	etwas loswerden
~ **a word in edgeways**	zu Wort kommen

Everyone was talking so fast I couldn't get a word in edgeways.
~ **cracking** (Sl.)	etwas Dampf machen, loslegen

We'll never finish the job in time if we don't get cracking.
~ **down to brass tacks** (Sl.)	Tacheles reden
~ **down to the nitty-gritty**	zur Sache kommen

~ goose bumps (Am.)/goose pimples (Brit.)	eine Gänsehaut bekommen
~ mad	wütend werden
~ mad at s.o.	sich über jdn. ärgern
I got so mad with my daughter, I wanted to slap her.	
~ off scot-free	ungeschoren davonkommen
~ on s.o.'s nerves	jdm. auf die Nerven gehen
~ on with it! (Sl.)	Wach auf! Gib dir einen Ruck!
~ one's act together (Sl.)	Ordnung in die Sache bringen, sich am Riemen reißen
I must get my act together before I present my project to the committee.	
~ one's fingers burned	sich die Finger verbrennen
~ s.th. under one's belt (Sl.)	sich etwas 'reinziehen
I'm so hungry, I'd feel much better if I got a good meal under my belt.	
~ the boot	den Laufpass kriegen
~ the cold shoulder	die kalte Schulter gezeigt bekommen
~ the hang of s.th. (Sl.)	herauskriegen, wie etwas funktioniert
~ the sack (Sl.)	entlassen werden
~ up on the wrong side of the bed	mit dem falschen Fuß aufstehen
~-up-and-go	Energie, Tatkraft, Motivation
Just look at John, he can't wait to start the game. He's full of get-up-and-go.	

ghost:

give up the ~	den Geist aufgeben
not have a ~ of a chance (Sl.)	nicht die geringste Chance haben

gift:

a ~ from the gods	unerwarteter Vorteil, Gottesgeschenk
to have the ~ of the gab	redegewandt sein
don't look a ~ horse in the mouth	einem geschenkten Gaul schaut man nicht ins Maul

gild:
~ the lily	des Guten zu viel tun
~ the pill	die bittere Pille versüßen
~ed youth	sorglose Jugendliche

a ginger group — Aktionsgruppe

give:
~ the alarm	Alarm auslösen
~ s.b. the all-clear	jdm. Entwarnung geben
~ as good as one gets	es jdm. mit gleicher Münze heimzahlen

Peter can take care of himself in an argument. He can give as good as he gets.

~ birth to	zur Welt bringen
~ cause for	Grund geben für
~ chase	verfolgen
~ credit where credit is due	Ehre wem Ehre gebührt

Let's give credit where credit is due, you have written a marvellous book.

~ ear to	anhören
~ s.o. free rein	jdm. freie Hand lassen

We gave the au-pair girl free rein with the care of the children.

~ in	aufgeben, nachgeben
~ it to s.o. straight (Sl.)	jdm. etwas klar und deutlich sagen
~ of one's best	sein Bestes geben
~ o.s. airs	sich aufspielen

Don't be so superior, stop giving yourself airs!

~ out	kaputtgehen

My washing-machine has finally given out on me, I must buy a new one.

~ rise to s.th.	etwas verursachen

The bad state of the building gave rise to much criticism.

~ s.o. a buzz (Sl.)	jdn. anrufen
~ s.o. a dirty look	jdn. böse anschauen

He gave his father a dirty look when he criticised him.
~ s.o. a hand with s.th.	jdm. bei etwas helfen

Will you give me a hand to move the furniture for the party?
~ s.o. a pain (Sl.)	jdn. ärgern, stören
~ s.o./s.th. away	jdn. verraten, etwas ausplaudern
~ s.o. the glad eyes (Sl.)	jdn. anschmachten
~ s.o. trouble	jdm. Schwierigkeiten machen
~ s.o. the green light	jdm. grünes Licht geben
~ s.o. what for (Sl.)	es jdm. geben
~ s.th. a lick and a promise (Sl.)	etwas oberflächlich tun

Shirley, you should clean your room properly, not just give it a lick and a promise.
~ the game away (Sl.)	einen Plan verraten
~ up the ghost (Sl.)	den Geist aufgeben, sterben
~ up a secret	ein Geheimnis preisgeben
~ way to	Platz machen

glad:
~ tidings	erfreuliche Neuigkeiten
to put one's ~ rags on	sich aufdonnern

glance:
~ at	einen Blick werfen auf
~ over s.th.	etwas überfliegen, den Blick schweifen lassen

He merely glanced over the paper, he didn't have time to read it carefully.

a gleam of hope	ein Hoffnungsschimmer
catch a glimpse of	nur flüchtig zu sehen bekommen

glove:
be hand in ~ with s.o.	mit jdm. unter einer Decke stecken
treat s.o. with kid ~s	jdn. mit Samthandschuhen anfassen
a glutton for work	immer zur Arbeit bereit

Josie is a real glutton for work, you can always find her in the office.

gnashing of teeth — Zähneknirschen

go:
a ~ — ein Versuch
have a ~ (Sl.) — 1. versuchen,
2. an die Reihe kommen

1. You can do it if you try, have a go.
2. It's my go to throw the bell.

~ a long way — wesentlich zu etwas beitragen
~ all out to do s.th. (Sl.) — alles dransetzen, etwas zu tun
~ about one's business — sich um seine eigenen Angelegenheiten kümmern
~ about s.th. — herangehen an, in Angriff nehmen
~ against the grain — gegen den Strich gehen

It goes very much against the grain to admit that my enemy is right.

~ ahead! — mach weiter!, nur zu!
~ along with s.o. (Sl.) — mit jdm. übereinstimmen
~ at each other — aufeinander losgehen, streiten
~ back on one's word — ein Versprechen/Wort nicht halten
~ bananas (Am./Sl.) — verrückt werden
~ behind s.o.'s back — jdn. hintergehen
~ beyond one's duty — seine Kompetenz überschreiten
~ by s.o.'s opinion — sich nach jds. Meinung richten
~ by the board — verloren gehen, kaputt gehen

Your plan has gone by the board, the trip has been cancelled.

~ by the rules — sich an die Regeln halten
~ cold turkey (Am./Sl.) — sofort aufhören, etwas abbrechen

When drug addicts go cold turkey they become very ill.

~ down fighting — bis zum bitteren Ende kämpfen
~ down in history — in die Geschichte eingehen

The last decade was a time of such tremendous change.
I'm sure it will go down in history.

~ **downhill**	sich rapide verschlechtern, abwärts gehen

He has gone downhill since his wife left him.

~ **down the drain**	schief gehen
~ **down well with s.o.**	bei jdm. gut ankommen
~ **easy on s.o.**	lieb/vorsichtig mit jdm. sein
~ **fly a kite!** (Am./Sl.)	Hau ab und lass mich in Ruhe.
~ **for s.th.** (Sl.)	sich um etwas bemühen
~ **from bad to worse**	immer schlechter werden
~ **haywire** (Sl.)	durchdrehen
~ **in for s.th.** (Sl.)	sich für etwas interessieren
~ **for nothing**	keine Anerkennung finden
~ **in one ear and out the other**	zum einen Ohr hinein, zum anderen hinaus gehen
~ **like clockwork** (Sl.)	wie am Schnürchen laufen
~ **off the deep end**	überstürzt, den Gefühlen gehorchend handeln

He has gone completely off the deep end with his new girl-friend.

~ **on and on**	immer weiter machen
~ **on at s.o.**	ständig mit jdm. herumschimpfen, ständig an jdm. herumnörgeln
~ **one better**	es besser machen
~ **places** (Sl.)	eine Zukunft haben

Cecilia is a very talented actress, she will obviously go places.

~ **sky high** (Sl.)	ins Unermessliche steigen, sehr hoch hinaufgehen

Everything is so expensive these days, prices have gone sky high.

~ **through thick and thin**	durch dick und dünn gehen

My friend and I were inseparable at school, we went through thick and thin together.

~ **through the roof**	vor Wut an die Decke gehen

John got so angry with his dog he almost went through the roof.

~ **to great lengths**	sein Möglichstes tun
~ **to pieces**	1. kaputt gehen, zu Bruch gehen, 2. zusammenbrechen

1. My ball-dress is so old it is going to pieces.

2. When she heard of his death she went to pieces.
~ to the dogs	vor die Hunde gehen
~ to town (Sl.)	1. hart/schnell arbeiten, 2. übertrieben viel Geld ausgeben

1. Just look how fast they are working, they really are going to town.
2. They really went to town about entertaining their friends.

it's no ~ (Sl.)	nichts zu machen
That just goes to show that ...	Das beweist nur, dass ...
That goes without saying.	Das versteht sich von selbst.
to be on the ~ (Sl.)	ständig unterwegs

God:
~ damn	Verdammt!
~ damn s.b.'s eyes	jmd. soll verdammt sein
~ forbid	da sei der Himmel vor
~ helps those who help themselves. (Sprichw.)	Hilf dir selbst, dann hilft dir Gott!
~ moves in a mysterious way (his wonders to perform). (Sprichw.)	Die Wege des Herrn sind unergründlich.

going:
a ~ concern	ein florierendes Geschäft
~, ~, gone	Zum ersten, zum zweiten, zum dritten!
the ~ rate	der übliche Preis
still ~ strong	nach wie vor aktiv oder erfolgreich
a gold mine	eine Goldmine

golden:
a ~ handshake	Geschenk zum Ruhestand
a ~ opportunity	eine hervorragende Gelegenheit
a ~ rule	eine goldene Regel

good:
the ~ book	Bibel
a ~ deal of	eine Menge
one's ~ deed for the day	die gute Tat des Tages

as ~ as it gets *I know everything is far from perfect, but I'm afraid this is as good as it gets.*	besser wird's nicht
~ for a laugh	erheiternd
It's no ~ crying.	Es nützt nichts, wenn du weinst.
~ for nothing	Tunichtgut, Taugenichts; zu nichts nütze
~ and proper	gründlich
~ gracious!	Du meine Güte!
~ riddance	Gut, dass wir das los sind!
for ~	für immer
~s and chattels	Besitztümer
My goose is cooked. (Sl.)	Das Ding ist gelaufen.
one's gorge rises	Ekel oder Übelkeit fühlen
grace and favour	guter Wille (im Gegensatz zu Verpflichtungen)
gracious living	Luxusleben
the grand manner	großartiges Auftreten
grasp the nettle	resolut mit einer Schwierigkeit umgehen
grass: **The ~ is always greener on the other side.** (Sprichw.)	Die Kirschen in Nachbars Garten sind süßer. Man hält immer das für besser, was man nicht hat.
~ widow	Strohwitwe
grease s.b.'s palms	jdn. schmieren, bestechen
Greek: **It's all ~ to me.**	Für mich sind das böhmische Dörfer.
The ~s had a name for it.	Etwas gibt es schon seit langer Zeit.

green:
go ~ with envy (Sl.)	gelb vor Neid
have ~ fingers	einen grünen Daumen haben
see any green in s.o.'s eye	jdn. für einen Dummkopf halten

grey:
a ~ eminence	eine graue Eminenz, jmd., der im Hintergrund die Fäden in der Hand hält
~ matter	Gehirn, Intelligenz

grin:
~ like a Cheshire cat	wie ein Honigkuchenpferd grinsen
~ and bear it (Sl.)	in den sauren Apfel beißen

grind one's teeth — mit den Zähnen knirschen

grip:
come to ~s with s.th.	etwas anpacken
take a ~ on oneself (Sl.)	sich zusammenreißen, sich einen Ruck geben

grist for s.b.'s mill — Wasser auf jds. Mühle

grit one's teeth — die Zähne zusammenbeißen
The only way to face something unpleasant is to grit one's teeth and bear it.

ground:
~ed (Sl.)	Stubenarrest haben
be dashed to the ~	am Boden zerstört sein
be well ~ed in	bewandert sein in

There's no doubt he'll pass the examination, he's so well-grounded in all the subjects.

gain ~	an Boden gewinnen
have one's feet on the ~	mit beiden Beinen fest auf der Erde stehen
lose ~	an Boden verlieren
stay one's ~	sich behaupten

grow:
~ in strength — stärker werden
~ out of s.th. — 1. aus etwas herauswachsen, 2. zu alt für etwas werden

1. John has grown out of his shoes yet again.
2. I'm twenty now and have grown out of such childish things.

~ old gracefully — würdevoll altern
~ on s.o. (Sl.) — mit der Zeit ans Herz wachsen

to bear s.o. a grudge — jdm. böse sein

guard:
~ against — sich hüten vor
on one's ~ — auf der Hut; vorbereitet

Be on your guard, they may still come and catch you.

guardian angel — Schutzengel

guiding light — leuchtendes Vorbild

guinea-pig — Versuchskaninchen

gun:
~ for s.o. (Sl.) — jdn. suchen, um ihm zu schaden/strafen

The headmaster is gunning for you, he knows you missed the cricket match.

a big ~ (Sl.) — ein wichtiger, einflussreicher Mensch

George is one of the big guns in his profession.

stick to one's ~s — seinen Standpunkt fest behaupten

the gutter press — Sensationspresse

H

habit:
break a ~ — sich etwas abgewöhnen
kick the ~ (Sl.) — abgewöhnen, aufgeben
make a ~ of s.th. — sich etwas zur Gewohnheit machen

hail:
within ~ — in Rufweite
~ from — ursprünglich herstammen/kommen

McGregor hails from Scotland.
I'm from New York. Where do you hail from?

hair:
keep one's ~ on — sich beherrschen
a ~ of the dog that bit you (Sl.) — ein Schluck Alkohol gegen den Kater

There's only one cure for a hangover and that is some of the hair of the dog that bit you.

let one's ~ down (Sl.) — aus sich herausgehen
split ~s — über unwichtige, banale Sachen streiten, Haarspaltereien betreiben

My ~'s standing on end. — Die Haare stehen mir zu Berge.
I was so afraid my hair stood on end.

hale and hearty — gesund

half:
~-baked — noch grün hinter den Ohren
by ~ — Ausdruck der Übertreibung
You must have a serious talk with John, he is too cheeky by half.
~ cut — angetrunken
~ seas over (Brit./Sl.) — betrunken
that's ~ the battle — damit ist viel gewonnen

too ... by ~	viel zu ...
~ a loaf is better than no bread. (Sprichw.)	Der Spatz in der Hand ist besser als die Taube auf dem Dach.
~ a mo (Sl.)	Moment!
do things by halves	halbe Sachen machen

hammer:

~ at s.th.	eifrig an etwas arbeiten
~ s.th. into s.b.	jdm. etwas einbläuen
It took the teacher all morning to hammer the theory into his pupils.	
~ and tongs	mit viel Lärm/Kraft/ Enthusiasmus
He may not be any good as a pianist but he certainly goes at it hammer and tongs.	
~ out (Brit./Sl.)	nach vielen Diskussionen zu einer Entscheidung kommen
We spent all weekend hammering out our plans for the future.	

a halfway house	Kompromiss
the hall of fame	die Ruhmeshalle

hand:

an old ~	ein Mensch mit viel Erfahrung
Let me help. I'm an old hand at mending things.	
at first ~	aus erster Hand
change ~s	den Besitzer wechseln
This house has changed hands many times.	
gain the upper ~	gewinnen
do s.th. off ~	etwas aus dem Stegreif tun, etwas nebenbei tun
~ down to	vererben, weitergeben an
lend a ~	helfen
on the other ~	andererseits
~ in glove with s.o.	sehr eng, nahe
The doctor and his nursing staff really work hand in glove.	
out of ~	außer Kontrolle

~-me-down	ein weitergereichtes Kleidungsstück
Why can't I have a new dress? I hate always wearing hand-me-downs.	
~ over fist	sehr schnell
What a good day we've had at the flea market. We took in money hand over fist.	
~ s.th. in	abgeben
have a ~ in s.th.	teilhaben an, die Finger in einer Angelegenheit haben
John knows all about the scheme. He must have had a hand in the planning.	
lay ~s on s.th.	etwas in die Finger bekommen
throw in one's ~	aufgeben
turn one's ~ to s.th. (Sl.)	sich einer Sache oder Tätigkeit zuwenden
wash one's ~s of s.th.	nichts mit einer Sache zu tun haben wollen
you have got to ~ to s.o. (Sl.)	das muss man jemandem lassen
handle with kid gloves	mit Samthandschuhen anfassen
hang:	
~ about	herumlungern
~ around	bleiben
~ back	zögern, sich sträuben
~ by a single thread	am seidenen Faden hängen
~ in the balance	unentschlossen sein
The whole issue will just have to hang in the balance until father returns.	
~ one's head	den Kopt hängen lassen
~ on!	Halt! Moment!
~ on s.b.'s lips/words	an jds. Lippen hängen
The child was fascinated by the story his grandmother was telling and hung on to her every word.	
~ out (Sl.)	1. hausen, sich aufhalten, 2. verkehren mit

1. I hang out in the East
End of London.
2. I'm afraid Mary might be
hanging out with the wrong people.
~ up   den Telefonhörer auflegen

happen:
~ on s.b.   zufällig auf jdn. treffen
*I walked into the library and
happened on John and David.*
~ what may! (Brit.)   Was auch immer geschieht!

happy:
a ~ coincindence   ein glückliches Zusammentreffen von Ereignissen
the ~ couple   ein frisch verheiratetes Paar
a ~ hunting ground   Paradies

hard:
~ by   in der Nähe von
be ~ one s.b.   jdm. schwer zusetzen
~ to come by   schwer zu bekommen
a ~ nut to crack   eine harte Nuss zu knacken
~ on s.o.'s heels   dicht hinterher
~ put to do s.th.   etwas mit Schwierigkeiten tun
~-to-get   sich zieren
~ up (Sl.)   blank, ohne Kohle
~ and fast   1. festgelegt, präzise,
2. mit Energie

1. *There are no hard and fast rules
for these occasions, you just have
to decide on the spot.*
2. *He played the game hard and
fast, but it was great fun.*
~ of hearing   schwerhörig

hare:
~-brained   dumm, unverantwortlich
**run with the ~ and hunt
with the hounds** (Sl.)   auf zwei Hochzeiten tanzen

be out of harm's way   außer Gefahr sein, keinen Unfug anrichten können

hash

make a hash of s.th.	Chaos anrichten, etwas in den Sand setzen
Make haste!	Beeile dich!

hat:
at the drop of a ~	ohne Weiteres
eat one's ~	einen Besen fressen
hatch a plot	einen Plan entwerfen
bury the hatchet	das Kriegsbeil begraben

hate:
~ s.b.'s guts	jdn. verabscheuen
~ the sight of s.b.	den Anblick von jdm. nicht ertragen können
haul s.o. over the coals	jdn. zur Schnecke machen

have:
~ a bone to pick with s.b.	mit jdm. ein Hühnchen zu rupfen haben
~ a brush with s.th.	mit etwas kurz in Kontakt/Berührung kommen

When I had pneumonia as a child I had a brush with death, but I got over it.

~ a close shave	glimpflich davonkommen
~ a fit (Sl.)	einen Wutanfall bekommen
~ a fling with s.o.	mit jdm. eine Affäre haben
~ a go at s.th.	etwas versuchen
~ a good command of s.th.	etwas beherrschen/gut können

He has a good command of English.

~ a good head on one's shoulders	ein kluger Kopf sein, intelligent sein
~ a hand in s.th.	die Hand im Spiel haben
~ a hold over s.b.	jdn. in der Hand haben
~ a lot on one's mind	viel im Kopf haben

I'm sorry I forgot to write you. I've had a lot on my mind recently.

~ a mind to	Lust haben zu
~ a near miss	knapp (mit dem Leben) davonkommen
~ a say in s.th.	mitreden, etwas zu sagen haben
~ a screw loose (Sl.)	eine Schraube locker haben
~ a sweet tooth	gern Süßes essen

Jane loves ice cream. She has a sweet tooth.

~ a swelled head (Am/Sl.)	eingebildet sein
~ a whale of a time (Sl.)	sehr viel Spaß haben
~ a word with s.o.	mit jdm. ein Wörtchen reden
~ ants in one's pants	unruhig sein, rastlos sein
~ bats in one's belfry (Sl.)	nicht alle Tassen im Schrank haben
~ had it (Sl.)	erledigt sein, am Ende sein, ausgespielt haben
~ had one's fill	gesättigt sein
~ it in for s.o. (Sl.)	es auf jdn. abgesehen haben
~ it out with s.o.	ausdiskutieren
~ one's feet on the ground	mit beiden Beinen auf dem Boden stehen
~ one's finger in the pie	mitmischen
~ one's head in the clouds	geistesabwesend sein
~ one's heart in one's mouth	sein Herz auf der Zunge tragen
~ one's nose in the air	hochnäsig sein
~ one's way	es machen, wie man will; sich durchsetzen
~ one's wits about one	alle seine Sinne beieinander haben

You have to have your wits about you when driving a car.

~ a row with s.o.	Streit mit jdm. haben
~ second thoughts	Zweifel bekommen
~ s.th. up one's sleeve	ein Geheimnis/eine Überraschung parat haben
~ s.th. wrapped up	etwas erklärt/erledigt haben
~ the courage of one's convictions	Zivilcourage haben
~ the gift of the gab (Sl.)	gut im Reden sein, überzeugend sein
~ the guts to do s.th. (Sl.)	den Mumm haben, etwas zu tun
~ the time of one's life	einen Mordsspaß haben

~ too many irons in the fire	zu viele Eisen im Feuer haben, zu viel auf einmal anpacken
~ what it takes	das gewisse Etwas haben
Make hay while the sun shines. (Sprichw.)	das Eisen schmieden, solange es heiß ist
to go haywire (Sl.)	durchdrehen

head:

be off one's ~ (Sl.)	verrückt sein
not make ~ or tail of s.th.	sich keinen Reim auf etwas machen können, aus etwas nicht klug werden

I can't make head or tail of what she's saying.

have a good ~ on one's shoulders	ein kluger Kopf sein
keep one's ~	einen kühlen Kopf bewahren
keep one's ~ above water	sich über Wasser halten können
be ~ over heels in love	bis über beide Ohren verliebt sein
talk one's ~ off	sich dumm und dusselig reden
talk over one's ~	jdn. sprachlich überfordern
take the ~	die Führung übernehmen
run ~ over heels	Hals über Kopf davonstürzen
~ and shoulders above	weit voraus/überlegen sein
have one's ~ screwed on the right way	intelligent/klug sein

John will make the right decision. He has his head screwed on the right way.

~ on	frontal

The two trains collided head on.

to be a headache (Sl.)	jdn. nerven

hear:

~ the last of s.b.	mit jdm. fertig sein
~ s.o. out	jdn. ausreden lassen
in my ~ing	in meiner Gegenwart
~ from s.o.	eine Botschaft/einen Brief von jdm. bekommen

heart:
~ to ~ — im Vertrauen, zwischen Freunden
after one's own ~ — nach dem eigenem Geschmack
break s.o.'s ~ — jdm. das Herz brechen
find it in one's ~ to — es übers Herz bringen
I could not find it in my heart to tell him.
have a ~ — sei so nett
have one's ~ in one's boots (Sl.) — sehr deprimiert sein, Angst haben
have one's ~ in one's mouth — erschrocken sein
have the ~ to do s.th. — etwas übers Herz bringen
learn s.th. by ~ — etwas auswendig lernen
lose ~ — den Mut verlieren
It is very easy to lose heart when nothing goes right.
lose one's ~ to s.o. — sein Herz an jdn. verlieren
take s.th. to ~ — sich etwas zu Herzen nehmen
wear one's ~ on one's sleeves — aus seinem Herzen keine Mördergrube machen

hearth and home — Heim und Herd

in the heat of the moment — im Eifer des Gefechts

heaven:
~ on earth — ein himmlischer Ort
the ~s open — es regnet

heavy:
the ~ father — ein autoritärer Vater
~ going — eine schwierige oder mühsame Tätigkeit

Loading the car turned out to be heavy going.

heel:
dig one's ~s in — sich stur stellen
take to one's ~s — die Beine in die Hand nehmen, ausreißen

When I saw the bull in the field, I look to my heels and fled.

kick one's ~s	Zeit verschwenden/vertrödeln
the height of folly	der Höhepunkt der Dummheit

hell:
~-bent on doing s.th.	wild entschlossen, etwas zu tun
all ~ breaks loose	der Teufel ist los
~ for leather	mit größtmöglichem Tempo

help:
~ a lame dog over a stile	jdm. helfen, der in Schwierigkeiten steckt, jdm. in der Not beistehen
~ o.s. to s.th.	sich etwas nehmen, sich bedienen
~ s.b. with s.th.	jdm. bei etwas behilflich sein

here:
~ below	in diesem Leben
~ goes!	Jetzt geht's los!
~ and now	jetzt und hier
~ and there	an verschiedenen Orten
~, there and everywhere	an den unterschiedlichsten Orten, überall
~ today and gone tomorrow	heute hier, morgen vergangen
~'s to ...	Toast auf ...

Here's to Louise who is celebrating her birthday tonight!

hey presto	Abrakadabra! (Zauberwort)
the hidden persuaders	die Werbebranche

high:
be in ~ spirits	gute Laune haben
~ and dry	verlassen
~-handed	arrogant
~ jinks	Blödsinn, Scherze
~ and low	überall
~ and mighty	arrogant
~ summer	Hochsommer
~, wide and handsome	beeindruckend, optisch ansprechend

The ~er you climb the harder you fall. (Sprichw.)	Wer hoch steigt kann tief fallen.
fly ~	ehrgeizig sein
It's ~ time.	Es ist höchste Zeit.
Goodness, it's past ten o'clock. It's high time we went home.	

hint:
drop a ~	einen dezenten Hinweis geben
give a broad ~	einen Wink mit dem Zaunpfahl geben
take a ~	einen Wink verstehen

hit:
~-and-miss	unüberlegt, ziellos
~ at s.th.	nach etwas schlagen
~ back	zurückschlagen
~ bottom (Sl.)	einen Tiefpunkt erreichen
~ on	stoßen auf
~ or miss	auf gut Glück
~ it off with s.o.	mit jdm. schnell warm werden
As I have the same interests as Jane, we hit it off immediately.	
~ s.o. below the belt	jdn. unter der Gürtellinie treffen
~ the ceiling (Sl.)	in die Luft gehen (vor Wut)
~ the sack (Sl.)	sich aufs Ohr hauen, ins Bett gehen
~ the nail on the head	den Nagel auf den Kopf treffen
~ the roof	an die Decke gehen

hither and thither	ziellos von einem Ort zum anderen
They moved hither and thither for a few years before finally settling down in the city.	
to hog s.th. (Sl.)	etwas an sich reißen

hold:
have a ~ of s.th.	etwas beherrschen
~ in high regard	hoch achten, in Ehren halten
~ all the aces (Sl.)	alle Asse in der Hand halten, eine gute Ausgangsposition haben

hole

Don't ~ your breath.	Warte gar nicht erst darauf, dass es passiert!
~ forth	lang reden
Janet is incredibly boring. She can hold forth for ages on the most uninteresting subjects.	
~ good	gültig sein
~ one's own	sich behaupten
A shy person always has difficulty holding his own in an argument.	
~ one's peace	sich nicht einmischen, still/ruhig bleiben
~ one's tongue	nicht sprechen, den Mund halten
~ out	aushalten
He has lost a lot of blood in the car crash, I hope he can hold out till the ambulance gets here.	
~ the line!	Bleiben Sie bitte am Apparat!
~ true	sich bewahrheiten
keep ~ of s.th.	etwas festhalten
take ~ of s.th.	Besitz ergreifen von
~ water	stimmen, überzeugen
~ with s.th.	einverstanden sein

hole:

a ~ and corner business	eine zwielichtige Tätigkeit
a ~ in the wall	ein sehr kleiner Laden
be in a ~ (Sl.)	in der Klemme sitzen

holier than thou   selbstgerecht

hollow:

a ~ laugh	ein gezwungenes Lachen
to beat s.o. hollow	jdn. überlegen schlagen

holy:

~ war	heiliger Krieg
a ~ terror	eine furchteinflößende Person

home:

a ~ bird	ein Stubenhocker
drive s.th. ~ to s.b.	jdm. etwas klarmachen

It took me a long time to drive the point home to him, but I think he understood in the end.
hit ~	ins Schwarze treffen
make o.s. at ~	es sich bequem machen

Homer sometimes nods. (Sprichw.) — Irren ist menschlich.

honest to God — Ehrlich!

Honesty is the best policy. (Sprichw.) — Ehrlich währt am längsten.

honour:
a debt of ~	Ehrenschulden
a point of ~	Ehrensache
~ among thieves	Ganovenehre

hook:
on one's own ~	auf eigene Faust
by ~ or by crook	auf Biegen und Brechen
~, line and sinker	ganz und gar, komplett
off the ~	aus der Klemme

He's really to blame for getting himself into this situation, but we must see if we can get him off the hook.

play ~y (Am./Sl.)	Schule schwänzen
~ed on s.th. (Sl.)	einer Sache (Droge) verfallen sein, süchtig sein

Nobody cares two hoots about it. — Danach kräht kein Hahn.

hop:
keep s.b. on the hop	jdn. in Ruhe lassen
be ~ping mad (Sl.)	stinksauer sein
~ to it! (Sl.)	Beweg' dich! Mach schnell!

stir up a hornet's nest — in ein Wespennest stechen

horse:
back the wrong ~ auf das falsche Pferd setzen
have ~ sense einen gesunden Menschenverstand haben
sit on a high ~ auf einem hohen Ross sitzen
straight from the ~'s mouth direkt von der Quelle, aus erster Hand

~ play (Sl.) das Herumtoben

Reckon without one's host. Die Rechnung ohne den Wirt machen.

hot:
a ~ spot Brennpunkt
get into ~ water (Sl.) in Teufels Küche kommen
go like ~ cakes weggehen wie warme Semmeln
talk a lot of ~ air (Sl.) Blödsinn reden
~ and bothered aufgeregt, ängstlich
The witness grew hot and bothered when the judge asked him a question.
~ under the collar wütend, verlegen, durcheinander

house:
~ of cards Kartenhaus, instabile Konstruktion
bring down the ~ hervorragend spielen (Theater)
keep (an) open ~ ein offenes Haus haben, Leute zu jeder Zeit willkommen heißen
like a ~ on fire schnell, mit Elan
She was working away like a house on fire.
put one's ~ in order vor seiner eigenen Tür kehren

it's a household name das ist ein Begriff

how:
~ about ...? Wie wär's mit ...?
~ are things? Wie geht's?
~ come? Wieso das?
~ crazy can you get? Gibt es keine Grenzen der Verrücktheit?

~ dare s.b.	wie kann es jmd. wagen
~ on earth	wie zur Hölle
~'s the world been treating you?	Wie ist es dir ergangen?

hug o.s. about s.th. — sich selbst zu etwas beglückwünschen/gratulieren

howl:
a ~ of protest	ein Aufschrei der Entrüstung
a ~ing success	ein herausragender Erfolg
a ~ing wilderness	tiefe Wildnis

a hue and cry — Alarm, allgemeine Aufregung

humanly possible — menschenmöglich

have the hump — schlechte Laune haben

Hunger is the best sauce. (Sprichw.) — Hunger ist der beste Koch.

hunt:
~ for/up	suchen
~ after s.th.	etwas nachjagen
~ s.b. down	jdn. zur Strecke bringen

hurt:
~ s.b.'s feelings	jds. Gefühle verletzen
~ s.b.'s pride	jdn. kränken

hurry:
be in a ~	in Eile sein, es eilig haben
~ over s.th.	etwas hastig tun/erledigen
~ up!	Beeile dich!

hustle and bustle — geschäftiges Treiben

I

I:

~ ask you?	Hast Du so etwas schon einmal gehört?
~ beg to differ	ich bin leider anderer Ansicht
~'ll bet!	Ich glaube kein Wort!
~ can tell you!	(bekräftigend:) aber wie!
~ dare say ...	mir scheint sicher, dass ...
~ don't know what the world is coming to.	(oft iron.) Wo soll das noch hinführen!
~ don't mind if ~ do	Danke, herzlich gerne!
Cigarette? – I don't mind if I do!	
~ don't think	das bezweifele ich
~'ll eat my hat	ich fresse einen Besen
~ like that	Von wegen!
~ might add	ich sollte noch darauf hinweisen
~ should think so	Aber sicher!
~'ve had it.	Ich bekomme eins auf den Deckel. Dann kann ich's vergessen. Es ist um mich geschehen.
~ would if ~ could but ~ can't	ich würde ja gerne, aber es geht nicht
~ wouldn't touch it with a barge pole.	Das würde ich nicht mit der Kneifzange anfassen.

ice:

keep s.th. on ~	eine Sache auf Eis legen

idea:

the very ~	was für eine lächerliche Vorstellung
form an ~ of s.th.	sich von etwas eine Vorstellung machen
put ~s into s.o.'s head	jdm. Flausen in den Kopf setzen
What's the big ~?	Was soll das? Was hast du für einen Unsinn vor?

if:

~ any	wenn etwas da sein sollte

~ at all	wenn überhaupt
~ one believes that, one will believe anything	wer so dumm ist, diese Sache zu glauben, beweist damit seinen Mangel an Urteilsvermögen
~ the cap fits, wear it	Wen's juckt, der kratze sich. Man soll sich ruhig angesprochen fühlen, wenn die Kritik zutrifft.
~ need be	falls es wirklich nötig sein sollte
~ the worst comes to the worst ...	Wenn alle Stricke reißen, ... Wenn wirklich alles schief läuft, ...
~ you ask me	wenn du meine Meinung wissen willst
~ you can't beat them, join them	wen man nicht besiegen kann, mit dem muss man sich verbünden
~ you please	wenn du so freundlich wärst
~s and buts	zahlreiche Einwände und Vorbehalte, Wenn und Aber

ill:
~ at ease	unwohl (in der Haut), ängstlich, nervös

A person will often feel ill at ease before an interview.

~-assorted	inkompatibel, schlecht zueinander passend
It's an ~ bird that fouls its own nest. (Sprichw.)	Das eigene Nest beschmutzt man nicht.
~ weeds grow apace. (Sprichw.)	Unkraut vergeht nicht.

impose:
~ on s.b.	jdm. zur Last fallen
~ o.s. on s.b.	sich jdm. aufdrängen

improve:
~ the occasion	eine gegebene Situation zu seinem Vorteil nutzen
~ on s.th.	etwas besser machen

in:
~ a bad way	in schlechter Verfassung
~ a flash (Sl.)	schnell, sofort

~ a fog	geistesabwesend, unachtsam
~ a huff	eingeschnappt
~ a lather (Sl.)	aufgeregt, durcheinander, erhitzt
~ a month of Sundays	ewig lang

I haven't seen you in a month of Sundays, you look well.

~ a nutshell	knapp ausgedrückt, kurz gefasst
~ a quandary	konfus, durcheinander
~ a light spot	in Schwierigkeiten
~ a vicious circle	in einem Teufelskreis
~ apple-pie order (Am./Sl.)	in guter Verfassung, ordentlich
~ bad taste	geschmacklos

To laugh at a funeral is in very bad taste.

~ black and white	schriftlich, schwarz auf weiß
~ brief	ganz kurz
~ broad daylight	am helllichten Tag
~ cold blood (Sl.)	grausam, kaltblütig
~ confidence	im Vertrauen gesagt
~ deep (Am./Sl.)	in größten Schwierigkeiten, verschuldet
~ due course	zur richtigen Zeit, mit der Zeit
~ fine feather	gut gelaunt
~ full swing	voll im Gange

The party was in full swing when I arrived.

~ for a penny, ~ for a pound. (Brit./Sl.)	Wer A sagt, muss auch B sagen.
~ for it (Sl.)	vor Schwierigkeiten stehen

When I saw how angry my father was, I knew I was in for it.

~ for s.th. (Sl.)	etwas zu erwarten haben
~ good time	schnell, in kurzer Zeit
~ hot water (Sl.)	in Schwierigkeiten
~ less than no time	im Nu
~ no time (at all)	sehr schnell
~ one ear and out the other	zum einen Ohr hinein, zum anderen hinaus
~ one's cups	betrunken

He is likely to start a fight when he's in his cups.

~ one's mind's eye	vor dem inneren Auge
~ one's right mind	rational, geistig gesund

No one in their right mind would walk into a cage full of lions.

~ one's Sunday best	im Sonntagskleid/-staat
~ short supply	rar
~ the absence of ...	angesichts der Tatsache, dass etwas oder jmd. fehlt
~ the bag (Sl.)	gewiss, sicher

I've got the contract in the bag, nothing can stop me now.

~ the doghouse (Sl.)	in Schwierigkeiten
~ the long run	auf lange Sicht, endlich, zum Schluss
~ the middle of nowhere	dort, wo sich Fuchs und Hase „Gute Nacht" sagen

We can't go and see Ann very often, she lives in the middle of nowhere.

~ the near future	in naher Zukunft
~ the prime of life	im besten Alter
~ the twinkling of an eye	im Nu, im Handumdrehen

My aunt is an excellent cook. She can put a delicious meal on the table in the twinkling of an eye.

~ this day and age	heutzutage
~-laws	die angeheirateten Verwandten
~s-and-outs	alle Einzelheiten
industrial action	Streik
inside every fat man there is a thin man trying to get out	dicke Menschen haben das Gefühl, dass sie von der Welt falsch eingeschätzt werden
an interested party	diejenigen, die von einer Entwicklung profitieren
into the bargain	zusätzlich
iron:	
the ~ enters one's soul	jmd. wird verbittert
an ~ fist in a velvet glove	ein Wolf im Schafspelz

~ rations	die eiserne Reserve
strike while the ~ is hot	das Eisen schmieden, solange es heiß ist
have too many ~s in the fire	zu viele Eisen im Feuer haben, zu viel auf einmal anpacken
~ s.th./things out	ein Problem ausbügeln

it:

~ never rains but ~ pours. (Sprichw.)	Ein Unglück kommt selten allein.
~'s high time.	Es ist höchste Zeit.
~ beats me (Sl.)	ich komme mit etwas nicht klar
~ can't happen here	so etwas wird hier (oder uns) nie geschehen
~ figures ...	es erscheint vernünftig oder wahrscheinlich, dass ...
~ is all in a day's work	eine Aufgabe, an die man gewöhnt ist, macht einem nichts aus
~ is just as well ...	es ist ein Glück, dass ...
It was just as well we did not go out that night, as the weather took a turn for the worse.	
~ happens that ...	es trifft zufällig zu, dass ...
~ takes two to do s.th.	manche Dinge schafft man nicht alleine
It takes two to tango.	Es gehören immer zwei dazu.
~'s the thought that counts. (Sprichw.)	Der gute Wille zählt.
~'s a small world	wie klein die Welt ist
~'s all in the mind	das ist alles Einbildung
an ivory tower	ein Elfenbeinturm, abgeschottet von der wirklichen Welt
the Ivy league	die Gruppe der älteren und prestigeträchtigen amerikanischen Universitäten

J

Jack:
~ of all trades (and master of none) — ein Hansdampf in allen Gassen
~ is as good as his master. — Wie der Herr, so's G'schärr.
before you can say ~ Robinson — schneller, als du denken kannst

jack:
~ up s.o. (Am./Sl.) — jdn. motivieren
I guess I'll have to jack up the workmen to do the job properly.

~ up s.th. — 1. etwas mittels eines Hebers anheben, 2. Preis anheben
1. The mechanic jacked up the car to look underneath.
2. The telephone company jacked up the price of a call.

to hit the jackpot — das große Los ziehen

jam:
~ tomorrow — der Glaube daran, dass sich die Lage bessern wird
~ the brakes on — eine Vollbremsung machen
be in a ~ — in der Patsche sitzen

with a jaundiced eye — etwas zynisch betrachten

one's jaw drops — jdm. fällt die Klappe runter
John's jaw dropped when he saw the mess the dog had made.

jazz s.th. up (Sl.) — etwas aufpeppen, aufregend machen
Most classrooms could do with being jazzed up a bit.

back in a jiffy (Sl.) — gleich wieder da

the jig is up — alle Hoffnung ist dahin

job:
the ~ in hand	die Aufgabe, mit der man im Moment beschäftigt ist
a ~ lot	Warenposten
a ~ of work	eine schwierige oder unmögliche Aufgabe
be on the ~	bei der Arbeit sein
It's quite a ~.	Es ist keine einfache Sache. Das ist nicht einfach.
make a good ~ of s.th.	gute Arbeit leisten, etwas ordentlich tun
It isn't my ~.	Das ist nicht mein Bier. Das geht mich nichts an.

a Job's comforter — jmd., der durch seinen Trost die Situation nur verschlimmert

jog:
~ along — dahintrotten, weiterwursteln
How's life? Jogging along as usual?
~ s.b.'s arm/elbow — jdn. anstoßen, um seine Aufmerksamkeit zu erregen
~ s.o.'s memory — jdm. auf die Sprünge helfen (geistig)

John Bull — Personifizierung Englands

Johnny-come-lately — jmd., der sich einer Gruppe erst vor kurzem angeschlossen hat, und noch nicht wirklich dazu gehört

join:
~ hands with — sich die Hände reichen
~ up with s.o. — sich jdm. anschließen
~ forces with s.o. — seine Kräfte mit denen einer anderen Person/Gruppe vereinigen
~ the fray — sich an einer Auseinandersetzung beteiligen
care to ~ s.o. — sich jdm. anschließen

put s.o.'s nose out of joint (Sl.) — jdn. vor den Kopf stoßen, kränken

jolly:

a ~ good s.th.	sehr gut
That was a jolly good movie we saw last week.	
~ well	mit Sicherheit

jot:

~ down	notieren
~ or tittle	das kleinste Detail

journey's end	Tod

joy:

No ~!	Tote Hose
Any ~?	Erfolg gehabt?

a judgement of Solomon	eine weise Entscheidung
stew in one's own juices	im eigenen Saft schmoren lassen

jump:

~ all over s.o. (Am./Sl.)	jdn. wüst beschimpfen, jdn. zur Schnecke machen
~ at s.th.	sich auf etwas stürzen
~ the gun	vorzeitig mit etwas anfangen
~ the queue	sich vordrängeln
~ to one's feet	aufspringen
~ to conclusions	voreilige Schlüsse ziehen, vorschnell urteilen
~ down s.o.'s throat	jdm. über den Mund fahren
~ out of the frying pan into the fire. (Sprichw.)	Vom Regen in die Traufe kommen.
It's the high ~ for s.o.	jmd. kann sich auf etwas gefasst machen

just:

~ another s.th.	nur ein weiteres ... ohne besondere Merkmale
~ anybody	jeder Beliebige
~ as one is	unverändert
~ as soon do s.th.	etwas genauso gut/gerne tun
I'd just as soon go to England for my holiday.	
~ as you like	ganz wie du willst

~ for the ride	nur zum Spaß
~ in case	nur für den Fall
~ like that	einfach so
~ one of those things	eine dieser unvermeidlichen Sachen
~ the job	genau das, was man braucht
~ what the doctor ordered	genau das Richtige
but ~	eben erst
my ~ right	mein volles Recht

K

keen:
~ on doing s.th.	sehr für etwas sein
~ on s.th.	schätzen, gerne tun
~ on s.o.	für jdn. schwärmen

keep:
~ a civil tongue in one's head	höflich reden/bleiben
~ a close watch on s.b.	jdn. scharf beobachten
~ a stiff upper lip	kühl, unbewegt bleiben
~ abreast of	mithalten

We do what we can to keep abreast of scientific development.

~ after s.b.	jdn. verfolgen, jdm. nachstellen
~ an eye on s.o.	jdn. im Auge behalten
~ s.o. at arm's length	sich jdn. vom Leib halten
~ s.th/s.o. at bay	etwas/jdn. abwehren, fern halten

The soldier managed to keep the enemy at bay.

~ at 1. s.o/2. s.th.　　1. herumnörgeln. 2. bei etwas bleiben, festhalten an, darauf bestehen

1. My mother keeps at me to go to university.
2. You'll never learn to play the piano unless you keep at it.

~ coming back to s.th.	auf etwas beharren
~ company	verkehren mit

A person is always judged by the company he keeps.

~ close	wenig sprechen
~ dark	geheim halten

I'm leaving the firm next week, but please keep it dark.

~ going	dabei bleiben, weitermachen
~ one's fingers crossed	die Daumen drücken
~ in check	in Schranken halten, zügeln
~ in mind	etwas nicht vergessen, an etwas denken
~ in ignorance	in Unkenntnis lassen

kettle   **130**

~ in sight	im Auge behalten
~ in touch with	in Kontakt bleiben mit
~ late hours	lange aufbleiben, spät schlafen gehen

She is always late for class because she keeps late hours.

~ on doing s.th.	weiterhin etwas tun; fortfahren, etwas zu tun; etwas weiter tun
~ one's chin up	den Kopf hinhalten, tapfer handeln/tun
~ one's hair on (Brit./Sl.)	ruhig bleiben
~ one's hand off s.th.	die Finger von etwas lassen
~ one's head above water	sich über Wasser halten (finanziell)
~ one's nose out of s.th.	sich aus einer Sache heraushalten
~ one's temper	sich beherrschen
~ one step ahead of s.b.	jdm. einen Schritt voraus sein
~ pace with	Schritt halten mit
~ quiet	ruhig bleiben, sich ruhig verhalten
~ s.o. company	jdm. Gesellschaft leisten, bei jdm. bleiben
~ s.o. on tenterhooks	im Ungewissen lassen, jdn. zappeln lassen
~ track of s.b.	jdm. auf der Spur bleiben
~ up with the Joneses	mit jdm. Schrritt halten
~ up with the times	mit der Zeit gehen, sich auf dem Laufenden halten
~ your shirt on! (Sl.)	Hab Geduld! Warte einen Moment!

That's a pretty kettle of fish. (Brit./Sl.)   Das ist eine schöne Bescherung.

kick:

~ a habit (Sl.)	sich etwas abgewöhnen

The drug habit is probably the most difficult to kick.

~ one's heels	warten müssen
~ over the traces	über die Stränge schlagen
~ o.s. (for the doing s.th.) (Sl.)	sich in den Hintern beißen, etwas bedauern
~ s.o. out	jdn. hinauswerfen

~ s.o. upstairs (Sl.)	jdn. befördern
~ the bucket (Sl.)	den Löffel abgeben, abkratzen
~ up (a) dust/a fuss (Sl.)	Staub aufwirbeln
for ~s (Sl.)	zum Spaß
get a ~ out of s.th. (Sl.)	etwas aufregend finden, genießen
~ing and screaming	gegen starken Protest

kid:

~s' stuff (Sl.)	Kinderkram
to ~ s.o.	jdn. veralbern, jdn. ärgern
Don't ~ yourself!	Mach dir nichts vor!
No kidding?	Ehrlich?

kill:

~ the goose that lays the golden eggs	den Ast absägen, auf dem man sitzt
~ the fatted calf	ein Festessen geben, mit viel Aufwand bewirten
~ o.s. doing s.th.	sich mit etwas viel Mühe geben
dressed to ~	aufgetakelt wie eine Fregatte
~ s.o./s.th. off	jdm./etwas ein Ende bereiten
~ s.th. stone dead	eine Sache vollständig zerstören oder beenden
~ time	die Zeit totschlagen
~ two birds with one stone	zwei Fliegen mit einer Klappe schlagen
~ with kindness	jdn. mit Freundlichkeit überhäufen
make a ~ing	viel Geld scheffeln

kind:

~ of	in gewisser Weise, so in etwa
one of a ~	einmalig
two of a ~	zwei, die sich gesucht und gefunden haben

a kindred spirit	eine verwandte Seele
a King Charles's head	ein Thema oder Objekt, auf das sich jmd. dauernd bezieht, unabhängig, ob es mit dem Rest des Gesprächs zu tun hat

king:
~ of the castle	Anführer
a ~'s ransom	eine sehr große Summe

Kingdom come — Himmel, die nächste Welt

kiss:
~ **the Blarney stone** (Brit.) — die Fähigkeit, Leuten schmeicheln und sie überreden zu können

~ **of death** — der Todesstoß/-kuss

The judge's decision was the kiss of death for our plan.

~ **of life** — Mund-zu-Mund-Beatmung

~ **the dust** (Sl.) — ins Gras beißen

a kitchen-sink drama — ein realistisches Theaterstück über das Leben der Unterklasse

knee-high to a grasshopper — ein kleines Kind

knit one's brows — die Stirn runzeln

knock:
~ **about** (Sl.) — herumreisen

He spent his holiday knocking about in Scotland.

~ against	dagegenschlagen
~ back a drink	ein Getränk runterkippen
~ it off! (Sl.)	Hör auf!
~ out	bewusstlos schlagen
~ s.o.'s block off (Sl.)	jdn. fest auf den Kopf schlagen
~ s.o. into a cocked hat (Sl.)	jdn. locker in die Tasche stecken
~ s.th. (Sl.)	mäkeln, kritisieren
~ the stuffing out of s.o. (Sl.)	jdn. umhauen
a ~ing shop	Bordell

knock-on effect — Kettenreaktion

know:
~ all the answers	immer alles besser wissen
~ all the tricks of the trade	sich gut auskennen, gerissen sein

~ one's stuff (Sl.)	sich in seinem Fach gut auskennen

She is not the right person for the job, she doesn't know her stuff.

~ a good thing when one sees one	klug genug sein, den Wert einer Sache beurteilen zu können
~ a hawk from a handsaw	intelligent
~ a thing or two (Brit./Sl.)	schlau sein, weise sein

John is a smart man; he knows a thing or two.

~ how many beans make five	vernünftig in praktischen Dingen
~ s.th. inside out	etwas in- und auswendig kennen
~ the ropes (Sl.)	wissen, wie etwas läuft/wie eine Sache funktioniert
~ what's what	im Bilde sein
~ which side one's bread is buttered on	wissen, wo seine Interessen liegen
be in the ~	Bescheid wissen
make ~n	bekannt machen
~n all over the place (Sl.)	bekannt wie ein bunter Hund

L

labour:
~ a point — etwas übermäßig betonen
I understand what you mean, you don't need to labour the point.
a ~ of love — eine Aufgabe, die man aus Liebe zur Sache übernimmt
~ over s.th. — sich mit etwas abmühen
~ under a delusion — sich täuschen

lag behind — trödeln
Going for a walk with small children is no fun. They quickly lose interest and lag behind.

laid:
~ back (Sl.) — gelassen
~ up — 1. im Bett (krank), 2. außer Dienst (Reparatur)

1. I've been laid up all week with a bad cold.
2. My car is laid up, it needs a new gearbox.

a lame duck — eine Niete

land:
a ~ flowing with milk and honey — ein Land in dem Milch und Honig fließen; ein Land mit einem Übermaß an natürlichen Ressourcen
the ~ of Nod — im Tiefschlaf
~ on one's feet — auf die Füße fallen
~ s.b. in a mess — jdn. in Schwierigkeiten bringen
~ up as ... — als ... enden
see how the ~ lies — die Lage peilen, sich (diskret) erkundigen

be at large — auf freiem Fuß sein

larger than life — dramatisch übertrieben

last:

~ but not least	und nicht zuletzt, und nicht zu vergessen
~ night	gestern Abend
the ~ gasp	der letzte Atemzug
the ~ rites	Sterbesakramente
of the ~ importance	von äußerster Wichtigkeit
the ~ but one	der Vorletzte
be on one's ~ legs	auf dem letzten Loch pfeifen
It's the ~ straw that breaks the camel's back. (Sprichw.)	Das ist der Tropfen, der das Fass zum Überlaufen bringt.
at long ~	endlich
the ~ thing at night	vor dem Schlafengehen
the ~ thing one wants	das, was man wirklich nicht will

late:

~ in life	im fortgeschrittenen Alter
her ~ husband	ihr verstorbener Ehegatte
of ~	in letzter Zeit
better ~ than never	besser zu spät als gar nicht

laugh:

~ up one's sleeve (Sl.)	sich ins Fäustchen lachen
have the last ~	das letzte Wort haben
~ at s.b.	jdn. auslachen
~ s.th. off	mit einem Lachen über etwas hinweggehen
~ like a drain	sich ausschütten vor Lachen
~, and the world ~s with you weep, and you weep alone. (Sprichw.)	Lache und die Welt ist dein, weine und du bist allein.
You'll ~ on the other side of your face.	Dir wird das Lachen schon vergehen.
He ~s best who ~s last. (Sprichw.)	Wer zuletzt lacht, lacht am besten.

just for ~s nur zum Spaß

the laughing academy Irrenanstalt

rest on one's laurels sich auf seinen Lorbeeren ausruhen

lay:

~ by for a rainy day	einen Notgroschen beiseite legen
~ aside one's worries	seine Sorgen hinter sich lassen
~ claim to s.th.	auf etwas Anspruch erheben
~ a trap for s.b.	jdm. eine Falle stellen

The police laid a trap for the criminal and he walked into it.

~ hold of s.th.	etwas in die Hand nehmen, anpacken

I can't wait to lay hold of that spade and help you dig the garden.

~ it on thick	übertreiben

I don't believe half of what you say. You always lay it on thick.

~ in food supplies	Hamsterkäufe tätigen, Essensvorräte anlegen
~ off s.o. (Sl.)	jdn. in Ruhe lassen
~ s.o. off	jdn. entlassen
~ plans	Pläne machen
~ on a party	eine Party veranstalten
~ one's cards on the table	die Karten auf den Tisch legen
~ one's hands on s.th.	etwas in die Hände bekommen, erwischen

I'll really tell him off when I lay hands on him.

~ s.th. on thick	etwas dick auftragen
~ s.th. at s.b.'s door	jdm. die Schuld für etwas anlasten
~ s.th. bare	eine Sache aufdecken
~ stress on s.th.	etwas betonen
~ the blame for s.th. on s.b.	jdm. die Schuld für eine Sache in die Schuhe schieben

lead:

~ a dog's life	ein Hundeleben führen
~ astray	auf den falschen Weg führen, fehlleiten
~ a busy life	beschäftigt sein, viel zu tun haben
~ s.b. a dance	jdn. an der Nase herumführen
~ off	die Führung übernehmen, den Anfang machen

~ on	ermutigen, aufmuntern
~ up the garden path	jdn. an der Nase herumführen
~ up to	anleiten, überleiten zu, nach sich ziehen
~ the life of Riley (Sl.)	in Luxus leben
~ two lives	ein Doppelleben führen
~ the way	jdm. den richtigen Weg zeigen
a ~ing light	eine herausragende Persönlichkeit

leaf:

shake like ~	wie Espenlaub zittern
~ through	durchblättern
take a ~ out of s.o.'s book	jdm. etwas nachmachen, wie jdn. handeln
turn over a new ~	ein neues Leben anfangen

lean over backwards to do s.th.	sich die größte Mühe geben, etwas zu tun; sich fast umbringen, etwas zu tun

leap:

~ at the chance	die Gelegenheit beim Schopf ergreifen
by ~s and bounds	sprunghaft

learn:

~ a lesson	etwas aus Erfahrung lernen
~ by heart	auswendig lernen
~ by rote	auswendig lernen
~ s.th. the hard way	aus (bitterer) Erfahrung lernen

enjoy a new lease of life	neu aufleben

least:

the ~ one can do	das Mindeste, was man tun kann
~ said, soonest mended. (Sprichw.)	Reden ist Silber, Schweigen ist Gold.

be tough as old leather	zäh wie Leder sein

leave:

~ alone	in Ruhe lassen
~ a lot to be desired	sehr viel zu wünschen übrig lassen
~ no stone unturned	nichts unversucht lassen
~ off	aufhören, ablassen
~ s.b. to himself/to his own devices	jdn. sich selbst überlassen
~ s.o. in the lurch	jdn. im Stich lassen
~ s.o. out in the cold	jdn. ausschließen
~ s.th. to chance	etwas dem Zufall überlassen
~ it at that	es dabei belassen
~ it out! (Sl.)	Kommt nicht in Frage!
~ word with s.o.	eine Nachricht hinterlassen
take one's ~	seinen Abschied nehmen
take ~ of one's senses	von allen guten Geistern verlassen sein

Hove you taken leave of your senses, driving my car into the ditch!

left:

~ and right	in alle Richtungen
~, right and centre	überall
a ~-handed remark/compliment	ein zweifelhaftes, fragwürdiges Kompliment

leg:

not to have a ~ to stand on	etwas nicht entschuldigen können
to be on one's last ~	am Ende sein

lend:

~ one's ear	ein Ohr leihen, zuhören
~ s.b. a hand	jdm. zur Hand gehen
~ o.s. to s.th.	sich zu etwas hergeben, bei etwas mitmachen

This kind of plan is not one I could lend myself to.

length:

the ~ and breadth of s.th.	das ganze Gebiet
at great ~	lang und breit, ausführlich

The professor always spoke at great length about nothing at all.

at ~ *At length, he got up and left the room.*	nach einiger Zeit, mit der Zeit
For what ~ of time?	Für wie lange?
go to any ~s *He will go to any lengths to get what he wants.*	über Leichen gehen
the lesser of two evils	das Geringere von zwei Übeln
let:	
~ alone	1. nicht berühren, sich nicht einmischen, 2. geschweige denn
1. Let it well alone. That's none of our business. *2. I didn't ask Mary, let alone the rest of the family.*	
~ a person off s.th.	jdm. etwas erlassen, jdn. entbinden von
Let bygones be bygones. (Sprichw.)	Schwamm drüber; lass die Vergangenheit ruhen
~ grass grow under one's feet *John is always busy, he doesn't let the grass grow under his feet.*	still stehen, nichts tun
~ off steam	Dampf ablassen, explodieren
~ down	1. enttäuschen, im Stich lassen, 2. die Luft aus den Reifen lassen
1. He promised never to let her down. *2. He let the tyre of her bicycle down.*	
~ go!	Lass los!
~ it go at that	es dabei bewenden lassen
~ o.s. in for s.th.	sich auf etwas einlassen
Let sleeping dogs lie. (Sprichw.)	Schlafende Hunde soll man nicht wecken.
~ s.o. off the hook	jdn. verschonen
~ s.th. slide (Sl.)	etwas vernachlässigen
~ s.th. slip	eine Bemerkung fallen lassen, etwas verraten
~ the cat out of the bag	ein Geheimnis lüften, die Katze aus dem Sack lassen

I wasn't supposed to know about the party but my sister let the cat out of the bag.

the letter of the law   der Wortlaut des Gesetzes

level:
do one's ~ best   sein Möglichstes tun
have/keep a ~ head   einen kühlen Kopf haben/behalten
on the ~   ehrlich
~ with s.o. (Sl.)   zu jdm. ehrlich sein

lick:
~ s.b.'s boot   jdm. die Stiefel küssen
~ one's lips   sich die Lippen lecken
a ~ of paint   eine Schicht Farbe
~ one's wounds   sich die Wunden lecken
~ s.th. into shape (Sl.)   etwas formen, salonfähig (vorzeigbar) machen

The garden looks a terrible mess, but we'll soon lick it into shape.

lie:
~ awake   wach liegen
~ doggo (Sl.)   sich verstecken
~ down on the job   nicht aufpassen, etwas schlecht erledigen

I have to keep an eye on the workmen, I don't want them lying down on the job.

~ low (Sl.)   sich ruhig und unauffällig verhalten

tell a ~   lügen
~ through one's teeth   dreist lügen (überzeugend)
give the ~ to   absolut widersprechen
His behaviour gave the lie to what he said.
~ at s.o.'s door   für etwas verantwortlich sein
~ in store for   auf jdn. warten
a white ~   eine harmlose Lüge

life:

~ begins at forty. (Sprichw.)	Mit vierzig fängt das Leben an.
~ is not a bed of roses	das Leben ist nicht einfach
~ is worth living	man genießt das Leben

Sitting there on the beach with a drink in his hand, life certainly was worth living.

for ~	lebenslänglich
have the time of one's ~	etwas sehr genießen, eine wunderbare Zeit haben
not for the ~ of me	nicht um alles in der Welt
not on your ~!	nie und nimmer! auf gar keinen Fall!
seek s.o.'s ~	jdm. nach dem Leben trachten
be the ~ and soul of the party	der Mittelpunkt des Festes sein
in the prime of ~	im besten Alter
as large as ~	in voller Größe

lift:

give s.b. a ~	jdn. (per Anhalter) mitnehmen
~ a hand against s.o.	jdm. Schläge androhen
not ~ a finger	keinen Finger rühren

He never even lifted a finger to help me.

light:

the ~ of day	bei Tageslicht
cast some ~ on s.th.	erklären, Licht in eine Sache bringen
come to ~	ans Tageslicht kommen, aufgedeckt werden

His treachery only came to light after his death.

in a good ~	günstig, in günstigem Licht
in the ~ of	in Anbetracht ...
~ upon	durch Zufall entdecken
make ~ a work of s.th.	ein anderes Licht auf etwas werfen
make ~ of	bagatellisieren

He always makes light of his disability.

to see the ~	die Wahrheit erkennen, Erleuchtung erlangen (oft iron.)

lighten up (Sl.)   entspannen, etwas nicht so schwer nehmen

like:
and one's ~	seinesgleichen
and the ~	und Ähnliches
The farmer gave us fresh bread, butter, apples, pears and the like.	
~ anything!	(bekräftigend:) Aber wie!
~ a bat out of hell	wie ein geölter Blitz
~ billy-o (Sl.)	energisch, erfolgreich
~ blazes	so stark wie möglich
~ a bolt out of the blue (Sl.)	wie ein Blitz aus heiterem Himmel
~ a bull at the gate	aggressiv, direkt
~ a bull in a china shop	wie ein Elefant im Porzellanladen
~ calls to ~	Gleich und gleich gesellt sich gern.
~ a cat on hot bricks	wie die Katze auf dem heißen Blechdach
~ the cat that stole the cream	selbstzufrieden
~ Caesar's wife	keusch, anständig
~ the clappers	geräuschvoll
~ the curate's egg	eine Sache hat gute und schlechte Teile
~ a dog with two tails	begeistert, zufrieden mit sich selbst
~ father, ~ son. (Sprichw.)	Wie der Vater, so der Sohn.
~ a fish out of water	fehl am Platz, ungeschickt
~ a fishwife	laut, vulgär
~ a fly in amber	unverändert erhalten
~ greased lightning	wie ein geölter Blitz
~ hell it is	so ist es absolut nicht
It is all right!	
Like hell it is!	
~ it or lump it (Sl.)	Vogel friss oder stirb, eine Sache entweder akzeptieren/ einsehen oder einfach hinnehmen
~ a hot knife through butter	ohne jeden Widerstand
~ a lamb	ohne Protest, brav
~ nobody's business	mit größter Intensität
as ~ as two peas in a pod	wie ein Ei dem anderen gleichen

~ a sack of potatoes	wie ein Sack Kartoffeln
~ a stuck pig	wie ein angestochenes Schwein
~ a ton of bricks	mit großer Wucht oder Ernsthaftigkeit
~ water off a duck's back	ohne sichtbaren Erfolg, ohne Eindruck zu machen
~ wildfire	weitreichend und mit großer Geschwindigkeit
That's just ~ him.	Das sieht ihm ähnlich.
That's more ~ it.	Das ist doch schon besser!
There is nothing ~ ...	Es geht nichts über ...
What is she ~?	Wie ist sie?
a likely story	(iron.) eine unwahrscheinliche Geschichte

likes:

~ and dislikes	Vorlieben und Abneigungen
the ~ of s.b.	Leute wie ...

The likes of the Harveys do not go to church unless they can be sure of an audience, you know.

That's about the limit. (Sl.)	Das ist der absolute Hammer.

line:

~ one's own pockets	auf unredliche Weise Geld verdienen
be in ~ with	übereinstimmen mit
fall into ~ with s.b.	sich jdm. anschließen
~ up	sich anstellen
put s.th. on the ~	Klartext über eine Sache reden
stand in ~	in einer Reihe stehen
take the ~ of least resistance	den Weg des geringsten Widerstandes gehen
way out of ~	absolut nicht in Ordnung

lion:

the ~ lies down with the lamb	Frieden und Ruhe herrschen
the ~'s share	der Löwenanteil

live:

~ it up	sich ein schönes Leben machen

~ like a lord (Sl.)	auf großem Fuß leben
~ above/beyond one's means	über seine Verhältnisse leben
~ and let live	leben und leben lassen
~ on	sich ernähren von
~ through s.th.	etwas durchmachen
~ to see the day	etwas noch erleben
You have to ~ with it.	Du musst dich damit abfinden/ damit leben.
~ up to s.th.	Erwartungen erfüllen, sich als würdig erweisen

You have just given me such a good reference, I hope I can live up to it.

lo and behold! — Sieh da!

a load of rubbish — Unfug

lock:
~ the stable door after the horse has bolted	Wer zu spät kommt, den bestraft das Leben.
~, stock and barrel	alles, mit allem Drum und Dran

I finished the job at last, lock, stock and barrel.

Lombard street to a China orange — die Wahrscheinlichkeit ist deutlich in einer bestimmten Richtung

a lone wolf — ein einsamer Wolf; jmd., der so weit wie möglich ohne andere Menschen lebt oder arbeitet

Lonely Hearts — einsame Herzen

long[1]:
the ~ arm of the law	die weitreichende Autorität des Gesetzes
in the ~ run	letztendlich
~ ago	vor langer Zeit
~ time no see. (Sl.)	Lange nicht gesehen!
a ~ shot	nur eine Vermutung, nicht sehr wahrscheinlich

by a ~ shot	bei Weitem
the ~ and the short of it	kurz und gut
The long and the short of it is that you just can't hope to win.	
~-standing	lang geplant/ausgemacht
I have a long-standing invitation to a concert this evening.	
~-suffering	geduldig, ausdauernd
~-winded	langatmig
so ~ (Sl.)	bis dann, später

long²:

~ for s.th.	sich nach etwas sehnen

look:

~ as if butter would not melt in s.b.'s mouth	sehr korrekt wirken
~ as if one has been dragged through a hedge backwards	unordentlich, verwüstet
have a good ~ at s.th.	sich etwas genau ansehen
~ s.o. in the eye	jdm. ins Gesicht sehen
I don't like the ~ of it.	Die Sache gefällt mir ganz und gar nicht.
it ~s like	es sieht so aus, als ob
~ after s.b.	sich um jdn. kümmern
~ ahead	in die Zukunft blicken
~ daggers at s.o. (Sl.)	jdn. böse anschauen
~ down on s.b.	auf jdn. herabsehen
~ for	suchen nach
~ forward	sich freuen auf
~ for trouble (Sl.)	Schwierigkeiten heraufbeschwören
The policeman told me to leave, unless I was looking for trouble.	
~ here!	Na hören Sie mal!
~ into s.th.	einer Sache nachgehen
The headmaster promised to look into the matter.	
~ in on s.o.	bei jdm. vorbeischauen
~ s.th. up	etwas nachschlagen
~ on s.b. as	jdn. betrachten als, jdn. halten für
I look on him as a friend.	

~ down one's nose at s.o.	auf jdn. herabsehen
~ out!	Vorsicht! Pass auf!
~ out for s.b.	nach jdm. Ausschau halten
Look out for John when you're in London.	
~ over s.th.	etwas durchsehen
~ the other way	angestrengt wegsehen
~ up to s.o.	zu jdm. aufblicken

loose:
~ ends	offene Probleme
~ talk	Klatsch und Tratsch
at a ~ end	faul, untätig, ohne bestimmtes Ziel
have a ~ tongue	eine lose Zunge haben
have a slate ~	eine Schraube locker haben

lord:
~ it over s.o.	sich arrogant benehmen, wichtig tun
The head of department lords it over his assistants.	
~ and master	Herrscher, Befehlshaber
the ~s of creation	1. die Menschheit, 2. Männer (im Gegensatz zu Frauen)

lose:
~ face	das Gesicht verlieren, sich blamieren
~ it (Sl.)	wirr/wütend werden
~ one's cool (Am./Sl.)	böse/wütend werden
~ heart	den Mut verlieren
~ it's looks	schlechter aussehen als vorher
~ one's marbles (Sl.)	verrückt werden
~ one's mind	verrückt werden
~ one's rag	unbeherrscht reagieren, seinen Ärger offen zeigen
~ one's shirt (Sl.)	sein letztes Hemd verlieren
~ one's temper	wütend werden
~ one's train of thought	den Faden verlieren
~ one's tongue	sprachlos sein, es verschlägt einem die Sprache
~ sight of	aus den Augen verlieren

~ touch with	nicht mehr auf dem Laufenden sein, den Kontakt verlieren
be at a loss	in Verlegenheit sein

lost:
a ~ cause	eine verlorene Sache
a ~ soul	die Seele eines Sünders
~ in thought	in Gedanken verloren/vertieft

a lot of water has run under the bridge	viel Wasser ist den Bach heruntergeflossen

loud:
~ and long	laut und anhaltend
~ and clear	klar und deutlich

love:
~ is blind. (Sprichw.)	Liebe macht blind.
~ me, ~ my dog	Wer mich liebt, liebt auch meinen Hund.
fall in ~	sich verlieben
Give my ~ to …!	Grüße bitte … von mir.
~ doing s.th.	etwas sehr gerne tun
play for ~	nicht um Geld spielen
~ at first sight	Liebe auf den ersten Blick
The ~ of money is the root of all evil. (Sprichw.)	Geldgier ist die Wurzel allen Übels.
not for ~ or money	nicht für Geld und gute Worte, keineswegs, überhaupt nicht

I've tried all the libraries, but I can't find the book for love or money.

no ~ lost between	sich nicht grün sein/mögen
a low profile	unauffällig
lower one's sights	seine Ansprüche senken

luck:
bad ~!	So ein Pech!
It's the ~ of the draw.	Man muss es so nehmen, wie's kommt.

Just my ~! — Pech gehabt, wie immer!

lucky:
~ at cards, unlucky in love. (Sprichw.) — Glück im Spiel, Pech in der Liebe.
a ~ dip — Glückstopf

lumber s.o. with s.th. (Sl.) — jdn. mit etwas belasten

If you don't like it, you can lump it! — Damit wirst du dich abfinden müssen.

out to lunch (Sl.) — verrückt

mad:

~ about s.th.	verrückt nach etwas sein
~ as a hatter	vollkommen übergeschnappt
like ~ (Sl.)	wie verrückt

He's been playing tennis like mad all morning.

drive s.o. ~	jdn. verrückt machen
be ~ on/about s.o./s.th.	verrückt nach jdm. sein, etwas sehr gerne tun
go ~	wahnsinnig werden

make:

~ answer	antworten
~ an appearance	auftauchen, präsent sein
~ a beginning	einen Anfang machen
~ a beeline for	auf jdn./etwas geradewegs zugehen

He entered the room and made a beeline for his wife.

~ bold to do s.th.	etwas wagen
~ both ends meets	sich nach der Decke strecken
You can't ~ bricks without straw. (Sprichw.)	Mit nichts kann man kein Haus bauen.
~ a cat laugh	außergewöhnlich komisch sein
~ certain	sicherstellen
~ a change	1. etwas ändern 2. eine Abwechslung bieten

1. He made changes in the department as soon as he was appointed.
2. The new theatre certainly made a change in the cultural environment.

~ s.th. clear	deutlich machen
~ a deal with	ein Abkommen treffen mit
~ an example of s.b.	an jdm. ein Exempel statuieren
~ a face	Grimassen schneiden
~ fast	befestigen, anbinden
~ one's fortune	reich werden

~ a fuss about s.th.	viel Aufhebens um etwas machen
~ a go of s.th. (Sl.)	etwas erfolgreich tun
~ a good job of s.th.	gute Arbeit leisten
~ a good showing	sich ordentlich benehmen, den Erwartungen entsprechen
~ great strides	sich deutlich verbessern
~ a habit of s.th.	sich etwas zur Gewohnheit machen
~ a mountain out of a molehill. (Sprichw.)	Aus einer Mücke einen Elefanten machen.
~ a name for o.s.	sich einen Namen machen, bekannt werden
~ a song and dance of s.th.	ein fürchterliches Theater wegen etwas machen
~ do with s.th.	sich mit etwas behelfen
~ eyes at s.o.	jdm. schöne Augen machen
~ friends with	sich anfreunden
~ good money	gut verdienen
~ good use of s.th.	etwas richtig anwenden/ einsetzen
~ haste!	Beeil dich!
~ it	einen Termin schaffen
~ light of s.th.	etwas verniedlichen, herunterspielen
~ one's way in the world	seinen Weg machen
~ peace	Frieden schließen
~ shift with	sich behelfen mit
~ s.th. a rule	sich etwas zur Regel machen
~ s.th. up	etwas erfinden, sich etwas ausdenken
~ s.th.	es schaffen, zu etwas zu kommen (zu einer Einladung, Verabredung etc.)

We were sorry you couldn't come to the party but hope you'll make it next time.

~ the best of a bad job	gute Miene zum bösen Spiel machen
~ the grade	es schaffen, Erwartungen entsprechen

It is very important to make the grade if you want to be successful in business.

~ the most of one's life	das Beste aus seinem Leben machen, sein Leben in vollen Zügen genießen
~ tracks for home	sich auf den Heimweg machen
~ up for lost time	verlorene Zeit wieder wettmachen
~ up one's mind	sich entschließen, eine Entscheidung treffen
~ way for	vorbeigehen lassen, Platz machen
~ one's way	vorankommen

man:
~ and beast	Mensch und Tier
~ and boy	sein ganzes Leben lang, von Kindheit an

I have been living in this part of town, man and boy, for thirty-nine years now.

the ~ for the job	für eine Aufgabe geeignet
the ~ in the street	der Mann von der Straße
a ~ of few words	schweigsam
a ~ of God	Geistlicher
the ~ of the house	Hausherr
a ~ of letters	Dichter, Schriftsteller
a ~ of many parts	vielseitig begabt
a ~ of substance	wohlhabend
a ~ of the world	ein Mann von Welt
Man proposes but God disposes. (Sprichw.)	Der Mensch denkt, Gott lenkt.
~'s inhumanity to ~	die Bereitschaft der Menschen, einander Böses zu tun

many:
~ a one	manch einer
~ a long day	eine lange Zeit, eine Ewigkeit

We have not seen them for many a long day.

~ are called but few are chosen	Viele sind berufen, aber wenige sind auserwählt.
~ hands make light work.	Viele Hände, wenig Arbeit.
~ happy returns of the day	herzlichen Glückwunsch zum Geburtstag
~ a little makes a mickle. (Sprichw.)	Kleinvieh macht auch Mist.

~ a time	regelmäßig, oft
off the map (Sl.)	hinter dem Mond, abgelegen
a mare's nest	ein Reinfall
Tell that to the Marines. (Sl.)	Das mach' einem anderen weis.
mark:	
overstep the ~	zu weit gehen
up to the ~	gesundheitlich in Ordnung
~ time	auf der Stelle bleiben, nicht voran kommen
~ my words	erinnert euch daran, was ich sage
a marked person	auf der schwarzen Liste stehen
marriage:	
a ~ of convenience	eine Hochzeit aus Vernunftsgründen
a ~ of true minds	eine geistige Ehe
marry:	
~ in haste, repent at leisure. (Sprichw.)	Heiraten in Eile bereut man mit Weile.
~ money	reich heiraten
matter:	
a ~ of s.th.	es ist eine Frage von
a ~ of concern	Anlass zur Sorge
as a ~ of course	entsprechend der üblichen Abläufe
What's the ~?	Was ist los?
as a ~ of fact	in der Tat
a ~ of the moment	ein Problem von erheblicher Wichtigkeit
a ~ of opinion	Ansichtssache
a ~ of time	eine Frage der Zeit
no ~ what	egal was
it doesn't ~	das macht nichts
~-of-fact	hart, geschäftsmäßig, ohne Gefühle

He broke the sad news in a very matter-of-fact voice.
not mince ~s   kein Blatt vor den Mund nehmen

mean:
~ business   es ernst meinen
by all ~s   aber bitte sehr (als wohlwollende Zusage), unter allen Umständen
by no ~s   auf keinen Fall
~ well   es gut meinen
~ to do s.th.   vorhaben, etwas zu tun
I have been meaning to phone you all week.

the means to an end   die nötigen Mittel, um ein bestimmtes Ergebnis zu erzielen

meanwhile, back at the ranch   um zu der eigentlichen Geschichte zurückzukehren

measure one's length   der Länge nach hinfallen

meet:
~ one's end   sterben
~ with   bekommen, erhalten
He met with great sympathy when his wife died.
~ one's maker   sterben
~ one's match   seinen Meister finden
make ends ~   sich nach der Decke strecken
No matter how much I save, I don't seem to be able to make ends meet.
more than ~s the eye   mehr, als man auf Anhieb erkennen kann
~ s.b. halfway   jdm. auf halbem Weg entgegenkommen
~ s.b.'s eye   den Blick erwidern
~ with an accident   verunglücken

s.b.'s memory is green   jmd. ist nach seinem Tode nicht vergessen

mend:
~ one's ways	sich bessern (im moralischen Sinne)
~ one's manners	seine Manieren verbessern

Don't mention it! — Schon gut, nicht der Rede wert!

mess:
be in a ~ (Sl.)	in der Tinte sitzen
~ about with s.th.	an etwas herumbasteln
~ s.th. up (Sl.)	Mist machen
~ s.o. about (Sl.)	jdm. die Zeit stehlen
~ s.o. up (Sl.)	jdn. verprügeln

take the micky (Sl.) — jdn. veralbern

might:
~ as well	auch gleich

If you are going shopping, you might as well take the dog.

~ is right.	Wer die Macht hat, der hat auch das Recht.

a mile off — weit weg

milk:
~ s.o. dry	jdn. nach Strich und Faden ausnehmen
the ~ of human kindness	Güte
~-and-water	seicht, verwässert
a millstone round s.o.'s neck (Sl.)	ein Klotz am Bein
run of the mill (Sl.)	08/15, alltäglich

mind:
a ~ to	Wunsch, Bedürfnis

I've a good mind to complain to the company.

be in two ~s about s.th.	sich über etwas im Unklaren sein
Do you ~!	Muss das denn sein!
give s.o. a piece of one's ~ (Brit.)	jdm. gehörig die Meinung sagen
have s.th. in ~	etwas vorhaben, einen Plan haben

know one's ~	wissen, was man will
make up one's ~	sich entschließen
Never ~!	Das macht nichts!
read s.b.'s ~	jds. Gedanken lesen
speak one's ~	sagen, was man denkt
~ one's own business	sich um die eigenen Angelegenheiten kümmern

have a one-track ~ — immer nur das eine im Sinn haben
The only thing Eric thinks about is money, he has such a one-track mind.

~ one's P's and Q's	sich anständig benehmen
out of one's ~	wahnsinnig, von Sinnen
~ you	aber andererseits (im Sinne einer Einschränkung)

a mine of information — eine Quelle des Wissens

miss:

A ~ is as good as a mile. (Sprichw.)	Knapp daneben ist auch vorbei.
~ the boat (Sl.)	der Zug ist abgefahren, den Anschluss verpassen
~ the mark	daneben liegen, falsch liegen
~ the train	den Zug verpassen
~ one's footing	ausrutschen, stolpern
~ the point	nicht verstehen, worum es geht
give s.th. a ~	die Finger von etwas lassen

It's a mixed blessing. — Das ist ein zweischneidiges Schwert

just a mo' (Sl.) — sofort, gleich

moan and groan — sich beschweren

moment:

the ~ of truth	die Stunde der Wahrheit
in a ~	bald, gleich
unguarded ~	ein unachtsamer Augenblick

In an unguarded moment, he gave his secret away.

money:
~ is no object.	Geld spielt keine Rolle.
for my ~	meiner Ansicht nach
pocket-~	Taschengeld
put one's money where one's mouth is	seinen Worten Taten folgen lassen

monkey:
~ business	Unfug
not to give a ~'s about s.th. (Sl.)	sich einen Dreck um etwas scheren

a moonlight flit — bei Nacht und Nebel ausziehen
Why are you packing your suitcases? Are you thinking of a moonfight flit?

a moot point — ein strittiger Punkt

more:
the ~ the merrier	je mehr desto besser
~ royalist than the king	katholischer als der Papst
~ sinned against than sinning	jmd. hat mehr Unrecht erlitten als begangen
~ or less	mehr oder weniger
to be ~ to s.th. than ...	an etwas ist mehr dran, als ...

morning:
the ~-after feeling	die Katerstimmung am nächsten Morgen
~, noon and night	immer wieder; morgens, mittags, abends

the most one can say — das Beste, was man sagen kann

mother:
be tied to one's ~'s apron-strings	der Mutter am Rockzipfel hängen
a ~'s boy	ein Muttersöhnchen

mountain:
The ~ labours and brings forth a mouse.	Viel Mühe, wenig Nutzen.

If the ~ will not come to Mohammed, then Mohammed must go to the ~. (Sprichw.)	Wenn der Prophet nicht zum Berg kommt, kommt der Berg zum Propheten.

mouth:
one's ~ waters	jdm. läuft das Wasser im Munde zusammen
down in the ~	niedergeschlagen

move:
Get a ~ on!	Spute dich!
~ heaven and earth	Himmel und Hölle in Bewegung setzen
~ house	umziehen
~ up in the world	erfolgreich sein, avancieren

Mr Right	Märchenprinz
Mrs Grundy	eine engstirnige und humorlose Person
Mrs Mop	Putzfrau

much:
~ good as it may do	möge es ihm nützen
~ mistaken	im Irrtum
~ of a muchness	sehr ähnlich
I'm not ~ of a ...	Ich bin kein großer ...

Mud sticks. (Sprichw.)	Etwas bleibt immer hängen.
That's a mug's game!	Das ist doch schwachsinnig!

mum:
~'s the word!	Kein Wort darüber!
to keep ~	den Mund halten

N

nail:
be a ~ in s.b.'s coffin — ein Nagel zu jds. Sarg sein, das Ende oder Scheitern von jdm. beschleunigen

~ s.o. down — jdn. festnageln
I tried to nail him down as to the time of his arrival.

as hard as ~s — knallhart
hit the ~ on the head — den Nagel auf den Kopf treffen
on the ~ (Sl.) — pünktlich, sofort

have a narrow escape — gerade noch davonkommen

one's native heath — Heimatort

near:
be ~ at hand — in der Nähe/in Reichweite/zur Hand sein

a ~ thing — gerade noch mal Glück haben, ein knappes Entkommen
That was a near thing. You almost dropped that antique vase.

draw ~ — es geht auf ... zu
Christmas draws near, we must buy a tree and decorate it.

~ the mark — beinahe richtig
That wasn't quite the right answer but it was very near the mark.

be ~ and dear — jdm. nahe stehen
one's ~est and dearest — Familie
the ~est offer — der höchste gebotene Preis

a necessary evil — ein notwendiges Übel

Necessity is the mother of invention. (Sprichw.) — Not macht erfinderisch.

neck:
~ and ~ — Kopf an Kopf

get it in the ~ (Brit./Sl.)	bestraft werden
~ and crop	vollständig
~ or nothing	Kopf und Kragen für den Erfolg riskieren

need:
~ one's head examined	nicht ganz bei Trost, dumm
~ s.th. like one ~s a hole in the head	etwas brauchen wie einen Kropf
~ a long spoon to eat with the devil.	Wer mit dem Teufel essen will, muss einen langen Löffel haben.
~ no introduction	als bekannt voraussetzen können

a needle in a haystack	die Nadel im Heuhaufen

neither:
~ here nor there	das spielt keine Rolle
~ hide nor hair of s.b.	keine Spur von jdm.

nerve:
You have got a ~! (Sl.)	Du hast vielleicht Nerven!
have the ~ to do s.th.	die Frechheit besitzen, etwas zu tun

a nervous wreck	mit den Nerven am Ende
the net result	das Endergebnis

never:
~ fear	nur keine Bange
~ mind!	Lass gut sein, vergiss es!
well, I ~!	kaum zu glauben!

new:
~ blood	Anfänger, neue Leute
A ~ broom (sweeps clean).	(Sprichw.) Neue Besen kehren besser.
a ~ deal	ein gesellschaftliches oder politisches Reformprogramm

news:
be ~ to s.o.	jdm. noch nicht bekannt sein
be bad ~	Ärger bringen

~ from nowhere	nichts Neues, bereits bekannt
the good ~ is	die gute Nachricht ist

next:
the ~ best thing to s.th.	fast so gut wie
the ~ but one	der Übernächste
~ to nothing	fast nichts, sehr wenig

nice:
~ one, Cyril	Nicht schlecht gemacht!
~ weather for ducks	Regenwetter
~ work if you can get it	Ausdruck von Neid auf etwas, das jmd. anderes erhalten hat

nick:
in the ~ of time	gerade noch rechtzeitig
to ~ s.o. (Sl.)	jdn. verhaften
to ~ s.th. (Sl.)	etwas stehlen

night:
make a ~ of it	die Nacht durchmachen
a ~ out	ein Abend unterwegs

nine:
~ times out of ten	fast immer
a ~ to five job	eine geregelte Tätigkeit

nip:
It was ~ and tuck.	Das war eine knappe Sache.
~ in	bei jdm. vorbeischauen
~ s.th. in the bud	im Keim ersticken

get down to the nitty-gritty	zur Sache kommen

no:
~ doubt	sicher, ohne Zweifel
~ laughing matter	eine ernste Sache
To lose one's wallet on the underground is no laughing matter.	
~ skin off s.o.'s back	kein Problem sein

none:
~ the less	trotzdem

~ other than	kein anderer als
~ so blind as those who will not see. (Sprichw.)	Keiner ist blinder als der nicht sehen will.
~ too	nicht sehr
The dog was none too bright, but it would serve to play with the kids.	
~ too soon	im letzten Moment

nooks and crannies	kleine Ecken und Winkel

nose:	
~ about	schnüffeln
follow one's ~	immer der Nase nach
~ s.th. out	etwas aufstöbern/aufdecken
turn one's ~ up at s.th.	die Nase über etwas rümpfen
My cat turns up its nose at tinned food, it only eats fresh meat.	
under s.o.'s ~	vor der Nase von jdm.
~ for s.th.	nach etwas schnüffeln
~ around	herumschnüffeln, Nachforschungen anstellen

not:	
~ see wood for trees	vor lauter Bäumen den Wald nicht sehen
~ born yesterday	nicht von gestern
~ hold water (Sl.)	keinen Sinn ergeben
Your argument doesn't convince me, it doesn't hold water.	
~ sleep a wink	kein Auge zutun

strike the note	den richtigen Ton anschlagen

nothing:	
~ in particular	nichts Besonderes
~ doing! (Sl.)	Nichts da! Kommt nicht in Frage!
~ of the kind	absolut nichts, nichts dergleichen
~ short of	absolut
~ to it	einfach, leicht
~ to write home about (Sl.)	nichts Aufregendes/Besonderes
I can make ~ of it.	Damit kann ich nichts anfangen.

now:
- ~ and again — hin und wieder, von Zeit zu Zeit
- ~ or never — jetzt oder nie
- ~ it can be told — inzwischen kann man es offen sagen
- ~ you're talking! — Stimmt! Gute Idee!

nowhere:
- ~ to be seen — nirgends zu sehen
- ~ special — irgendwo

the nub of the matter — der springende Punkt

make o.s. a nuisance — lästig werden, zu einer Plage werden

null and void — wirkungslos, nicht bindend

number one — die eigene Person
Jack was busy looking after number one, so of course he could not help us!

nurse a grievance — lange über einem ärgerlichen Anlass brüten

nut:
- go off one's ~ — verrückt werden
- a hard ~ to crack — eine harte Nuss
The detective was having difficulty with a case. It was a hard nut to crack.

nuts:
- drive s.b. ~ — jdn. verrückt machen
- ~ about s.o. — nach jdm. verrückt sein
- **in a nutshell** — kurz zusammengefasst

nutty as a fruitcake (Sl.) — total verrückt

O

object:
an ~ lesson — praktische Unterweisung
the ~ of one's affection — Geliebte(r)

be obliged to s.o. — jdm. sehr verbunden sein

occur to s.o. — jdm. einfallen

odd:
~s and ends — Kleinkram
an ~ bird — eine exzentrische Person
~ jobs — verschiedene Aufgaben
~s and sods — wertloses Zeug
against all ~s — entgegen aller Erwartungen
be at ~s with s.b. — mit jdm. auf Kriegsfuß stehen
s.th. makes no ~s — etwas spielt keine Rolle
the ~ man out — Außenseiter, das fünfte Rad am Wagen

The ~s are against you. — Die Chancen stehen schlecht für dich. Du bist im Nachteil.

What's the ~s? (Sl.) — Was macht das schon?

of:
~ all the nerve! — So eine Frechheit!
~ academic interest — ohne praktischen Wert, bedeutungslos
~ course (not) — selbstverständlich (nicht)
~ the first magnitude — von äußerster Wichtigkeit
If that should happen, it would truly be a catastrophe of the first magnitude.

~ good standing — mit einem guten Ruf
~ late — in letzter Zeit
~ no avail — ohne Ergebnis
~ necessity — notwendigerweise, gezwungenermaßen
~ note — bekannt
~ the old school — vom alten Schlag
~ the order ~ — etwa

A saving in fuel of the order of at least ten per cent is expected.

~ one's own accord	spontan, freiwillig
~ the same stripe	zur gleichen Gruppe gehörig

off:

~ and on	gelegentlich
~-day (Sl.)	Pechtag
~ duty	dienstfrei
~-hand	leichthin, lässig
~ limits	Zutritt verboten
~-putting	unsympathisch, unkooperativ
~ the map	am Ende der Welt
~ the record	im Vertrauen
~ the beaten track	abseits, abgelegen
~ the cuff	spontan, ohne Übung
~ to (Sl.)	unterwegs nach
be ~ sick	sich krankgemeldet haben
on the ~-chance	in der leisen Hoffnung
tell s.o. ~	jdn. zusammenstauchen

oil:

~ s.b.'s palm	jdm. Schmiergelder zukommen lassen, jdn. bestechen
pour ~ on the flames	Öl ins Feuer gießen
~ and water do not mix. (Sprichw.)	Wasser und Feuer werden nicht Freunde.

old:

an ~ bag (pej.)	eine alte Schachtel
~ before one's time	schwächer, als das Lebensalter vermuten ließe
~ beyond ons's years	reifer, als in dem Alter üblich
~ boy!	Alter Junge!
the ~ buffer	alter Mann
~ enough to be s.b.'s father/mother	alt genug sein, um jds. Vater/Mutter zu sein
an ~ flame	eine ehemalige Beziehung, eine alte Flamme
an ~ fogey	ein alter Kauz
~ hat	aus der Mode; ein alter Hut
an ~ maid	eine alte Jungfer
~, unhappy, far-off things	Sorgen der Vergangenheit

an ~ wives' tale — Legende, Märchen

the oldest profession — das horizontale Gewerbe

an olive branch — ein Friedensangebot

on:
~ and off — gelegentlich
~ cloud nine (Sl.) — im siebten Himmel, sehr glücklich

~ edge — nervös
You can't have been sleeping well lately, you are so on edge.
~ one's toes — aufmerksam
~ second thoughts — nach reiflicher Überlegung
~ the spur of the moment (Sl.) — Hals über Kopf, plötzlich
~ the face of it — offensichtlich, anscheinend
~ the got — beschäftigt
~ the one hand — einerseits
~ the verge of ... — kurz davor sein ...
~ the wrong track — auf der falschen Fährte
have had s.o. ~ about s.th. (Sl.) — jdn. wegen einer Sache gesprochen haben

have s.th. ~ — etwas vorhaben
that's not ~ — das kommt nicht in Frage
what's ~? (Sl.) — Was gibt es? Wie sieht es aus?

once:
~ again — noch einmal
~ bitten, twice shy. (Sprichw.) — Gebranntes Kind scheut das Feuer.
~ and for all — ein für alle Mal
~ in a blue moon — alle Jubeljahre
~ in a while — gelegentlich
~ learnt, it isn't easily forgotten. — Was man einmal gelernt hat, vergisst man nicht so leicht.

~ too often — einmal zu viel
I tell you, you will be late once too often and then you will be out of a job!
~ upon a time — es war einmal
give s.o. the ~-over (Sl.) — jdn. kurz betrachten

one:

~ after the other	einer nach dem anderen
~ and all	jeder
~ day	eines Tages
~ for the road	ein letztes Glas vor dem Aufbruch
~ good turn deserves another. (Sprichw.)	Hilfst du mir, so helf ich dir. Eine Hand wäscht die andere.
~ of these days	irgendwann, gelegentlich
a ~-horse town	ein Kaff
~ in the eye for s.b.	ein Schlag ins Gesicht
~ in a million	einzigartig
a ~-man band	eine Einmannband
be ~ up on s.o. (Sl.)	jdm. voraus sein
~ man's loss is another man's gain.	Des einen Verlust ist des anderen Gewinn.
~ man's meat is another man's poison. (Sprichw.)	Was einem schadet, nützt dem anderen.
~ and only	absolut einzigartig
~ swallow does not make a summer. (Sprichw.)	Eine Schwalbe macht noch keinen Sommer.
~ thing and another	verschiedene Dinge/ Angelegenheiten
~ way or the other	auf die eine oder andere Weise
I for ~	ich zum Beispiel
~ on ~ (Sl.)	unter vier Augen

only:

an ~ child	Einzelkind
~ fair	nur recht und billig
~ just	nur ganz knapp
~ too conscious of s.th.	man ist sich einer Sache nur zu sehr bewusst, man weiß etwas ganz genau

the onus is on ... die Verantwortung liegt bei ...

ooh and aah lauthals Begeisterung oder Erschrecken äußern

The people oohed and aahed when the clown entered the cirus.

open:

~ and above board	offen und ehrlich

~ the floodgates	Tür und Tor öffnen
~ Pandora's box	die Büchse der Pandora öffnen, unbedacht Unheil verursachen
an ~ question	eine noch ungeklärte Frage
~ season for	Jagdsaison
~ up to s.o.	mit jdm. offen reden
the operative word	der springende Punkt
the opium of the people	Opium des Volkes, Religion
opposite number	Gegenstück

or:

~ else	oder etwas Unangenehmes wird geschehen
~ I'm a Dutchman	ich bin mir absolut sicher
~ rather	oder um es genauer zu sagen
~ so	oder so, etwa
ordeal by fire	Prüfung der Standhaftigkeit (eigentlich: Gottesurteil)
the order of the day	1. Planung oder Programm für den Tag, 2. üblich

other:

the ~ side of the coin	die Kehrseite der Medaille
~ things being equal	wenn sich die Lage ansonsten nicht ändert
every ~	jeder zweite
the ~ day	neulich
our man in	unser Vertreter an einem bestimmten Ort

out:

~ cold	bewusstlos
The boxer knocked his opponent out cold.	
~ of all proportion	maßlos übertrieben, in keinem Verhältnis
~ and about	wieder auf den Beinen

I'm pleased to see you out and about after your illness.	
~ **and** ~	gänzlich
The girl is an out-and-out genius.	
~ **for the count**	bewusstlos
~ **of date**	altmodisch
~ **of order**	außer Betrieb, kaputt
~ **of print**	vergriffen
~ **of the corner of one's eye**	aus dem Augenwinkel
~ **of the frying pan, into the fire**	vom Regen in die Traufe
~ **of the woods** (Sl.)	nicht mehr in der kritischen Phase
be ~	nicht zu Hause sein
have it ~ **with s.o.**	sich mit jdm. aussprechen
pull ~	sich zurückziehen
take it ~ **on s.b.**	etwas an jdm. auslassen
the ins and ~**s**	die Einzelheiten
outstay one's welcome	länger bleiben, als dem Gastgeber lieb ist

over:

all ~	aus und vorbei
~ **and above s.th.**	über etwas hinaus
~ **and done with**	aus und vorbei
~ **my dead body!**	Nur über meine Leiche!
~ **one's head**	zu hoch für jdn.
~ **s.o.** (Sl.)	über jdn. hinweg sein
overshoot the mark	über das Ziel hinausschießen
overstep the mark	eine Grenze überschreiten, übertreiben
owe s.b. a debt of gratitude	jdm. Dank schuldig sein

own:

hold one's ~	sich behaupten
on one's ~	allein, selbstständig
~ **up to s.th.**	sich zu etwas/einer Tat bekennen
The boy owned up to having stolen the apples.	
get one's ~ **back**	sich rächen

P

pack:
~ one's bags — sein Bündel schnüren, abreisen
~ it in! (Sl.) — Hör auf damit!
~ s.o. off somewhere — jdn. fortschicken, fortjagen
Mother packed the boys off to the beach so she could go shopping.

~ed like sardines — wie die Heringe, sehr eng
We were packed like sardines in the coach to London.

a ~ of lies — lauter Lügen
The story he told was nothing but a pack of lies.

send s.o. ~ing — jdn. kurzfristig entlassen, jdn. abservieren, jdn. kurz abfertigen

paddle one's own canoe — auf eigenen Füßen stehen

pain:
be a ~ in the neck (Sl.) — einem auf die Nerven gehen
take ~s to do s.th. — sich bei etwas große Mühe geben
He took great pains to help her settle in.

paint:
~ a gloomy picture of s.th. — ein düsteres Bild von etwas malen
~ the town red — die Stadt unsicher machen, feiern

beyond the pale — jenseits des Zumutbaren

palm s.th. off (Sl.) — jdm. etwas andrehen

a paper tiger — Papiertiger

par:
~ excellence — ganz besonders

~ **for the course** (Am.)	typisch, was man erwarten konnte
His performance at tennis was quite par for the course.	
up to ~	dem erwarteten Niveau entsprechend
a paragon of virtue	ein Muster/Ausbund an Tugend (iron.)
the parish pump	Klatsch und Tratsch in einer ländlichen Gemeinde
Once he had retired, his interests in life revolved mostly around the parish pump.	

part:

~ and parcel of s.th.	fester Bestandteil; samt und sonders
A glittering tree, presents and good food are all part and parcel of Christmas.	
He packed his family off part and parcel to spend a holiday in the country.	
for my ~	was mich betrifft
for the most ~	weitgehend, meistens
take in good ~	nicht beleidigt sein
take ~ in	teilnehmen an
take s.b.'s ~	Partei ergreifen für jdn.
~ with s.o. or s.th.	sich von jdm. oder etwas trennen
be partial to	mögen, gern haben
I am rather partial to roast beef and Yorkshire pudding.	
a party piece	ein besonderes Glanzstück

pass:

~ away/on	sterben
~ a remark	eine Bemerkung machen
~ for	gelten als

~ judgement	ein Urteil fällen
~ off	1. vorgeben, dass, 2. einen falschen Eindruck erwecken, 3. langsam weniger werden

1. She disliked his bad manners, but tried to pass them off as a joke.
2. The girl liked to pass herself off as much older than she was.
3. A feeling of nausea overcame her, but it soon passed off.

~ on	weitergeben
~ one's/the time	sich die Zeit vertreiben
~ out	ohnmächtig werden
~ over s.th./s.o.	über etwas/jdn. hinweggehen
~ the buck (Sl.)	jdm. den schwarzen Peter zuschieben
~ the time of day	jdm. Guten Tag sagen

past:

not to put it ~ s.o. jdm. etwas durchaus zutrauen

I wouldn't put it past John to take his girlfriend along on a business trip.

~ caring sich nicht mehr um etwas kümmern

patch:

not to be a ~ on s.th. (Sl.) sich nicht mit etwas messen können

to hit a bad ~ (Sl.) eine Pechsträhne haben

Patience is a virtue. (Sprichw.) Geduld ist eine Tugend.

pay:

the devil to ~ (Brit./Sl.) ein fürchterlicher Aufruhr

If you don't do as he says, there'll be the devil to pay.

~ attention	aufmerksam zuhören
~ back	1. zurückzahlen, 2. heimzahlen

1. He paid back the money he owed.
2. I'll pay you back one day for the harm you have done me.

~ s.o. a visit	jdn. besuchen
~ **through the nose for s.th.** (Sl.)	einen Haufen Geld für etwas bezahlen
He who pays the piper calls the tune. (Sprichw.)	Wer die Musik bezahlt, bestimmt die Melodie.
the pearly gates	die Himmelstür
as like as two peas in a pod (Sl.)	sich gleichen wie ein Ei dem anderen
pecking order	Hierarchie, Hackordnung
a peeping Tom	ein Spanner
take s.o. down a peg or two (Sl.)	jdm. einen Dämpfer verpassen
pen:	
The ~ is mightier than the sword. (Sprichw.)	Die Feder ist mächtiger als das Schwert.
a ~ **portrait**	eine schriftliche Beschreibung
penny:	
a pound to a ~	wahrscheinlich
cost a pretty ~	eine hübsche Summe Geld kosten
in for a ~**, in for a pound**	wenn schon, denn schon
spend a ~ (Sl.)	die Toilette aufsuchen
perfidious Albion	die verräterischen Engländer
Perish the thought!	Gott bewahre!
a phoenix from the ashes	Phoenix aus der Asche
pick:	
~ **a quarrel with s.b.**	jdn. kritisieren, sticheln
~ **and choose** (Brit.)	vorsichtig aussuchen
~ **on s.o./s.th.**	kritisieren, herumnörgeln
~ **holes in s.th./s.o.**	etwas/jdn. kritisieren
~ **one's way**	seinen Weg suchen
~ **one's words** (Brit.)	sich vorsichtig ausdrücken

~ out	auswählen, herausfinden
~ o.s. up	wieder aufstehen, sich erheben, sich aufraffen
~ s.b.'s brains	Ideen übernehmen, jdn. aushorchen
~ s.b. up	jdn. abholen, treffen
~ s.th. up	etwas aufschnappen
~ up (Sl.)	sich erholen
be in a pickle (Brit./Sl.)	in der Patsche sitzen
it's no picnic	Das ist kein Honigschlecken.

picture:

see ~s in the fire	in die Flammen schauen
put s.o. in the ~	jdn. ins Bild setzen über, jdn. einweisen

Let me put you in the picture: the train will be late due to mechanical problems at the next station.

that's all ~s in the sky	das sind nur verrückte Ideen

piece:

a ~ of cake	ganz einfach, keine Herausforderung
be of a ~ with s.th.	genau zu etwas passen
give s.o. a ~ of one's mind (Brit./Sl.)	jdm. den Kopf waschen, jdm. gründlich die Meinung sagen

pig:

~ in the middle	zwischen zwei Stühlen
buy a ~ in a poke (Brit./Sl.)	die Katze im Sack kaufen
happy as a ~ in muck	rundum zufrieden

pile:

make one's ~ (Brit./Sl.)	einen Haufen Geld verdienen
~ it on (thick)	übertreiben
~s of s.th. (Sl.)	haufenweise
~ up	sich anhäufen

My work is piling up, I must spend more time on it.

pillar:
a ~ of society	eine Stütze der Gesellschaft
from ~ to post	von Pontius zu Pilatus

pin:
~ down	festnageln, festmachen
~ money	Taschengeld
~ s.o. down to s.th.	jdn. auf etwas festnageln
~ s.o.'s ears back (Am./Sl.)	jdn. schelten, schlagen
~ up	anstecken, feststecken

see pink elephants	weiße Mäuse sehen

pipe:
~ down!	Red' nicht so viel!
put that in your ~ and smoke it (Sl.)	Das kannst du dir hinter die Ohren schreiben.
~ up	dazwischenreden, unterbrechen

piping hot	kochend heiß
pitch and toss	Kopf oder Zahl, hin- und herschaukeln

pity:
What a ~!	Schade!
take ~ on	Mitleid empfinden für, jdm. helfen

place:
be going ~s (Sl.)	es zu etwas bringen, Erfolg haben
do a ~ up (Sl.)	renovieren
in the first ~	erstens, zuallererst
in ~ of	an Stelle von
out of ~	fehl am Platz, nicht geeignet
put o.s. in s.b.'s ~	sich in die Lage von jdm. versetzen

plain:
as ~ as the nose on your face (Sl.)	sonnenklar
~ dealing	offenes, ehrliches Handeln

~ speaking	Klartext reden
~ sailing	eine klare Sache
be ~ with s.b.	mit jdm. offen reden

play:

~ ball	kooperieren
bring s.th. into ~	etwas ins Spiel bringen
~ fast and loose with s.o. (Sl.)	mit jdm. (emotional) spielen

It was really not okay to play fast and loose with her feelings like that.

~ for time	Zeit herausschinden
~ the game	die Regeln einhalten, ehrlich spielen
~ hooky (Am./Sl.)/~ truant (Brit.)	die Schule schwänzen
~ it cool	ruhig bleiben
~ it safe	kein Risiko eingehen
~ into s.o.'s hands	jdm. in die Hände spielen
~ one's cards well	die Gelegenheit ausnutzen
~ s.th. down	etwas herunterspielen
~ with fire	ein Risiko eingehen, mit dem Feuer spielen
~ed out	erschöpft, ausgebrannt
plead guilty	sich schuldig bekennen
Please God	wenn Gott will
plenty of s.th.	reichlich
plight one's troth	sich die Treue schwören
plough a lone furrow	allein auf weiter Flur stehen
give s.th. a plug (Sl.)	für etwas werben

pocket:

have long ~s and short arms (Sl.)	geizig sein
put one's pride in one's ~	über seinen Schatten springen, klein beigeben
in one's ~	in der Tasche, unter Kontrolle
be out of ~	finanzielle Verluste erleiden

point:

be on the ~ of doing s.th.	kurz davor sein, etwas zu tun
make a ~ of s.th.	auf etwas Wert legen
He made a point of welcoming the late-comers very warmly.	
~ out	hinweisen auf, hervorheben
stick to the ~	bei der Sache bleiben, nicht abschweifen
come to the ~	auf den Punkt kommen
That's not the ~.	Darum geht es nicht.
The ~ is that …	Die Sache ist die, dass …
make a ~	zur Diskussion beitragen
not to put too fine a ~ on it	das Kind beim Namen nennen, nicht um etwas herumreden, etwas Wichtiges sagen
a sore ~	ein wunder Punkt
My going out to work is a sore point with my husband.	
stretch a ~	ein Zugeständnis machen
The librarian will stretch a point and let me have the book for another week.	
strong ~	Stärke
Cleaning the house is not my strong point.	
take s.o.'s ~	die Meinung von jdm. akzeptieren
~ of view	Meinung, Standpunkt

a poison-pen letter — anonymer Brief

poke:

~ fun at	sich lustig machen über
~ one's nose into s.th.	seine Nase in etwas stecken

pop:

~ down	mal schnell hingehen
I will just pop down to the shops for some biscuits.	
~ in	hereinplatzen, auf einen Sprung vorbeikommen
My neighbour is always popping in for a cup of tea.	
~ the question (Sl.)	einen Heiratsantrag machen

keep s.o. posted (Sl.)	jdn. auf dem Laufenden halten
postpone the evil hour/day	ein unerfreuliches Ereignis vor sich herschieben

pot:
The ~ calls the kettle back. (Sl.)	Ein Esel schilt den anderen Langohr.
go to ~ (Sl.) *If you don't paint your fence soon it'll go to pot.*	ganz kaputt gehen

pour:
It never rains but it ~s.	Ein Unglück kommt selten allein.
~ forth	drauflosreden
~ cold water on s.th.	dämpfend wirken
~ oil on troubled water	beruhigen, schlichten, die Wogen glätten

power:
be the ~ behind the throne	die graue Eminenz sein
the ~'s that be	„die da oben", die Mächtigen
a practical joke	ein Streich
Practice makes perfect. (Sprichw.)	Übung macht den Meister.
practise what one preaches	seine Lehren auch in die Tat umsetzen
precious few/little	nur sehr wenige/wenig
a pregnant silence	beredtes Schweigen
present company excluded	das Gesagte gilt nicht für die Anwesenden

press:
be ~ed for *I can't stop and talk to you now, I'm pressed for time.*	kaum genug haben
~ for	pochen auf, bestehen auf
~ forward/on with	vorankommen mit

I want to press on with the work on our book.

Prevention is better than cure. (Sprichw.)	Vorbeugen ist besser als heilen.
prick up one's ears	die Ohren spitzen
in the prime of life	in den besten Jahren
the primrose path	der Rosenpfad
small print	das Kleingedruckte

private:
one's ~ life — Privatleben
a ~ eye (Sl.) — ein Privatdetektiv

Procrastination is a thief of time. (Sprichw.) — Aufschieb ist ein Tagedieb.

the prodigal son — der verlorene Sohn

promise the moon — das Blaue vom Himmel versprechen

proof:
The ~ of the pudding is in the eating. (Brit. Sprichw.) — Probieren geht über Studieren.
put to the ~ — testen

prop s.th. up — etwas stützen (besonders: im finanziellen Sinne)

a proper Charlie — dumm, unfähig

prophet:
~ of doom — ein Schwarzseher
The ~ is without honour in his own country. (Sprichw.) — Der Prophet gilt nirgends weniger als im eigenen Land.

pros and cons — die wesentlichen Argumente dafür und dagegen; Pro und Kontra

Before bringing the meeting to a close, Robert once again reviewed the pros and cons and asked for a decision.

be proud of s.th.	stolz auf etwas sein
prove one's case	eine Behauptung beweisen
prunes and prisms	übermäßig korrekte Aussprache
You pseud!	Du Angeber!
a pub crawl (Sl.)	Kneipentour
puff and blow	vor physischer Erschöpfung pusten und schnaufen
a puffing billy	Dampflokomotive

pull:
~ **a fast one over s.o.**	jdn. reinlegen
~ **a long face** (Brit.)	ein langes Gesicht machen
~ **o.s. together**	sich zusammennehmen, zusammenreißen
~ **rank**	seine Position zu seinem eigenen Vorteil nutzen
~ **s.th. off** (Sl.)	etwas erreichen, schaffen
~ **s.o.'s leg**	jdm. einen Bären aufbinden, jdn. zum Besten halten
~ **s.o.'s socks up**	sich zusammenreißen
~ **strings**	die Fäden aus dem Hintergrund ziehen, Beziehungen spielen lassen

It's easy to get a job if you have a rich uncle to pull strings.

~ **the wool over s.o.'s eyes**	jdn. hinters Licht führen
~ **one's weight**	seinen Teil leisten
pure and simple	schlicht, genau so

push:
~ **home**	nach Hause eilen

put   180

~ s.o. (Sl.)	jdn. unter Druck setzen
~ing up the daisies (Sl.)	die Radieschen von unten wachsen sehen, tot sein

put:

~ a spoke in s.o.'s wheel	jdm. Knüppel zwischen die Beine werfen
~ about	1. besorgt, ängstlich, 2. in Umlauf bringen

1. *I was quite put about when I didn't hear from you.*
2. *The news of his arrival was immediately put about.*

~ above all else	vor alles andere stellen
~ an end to s.th.	einer Sache ein Ende bereiten
~ by	zurücklegen, beiseite legen, auf die hohe Kante legen
~ in a (good) word for	ein (gutes) Wort einlegen für
~ in an appearance	erscheinen, auftauchen
~ ideas into s.o.'s head	jdm. Flausen in den Kopf setzen
~ in order	in Ordnung bringen
~ into the shade	in den Schatten stellen
~ into force	in Kraft setzen
~ into words	in Worte fassen
~ it down to ignorance	etwas auf Unwissenheit zurückführen, als Dummheit auslegen
~ off one's stride	aus dem Tritt gebracht
~ on the shelf	an den Nagel hängen
~ on one's thinking cap	scharf nachdenken
~ on weight	zunehmen (Gewicht)
~ one's finger on s.th.	den Kern der Sache treffen
~ one foot before the other	einen Fuß vor den anderen setzen
~ one's oar in (Sl.)	seinen Senf dazugeben
~ one's heads together (Sl.)	die Köpfe zusammenstecken
~ o.s. forward	sich hervortun
~ o.s. in s.b.'s place	sich in jdn. hineinversetzen
~ out of action	außer Gefecht setzen
~ pressure on	Druck ausüben auf
~ s.b. off	1. aus der Fassung bringen, 2. jdm. absagen

1. *Your always being late really puts me off.*

2. I've got to go to the doctor this afternoon so I've had to put John off.

~ s.b. on his guard	jdn. warnen
~ s.th. on the scrap heap (Sl.)	etwas ausrangieren
~ s.b. through it	jdn. auf Herz und Nieren prüfen
~ s.o. down	jdn. fertig machen
~ s.o. through the hoop(s)	jdn. einer schweren Prüfung unterziehen
~ s.th. right	etwas richtig stellen
~ s.b. on the spot	jdn. in Verlegenheit bringen
~ s.b. up	jdn. beherbergen
~ s.o. wise to s.th.	jdn. über etwas informieren, jdm. Bescheid geben
~ the lid on s.th.	etwas die Krone aufsetzen
~ the blame on s.b.	jdm. die Schuld in die Schuhe schieben
~ the cart before the horse	das Pferd von hinten aufzäumen
~ the kibosh on s.th. (Sl.)	etwas ein jähes Ende bereiten
~ two and two together	sich einen Reim machen auf, zwei und zwei zusammen zählen
~ up with s.th.	sich etwas gefallen lassen
~ word into s.o.'s mouth	für jdn. ohne dessen Erlaubnis sprechen

a Pyrrhic victory   ein Pyrrhussieg

Q

quarter:
live in close ~s	eng beieinander wohnen
in all ~s	überall

Queen Anne is dead. — Das ist nichts Neues. Jeder weiß das.

queer:

a ~ card — ein Exzentriker

The man had lived on his own quite happily for years but was obviously a queer card.

~ s.b.'s pitch — jdm. einen Strich durch die Rechnung machen

I must see my bank manager about a loan quickly, if my boss talks to him first it might queer my pitch.

question:
the ~ of the hour	das Thema, das momentan am meisten beschäftigt
be out of the ~	außer Frage stehen, nicht in Frage kommen
beg the ~	auf eine Frage ausweichend reagieren, sich vor einer Entscheidung drücken
beyond all ~	ohne Frage, zweifellos
no ~s asked	keine dummen Fragen stellen
The ~ does not arise.	Die Frage stellt sich nicht.

quibble about s.th. — sich über Kleinigkeiten streiten

quick:
~ on the draw	schlagfertig
~ on the uptake	von rascher Auffassungsgabe
a ~ one	ein schnelles Glas zwischendurch
cut to the ~	tief betroffen, verletzt

I was cut to the quick when my fiancé broke off our engagement.

a quid pro quo etwas beruht auf Gegenseitigkeit

quiet:
on the ~ insgeheim, unter der Hand
~ down sich beruhigen

quite:
~ so! Ganz recht so!
~ a bit ziemlich viel
~ a few ziemlich viele
~ a number eine beträchtliche Zahl
~ a lot ziemlich viel/viele

R

race:
~ against time — Wettlauf mit der Zeit; gegen die Uhr arbeiten

rack:
~ one's brains — sich den Kopf zerbrechen
on the ~ — äußerst gespannt, auf glühenden Kohlen

(go to) ~ and ruin — verkommen, vor die Hunde gehen
His health is going to rack and ruin.

rag:
a ~ and bone man — Straßenhändler, Lumpenhändler

all the rage (Sl.) — der letzte Schrei

rain:
come ~ or come shine — in jedem Fall
It's ~ing cats and dogs. — Es regnet Bindfäden. Es gießt wie aus Kübeln.
It never ~s but it pours. — Ein Unglück kommt selten allein.
save up for a ~y day — auf die hohe Kante legen
The ~ falls on the just and the unjust. — Tugend schützt nicht gegen alles.

raise:
~ an objection (to) — einen Einwand erheben gegen
~ from the dead — jdn. von den Toten auferwecken
~ one's eyebrows — leicht schockiert sein
~ one's hat to s.o. — vor jdm. den Hut abnehmen, jdn. grüßen
~ one's voice against s.th. — seine Stimme gegen etwas erheben
~ to the surface — an die Oberfläche bringen
~ the devil with s.o. (Sl.) — jdn. fürchterlich beschimpfen

rant and roar — lauthals protestieren

a rare bird — selten

rat:
~s desert a sinking ship. (Sprichw.) — Die Ratten verlassen das sinkende Schiff.
smell a ~ — den Braten riechen

rate:
at any ~ — auf jeden Fall
to ~ s.o. — jdn. schätzen

a raving beauty — eine strahlende Schönheit

give s.o. a raw deal — jdn. schlecht behandeln

ray:
a ~ of sunshine — eine Aufmunterung
a ~ of hope — ein Hoffnungsschimmer

reach:
~ for the sky — hohe Ziele haben, nach den Sternen greifen
~ out for — greifen nach
out of ~ — unerreichbar
within easy ~ — leicht erreichbar

read:
~ between the lines — zwischen den Zeilen lesen
~ into — hineinlesen
~ out — laut vorlesen
~ s.th. up — etwas nachlesen
~ s.o. like a book — jdn. sehr gut kennen

ready:
~ for anything — zu allem bereit
~, steady, go — auf die Plätze, fertig, los

really and truely — ganz sicher

reap the benefits of s.th. — von etwas profitieren

red:
see ~ — rot sehen
be in the ~ — Schulden haben, in den roten Zahlen sein

like a ~ rag to a bull	wie ein rotes Tuch ...
~-handed	auf frischer Tat
The burglar was caught red-handed as he left the house with the stolen goods.	
the ~-light district	Rotlichtbezirk
see the ~ light	eine Warnung vor Schwierigkeiten erhalten
~ in the face	verlegen

regard:
as ~s me	was mich betrifft
have no ~ for	nicht berücksichtigen, keine Rücksicht nehmen

reign supreme	alles beherrschen

rein:
give ~	die Zügel locker lassen
keep a tight ~ on	zügeln
My aunt is very strict and keeps at tight rein on her teenage son.	
take the ~s	die Führung übernehmen
When her husband died Mary took the reins of the family business.	

relieve:
~ one's feelings	seinen Gefühlen freien Lauf lassen
~ s.b. of his money	jdm. das Geld wegnehmen, beklauen, betrügen

be reluctant to	etwas widerwillig tun

remark:
pass a ~ on	sich äußern über
The teacher passed a remark on the clothes his pupils were wearing.	
without ~	kommentarlos, stillschweigend

render a service	unterstützen, helfen

rest:
~ upon s.th.	sich auf etwas stützen
set s.b.'s fears at ~	jdn. beschwichtigen

The doctor set my fears at rest when he told me I wasn't seriously ill.

The responsibility ~s with you.	Du trägst die Verantwortung.
~ assured	beruhigt sein
~ on one's laurels	sich auf seinen Lorbeeren ausruhen

Revenge is sweet. (Sprichw.)   Rache ist süß.

There's neither rhyme nor reason in that.   Das hat weder Hand noch Fuß.

ride:
~ a tiger	etwas Dummes oder Gefährliches tun
~ one's hobby-horse	seinem Steckenpferd/Zeitvertreib nachgehen
~ roughshod	ohne Rücksicht weitermachen

The young man rode roughshod over his parents' arguments and refused to take their advice.

take s.o. for a ~	jdn. auf die Schippe nehmen

right:
put to ~	berichtigen
You are ~ to do so.	Du hast recht, dich so zu verhalten.
~ away	sofort

The lawyer said he would see his client right away.

by ~s	rechtens, nach dem Recht
serve s.o ~	jdm. recht geschehen

It serves you right if you are wet, you shouldn't have started splashing me.

~ as rain	auf dem Damm, in Ordnung

The doctor said I was as right as rain and could go back to school.

ring:

~ a bell with s.o.	jdm. bekannt vorkommen
give s.o. a ~	jdn. anrufen
~ s.b. up	jdn. anrufen
run ~s round s.o.	jdm. weit überlegen sein
~ with	widerhallen von

The hall rang with the happy laughter of the children at the party.

~ off	ein Telefonat beenden

He was obviously offended, as he rang off without saying a word.

rip s.o. off (Sl.)   jdn. übers Ohr hauen

rise:

~ and shine!	Aufwachen!
~ to the occasion	sich der Situation gewachsen zeigen

risk:

at one's own ~	auf eigene Gefahr
run a ~	ein Risiko eingehen
~ one's neck	Kopf und Kragen riskieren

roll:

~ up one's sleeves	die Ärmel hochkrempeln
Tears ~ down her cheeks.	Tränen laufen ihr die Wangen herunter.
The years ~ by.	Die Jahre vergehen.

room:

~ for improvement	verbesserungsfähig, nicht ganz einwandfrei
~ and to spare	viel Platz
~ with s.o.	mit jdm. eine Wohnung/Zimmer teilen

root:

~ and branch	komplett, vollständig
the ~ of the trouble	die Wurzel des Übels

rope:
~ s.o. into (doing) s.th.	jdm. eine Arbeit aufhalsen

My brother roped me into helping him to move about the furniture.

know the ~s	die Spielregeln kennen

rose:
see life through ~-tinted spectacles	das Leben durch die rosarote Brille sehen
~s all the way	uneingeschränkt angenehm

rough:
it is ~ on s.o.	es ist hart für jdn.
~ it	primitiv leben

When we go on holiday we don't stay in hotels, we like to rough it.

have a ~ time	eine schwere Zeit haben
take the ~ with the smooth	es nehmen, wie es kommt

round:
a long way ~	ein Umweg
go ~ to s.b.'s	jdn. besuchen

I'm going round to Mary's for the evening.

~ off	vollenden, fertig machen
~ on	jdm. die Schuld geben, beschimpfen

He rounded on his servant for losing the cases.

rub:
~ it in (Sl.)	jdm. unter die Nase reiben
~ s.o. up the wrong way	jdn. verärgern
~ shoulders with s.o.	mit jdm. in Kontakt kommen

rude health	stabile Gesundheit
rue the day	ein Ereignis bereuen
ruffle s.b.'s feathers	jdn. verärgern

rule:
as a ~	im Allgemeinen, generell

~ out	ausschließen
~ing passion	persönliche Vorliebe, Lieblingszeitvertreib

Her ruling passion was to tend to her garden.

run:

~ a temperature	Fieber haben
~ across	zufällig begegnen
~ up against s.th.	auf etwas stoßen
~ aground	(Schiff) auf Grund laufen
~ away with the idea	sich einbilden
~ counter to	im Widerspruch stehen zu

This completely runs counter to our plans.

five days ~ning	fünf Tage nacheinander
give s.o. a ~ for his money (Sl.)	jdn. fordern, Leistung abverlangen

James thought it would be easy beating Harold at squash, but he gave him a run for his money.

in the long ~	langfristig
in the short ~	kurzfristig
on the ~	auf der Flucht
~ out of ...	keine ... mehr haben

May I borrow some milk? I've run out and want to bake a cake.

~ s.o. over	jdn. überfahren
~ short of s.th.	knapp werden

We are running short of time, you have to hurry up.

~ner-up	der Zweite

Even though Jim won the race, Bill was the runner-up.

up and ~ning	in Betrieb, funktionierend
~-off	Wettkampf
give s.o. the run-down (Sl.)	jdn. über etwas informieren

Jack will give you the run-down on what happened in London last week.

rush:
- **~ one's fences** — etwas übers Knie brechen
- **~ headlong** — überstürzen
- **~ into doing s.th.** — etwas überstürzt tun
- **~ s.o. to hospital** — jdn. schnellstens ins Krankenhaus bringen

in a rut — in eingefahrenen Gleisen
What I am really afraid of in my job is to get into a rut.

S

get the sack (Brit./Sl.) — entlassen werden

a sacred cow — heilige Kuh
I would have liked to say something about the company uniform, but had been told in advance that it was a holy cow, so I kept my mouth shut.

saddle s.o. with s.th. — jdm. etwas aufbürden

safe:
a ~ bet — eine sichere Sache
a ~ job — ein sicherer Arbeitsplatz
be on the ~ side — auf der sicheren Seite sein
play it ~ — auf Nummer sicher gehen
~ and sound — gesund und munter

when all is said and done — unterm Strich, letzten Endes

sail close to the wind — sich an der Grenze des Zulässigen bewegen

sake:
for …'s ~ — um … willen, aus Liebe zu …
For God's ~! — Um Gottes willen!

one's salad days — unschuldige Jugendjahre

salt:
~ away — auf die hohe Kante legen
not worth one's ~ — nichts taugen
Her kitchen equipment was really not worth its salt.
~ of the earth — absolut integer
with a pinch of ~ — mit Vorbehalt nehmen, nicht für bare Münze nehmen

same:
the ~ again?	Nochmal das Gleiche?
same here (Sl.)	das sehe ich genauso
the ~ old story	eine bekannte Geschichte
the ~ the world over	es ist überall das Gleiche

What's sauce for the goose is sauce for the gander. — Was dem einen recht, ist dem anderen billig.

save:
~ one's breath — den Mund halten
You may as well save your breath, the children aren't listening.

~ s.b. from s.th.	jdn. vor etwas retten
~ the situation	die Lage retten
~ money	Geld sparen
~ up for (s.th.)	aufheben für, sparen für
~ s.o.'s bacon	jdm. die nackte Haut retten

say:
~ cheese	Bitte lächeln!
have little to ~ for oneself	nichts zu seiner Rechtfertigung vorbringen können
have no ~ in s.th.	in einer Angelegenheit nichts zu sagen haben
not able to ~ boo to a goose	ängstlich sein
no sooner said than done	gesagt, getan
~ one's piece	seine Meinung sagen
That goes without ~ing.	Das versteht sich von selbst.
that is to ~	das heißt, vielmehr
when all is said and done	letzten Endes, unterm Strich
~ s.th. in a roundabout way	etwas umständlich zum Ausdruck bringen
~ s.th. to s.o.'s face	jdm. etwas ins Gesicht sagen

make o.s. scarce — sich aus dem Staub machen

scare:
be ~d stiff	zu Tode erschrocken sein, eine Heidenangst haben
~ the living daylights out of s.o.	jdn. fürchterlich erschrecken
~ s.o. to death	jdn. zu Tode erschrecken

not my scene	nicht mein Geschmack
throw s.o. off the scent	jdm. Sand in die Augen streuen
scoop the pool	den Jackpot gewinnen

score:
on that ~	in dieser Hinsicht
settle an old ~	eine alte Rechnung begleichen

scrape:
get into a ~	in Schwierigkeiten geraten
~ the barrel	den letzten Rest auskratzen
~ acquaintance (with)	sich um eine Bekanntschaft bemühen

scratch:
~ the surface of s.th.	sich nur oberflächlich mit etwas auseinandersetzen
~ one's head	sich am Kopf kratzen
up to ~	den Anforderungen entsprechen
start from ~	ganz von vorne anfangen

scream blue murder	laut Protest schreien

screw:
put the ~ on s.b.	jdm. die Macht zeigen, jdn. zwingen
~ up one's courage	allen Mut zusammennehmen
~ up	etwas vermasseln

Scrub that! (Sl.)	Vergiss das!
the scum of the earth	wertloses Pack
seal s.b.'s fate	jds. Schicksal besiegeln

search:
~ me! (Sl.)	Was weiß ich! Frag' mich etwas Leichteres!
in ~ of	auf der Suche nach
~ after	streben nach
make a ~ for	suchen nach

second:
~ nature to s.o.	einfach/selbstverständlich für jdn.
~ to none	besser als alle(s) andere(n)
I ~ that	ganz meine Meinung
on ~ thoughts	nach reiflicher Überlegung

see:

~ eye to eye with s.o. on s.th. — in einer Angelegenheit voll mit jdm. übereinstimmen

Morton and I see eye to eye on the matter of expanding into new markets.

~ with half an eye	sofort/auf einen Blick sehen
~ how the land lies	sehen, wie der Hase läuft
~ s.th. done	dafür sorgen, dass etwas geschieht
~ about/to s.th.	sich kümmern um
~ s.o. across the street	jdn. über die Straße bringen
~ s.b. home	jdn. nach Hause bringen
~ s.o. off	jdn. verabschieden
~ s.b. through s.th.	jdm. in einer schwierigen Situation beistehen
~ s.th. through	etwas zu Ende führen
~ to it that	dafür sorgen, dass

seize:
be ~d with	ergriffen/befallen sein von (Anfall, fixe Idee etc.)
~ the opportunity	die Gelegenheit nutzen

s.o.'s usual self — wie immer

She was her usual happy self.

sell:
~ the pass	jdn. verraten
~ at a loss	mit Verlust verkaufen
~ like hot cakes	sich wie warme Semmeln verkaufen
~ s.b. down the river	jdn. verraten
~ s.o. a pup	jdn. übers Ohr hauen

send:
~ a boy to do a man's work	jdn. mit einer Aufgabe betrauen, die ihn überfordert

~ s.b. crazy	jdn. aufregen/wahnsinnig machen
~ for s.th.	nach etwas schicken
~ s.b. packing	jdn. fortjagen
~ word to s.o.	jdm. eine Nachricht schicken

I'll send word that we'll be catching the later train.

sense:

make ~	Sinn ergeben, sinnvoll sein
make ~ of s.th.	etwas verstehen/begreifen
talk ~	vernünftig sein/reden

serve:

~ as an excuse	als Entschuldigung dienen
~ its purpose	seinen Zweck erfüllen
That ~s them right.	Das geschieht ihnen recht.
at your service	zu Ihren Diensten

set:

~ a good example	ein gutes Beispiel abgeben
be hard ~	in großer Not sein
dead ~ against s.th.	absolut dagegen sein
~ a dog on s.b.	einen Hund auf jdn. hetzen
~-back	Rückschlag
~-to	ernsthafter Streit

They had a real set-to about whose job it was to do the dishes.

~ fire to	anzünden
~ foot in	eintreten
~ great store by	große Stücke halten auf
~ in	beginnen, einsetzen

It looks as if winter will set in early this year.

~ one's heart on	sich etwas von Herzen wünschen
~ one's mind to	sich etwas in den Kopf setzen
~ one's teeth on edge	durch Mark und Bein gehen
~ s.b. down	jdn. absetzen
~ to rights	in Ordnung bringen
~ to work	zu arbeiten beginnen
~ up (shop)	(ein Geschäft) etwas aufbauen/einsetzen/ins Leben rufen

The Prime Minister set up a committee to investigate the matter.

settle:
~ back — sich zurücklehnen
~ down — sich niederlassen, sesshaft werden, sich beruhigen
~ on s.th. — sich für eine Sache entscheiden
She settled finally on the pink dress, not the blue.
~ with s.o. — mit jdm. abrechnen
~ for s.th. — sich mit etwas zufrieden geben
~ up — die Zeche zahlen

seven:
the ~ deadly sins — die sieben Todsünden
~th heaven — der siebte Himmel, Paradies

all sewn up — alles unter Dach und Fach

shake:
~ one rigid — jdn. erschrecken
~ like a leaf — wie Espenlaub zittern
~ hands — sich die Hand geben
~ in one's shoes — vor Angst zittern
~ s.o. up (Sl.) — jdn. schockieren/aufregen

shall be nameless — jmd. oder etwas soll nicht namentlich erwähnt werden

Various members of our group, who shall be nameless, did not contribute as much as we had hoped.

shame:
~ on you! — Schäm dich!
put s.o. to ~ — jdn. in den Schatten stellen
What a ~! — Wie schade!

Shank's pony — zu Fuß

the shape of things to come — zukünftige Entwicklungen

share:
have a ~ in — teilhaben an, Anteil haben an
~ out among — verteilen unter

~ and ~ alike	zu gleichen Teilen (teilen)

sharp:
~ practice	unsaubere Geschäfte
~en one's wits	seinen Geist schärfen

That was a close shave.	Das wäre beinahe ins Auge gegangen.

shed:
~ blood	Blut vergießen
~ light on	Licht werfen auf
~ tears over	Tränen vergießen über

sheep:
a wolf in ~'s clothing	ein Wolf im Schafspelz
cast ~'s eyes at	verliebt/schmachtend ansehen

have a sheet in the wind (Sl.)	einen in der Krone haben
Tom really had a sheet in the wind when he came back from the pub last night.	

shift:
~ for s.b.	alleine zurechtkommen
The boys had to shift for themselves when their mother was ill.	
~ from one foot to the other	von einem Fuß auf den anderen treten
~ the responsibility on ...	die Verantwortung auf ... schieben
~ one's ground	die Meinung, den Standpunkt ändern

shine:
a shining light	sehr gut, auffallend
a shining example	ein leuchtendes Beispiel
~ like a good deed in a naughty world	positiv hervorstechen
make a ~ about	Aufhebens machen um
take the ~ out of	in den Schatten stellen
~ up to s.o. (Am.)	um die Gunst von jdm. bitten

shipshape and Bristol-fashion	in bester Ordnung

keep one's shirt on	ruhig bleiben
It gives me the shivers.	Es läuft mir kalt den Rücken herunter.
get the shock of one's life	einen Schock fürs Leben bekommen

shoe:
know where the shoe pinches	wissen, wo der Schuh drückt
be in s.o.'s ~s	in der Haut von jdm. stecken

shoot:
~ ahead	schnelle Fortschritte machen
~ a glance at	einen raschen Blick werfen auf

shop:
all over the ~	überall
~ around	einen Einkaufsbummel machen
talk ~	fachsimpeln

short:
fall ~ of s.th.	nicht den Erwartungen entsprechen
run ~ of	knapp werden, zur Neige gehen
~ of cash	knapp bei Kasse
two bricks ~ of a load (Sl.)	dämlich
just ~ of London	kurz vor London
cut s.o. ~	jdn. unterbrechen, jdm. über den Mund fahren

I was about to explain my reasons, but he cut me short.

~-lived	von kurzer Dauer, kurzlebig
~ with s.o.	kurz angebunden

shot:
~ in the dark	auf bloße Vermutung hin, ins Blaue hinein
~ in the arm	finanzielle Unterstützung
have a ~ at s.th.	etwas versuchen, ausprobieren
like a ~	blitzartig

straight from the shoulder	direkt, geradeheraus
shove off (Sl.) *Just shove off and leave me alone, will you?*	sich verziehen
show:	
~ **a clean pair of heels**	schneller sein als jmd. anderes
~ **off**	angeben, prahlen
~ **one's hand**	mit offenen Karten spielen
~ **one's mettle**	seinen Mut unter Beweis stellen
~ **up**	aufkreuzen
~ **promise**	vielversprechend wirken
run the ~	den Laden schmeißen
a shrinking violet	Mimose, Feigling
shrug one's shoulders	mit den Achseln zucken
shudder to think …	man mag sich gar nicht vorstellen, dass …
shut:	
~ **down**	(endgültig) schließen
~ **one's eyes to s.th.**	die Augen vor etwas verschließen
~ **up!** (Sl.)	Halt den Mund!
~ **the stable door when the horse has bolted**	den Brunnen zudecken, wenn das Kind schon ertrunken ist
sick:	
~ **at heart**	unglücklich
~ **of the sight of s.th. or s.b.**	jdn. oder etwas nicht mehr sehen können
I'm ~ and tired of it.	Das hängt mir zum Hals raus.
side: ~	
a bit on the … ~	ein wenig …
~ **with s.b.**	jdm. beistehen, für jdn. Partei ergreifen
~ **against s.b.**	gegen jdn. Partei ergreifen
~ **by ~**	nebeneinander, einträchtig
split one's ~s with laughter	vor Lachen umkommen

sight:
at first ~ — auf den ersten Blick
lose one's ~ — erblinden
~ for sore eyes — ein willkommener Anblick
not by a long ~ — bei weitem nicht

silence reigns — es ist vollkommen still

the silver screen — Kino, Filmbranche

sing:
~ a different song — seine Meinung ändern
~ s.b.'s praises — jdn. öffentlich loben

sink:
~ like a stone — ein Schlag ins Wasser
~ into oblivion — in Vergessenheit geraten, in der Versenkung verschwinden
~ into sleep — in tiefen Schlaf fallen
It's ~ or swim. — Vogel friss oder stirb.
~ing sand — Treibsand

sit:
~ back and do nothing — die Hände in den Schoß legen
~ on the fence — zwischen zwei Stühlen sitzen
~ s.th. out — bis zum Ende bleiben, etwas aussitzen
~ tight (Sl.) — ausharren, geduldig warten
~ up for s.b. — für jdn. aufbleiben, auf jdn. warten
a ~ting duck — ein leichtes Ziel
~ting pretty — es gut haben

six:
~ of one and half a dozen of the other — Jacke wie Hose, gehupft wie gesprungen
at ~es and sevens — durcheinander, konfus

the sixty-four thousand dollar question — die alles entscheidende Frage

a skeleton in the cupboard — eine Leiche im Keller

skin:
~ and bone	Haut und Knochen
by the ~ of one's teeth	mit Hängen und Würgen, mit knapper Not
save one's ~	seine eigene Haut retten

the sky's the limit — nach oben sind keine Grenzen gesetzt

slap-bang in the middle of — genau in der Mitte von

a slap-up meal — ein großes Essen

sleep:
~ rough	draußen schlafen
~ like a log	schlafen wie ein Murmeltier
~ tight	Gute Nacht!
not to ~ a wink	kein Auge zumachen
up one's sleeve	in der Hinterhand

sleight of hand — Fingerfertigkeit

slice:
a ~ of life	ein Ausschnitt aus dem Leben
a ~ of luck	eine Portion Glück

slip:
~ away	entwischen
~ into	hineinschlüpfen, sich hineinstehlen
~ s.th. on/over	sich etwas überziehen
~ through one's fingers	durch die Finger schlüpfen/rutschen
~ of the tongue	Versprecher
Freudian ~	Freud'scher Versprecher
give s.o. the ~	jdm. entkommen
~ up	Fehler machen

be on the slippery slope — auf der schiefen Bahn sein

the slough of despond — eine Phase der Verzweiflung

slow:
my watch is ~	meine Uhr geht nach

~ly but surely	langsam aber sicher
~ on the uptake	schwer von Begriff

small:
~ beer/potatoes	bedeutungslos
the ~ change of s.th.	die unwesentlichen Aspekte von etwas
the ~ print	das Kleingedruckte
the ~ screen	Fernseher
~ talk	(höfliche) Konversation

a smart alec	Klugscheißer
smell a rat	Lunte riechen

smoke:
~ like a chimney	viel rauchen, wie ein Schlot rauchen
a ~ screen	Tarnung, Täuschung

smooth:
~ s.b.'s path	jdm. den Weg ebnen
a ~ customer	ein ganz gerissener Kerl

That's the snag.	Da liegt der Hase im Pfeffer.

snap:
a cold ~	eine Kältewelle
a ~ vote	eine vorschnelle Entscheidung
~ at s.b.	jdn. barsch anfahren
~ out of (Sl.)	abwerfen, loswerden, sich aus etwas zurückziehen

I wish he would snap out of his present mood.

a snare and a delusion	etwas erscheint sicher, ist aber nicht so
not to be sneezed at	nicht zu verachten

so:
~ far, ~ good	so weit so gut, bis jetzt ist alles in Ordnung

~ help me God	so wahr mir Gott helfe
~ long (Sl.)	auf Wiedersehen
~ many words	nur Gerede
~ much the better	um so besser
~ there!	Aha!
~ what? (Sl.)	Na und?

sober:
~ facts	ungeschminkte Tatsachen
a ~ing truth	eine ernüchternde Wahrheit

soft:
~ in the head	schwachsinnig
a ~ job	eine leichte Arbeit
a ~ option	eine Entscheidung für den einfacheren Weg
~ pedal s.th.	sehr zurückhaltend und diskret vorgehen
~ soap	Schmeichelei

be sold down the river	verraten und verkauft

sole and heel	Schuhe reparieren

The gentleman has been soling and heeling in that little shop of his for as long as I can remember.

some time or other	gelegentlich
someone or other	einer von, jemand

something:
~ doing (Sl.)	etwas passiert
~ else again	eine ganz andere Sache
~ like (Sl.)	genau das, was man will
~ out of the ordinary	ungewöhnlich

somewhere, over the rainbow	im Reich der Fantasie

song:
for a ~	für 'n Appel und 'n Ei
make a ~ about	Aufhebens machen um

sooner:
~ or later
~ you than me

früher oder später, irgendwann
es ist mir lieber, es betrifft dich, als mich

soothe the savage beast
a sore point

Ärger oder Aufruhr besänftigen
ein kritisches Thema, ein wunder Punkt

sorry:
~ for oneself
in a ~ state

selbstmitleidig
in einem beklagenswerten Zustand

sort:
~ s.th. out

1. etwas in Ordnung bringen,
2. jdn. zurechtweisen

1. He sorted out his problems.
2. If you don't get this done, I will come over and sort you out!
~ed for s.th. (Sl.)
out of ~s

ausgestattet für
schlecht gelaunt

be the soul of politeness
Susan is the soul of politeness, I have never heard her utter an evil word to anybody.

die Freundlichkeit in Person sein

sound:
~ and fury
~ in wind and limb
~ the death knell of s.th.

leerer Schall, lautstarke Aktivität
gesund und munter
einer Sache den Todesstoß versetzen

The invention of television was widely regarded as sounding the death knell of radio.

be in the soup

in der Patsche sitzen

sow:
~ the dragon's teeth
~ one's wild oats

Zwietracht säen
sich die Hörner abstoßen

call a spade a spade	das Kind beim Namen nennen
throw a spanner in the works	jmd. einen Knüppel zwischen die Beine werfen
spare:	
~ no expense	keine Ausgaben scheuen
one's ~ time	Freizeit
speak:	
~ the same language	sich über etwas gut verständigen können, dieselbe Sprache sprechen
~ of the devil (and he appears).	Wenn man vom Teufel spricht, kommt er.
generally/roughly ~ing	im Großen und Ganzen, grob gesagt
not to ~ of	ganz zu schweigen von
nothing to ~ of	nichts Erwähnenswertes
so to ~	sozusagen
~ volumes	Bände sprechen
~ one's mind	seine Meinung sagen
~ up	lauter reden
~ up for s.o.	jdn. verteidigen, für jdn. sprechen
spead the parting guest	jdn. formell verabschieden
spend:	
~ one's force	seine Kraft erschöpfen
~ money as if it's going out of fashion	Geld mit vollen Händen ausgeben
~ money as like water	mit Geld um sich werfen
spick and span	tipptopp, geschniegelt und gebügelt
spike s.b.'s guns	jdm. den Wind aus den Segeln nehmen
spill the beans (Sl.)	ein Geheimnis verraten
cry over spilt milk	über Dinge jammern, die nicht mehr zu ändern sind

spin:
in a flat ~ — in Panik
~ a yarn — Seemannsgarn spinnen, eine erfundene Geschichte erzählen
~ out — in die Länge ziehen

The spirit is willing but the flesh is weak. (Sprichw.) — Der Geist ist willig, aber das Fleisch ist schwach.

spit:
be the ~ting image of s.o. — jdm. wie aus dem Gesicht geschnitten sein
~ it out! — Spuck's aus! Sag es endlich!

put a spoke in s.o.'s wheel — jdm. einen Knüppel zwischen die Beine werfen

sponge off s.o. — jdm. auf der Tasche liegen

be born with a silver spoon in one's mouth — reich auf die Welt kommen, mit einem goldenen Löffel im Mund geboren sein

spot:
a ~ of — etwas von, ein wenig
a soft ~ for — eine Schwäche für
be on the ~ — zur Stelle sein
~ on — ganz genau
knock the ~s off s.o. — jdn. in die Pfanne hauen

spread:
a good ~ — eine üppige Mahlzeit
~ like a wildfire — sich wie ein Lauffeuer verbreiten

spring clean — aufräumen, sauber machen

square:
~ the circle — das Unmögliche möglich machen
a ~ peg in a round hole — am falschen Ort zur falschen Zeit, absolut nicht passen

a stag party — Junggesellenabschied

stage:
- ~ and screen — Theater und Kino
- ~ a strike — einen Streik ausrufen

be at stake — auf dem Spiel stehen

stamp:
- a man of that ~ — ein Mann dieses Schlages
- set one's ~ on — seinen Stempel aufdrücken

stand:
- make a ~ — Widerstand leisten
- not to ~ for s.th — etwas nicht dulden
- ~ a chance — eine Chance haben
- ~ by — bereitstehen
- ~ corrected — seinen Fehler eingestehen, sich verbessern lassen

Frank stood corrected when Dan looked it up in the book.

- ~ for — repräsentieren, stehen für
- ~ in for s.o. — jdn. vertreten
- ~ in good stead — jdm. nützlich sein
- ~ on ceremony — sehr förmlich sein
- ~ out — hervorragen
- ~ together — zusammenhalten
- ~ up for — eintreten für
- ~ s.o. up — jdn. sitzen lassen
- ~ well with s.o. — mit jdm. gut stehen
- ~ for s.th. — etwas dulden

I will not stand for this kind of treatment.

- as it ~s — so, wie es im Moment aussieht
- It ~s to reason. — Es ist ganz klar und logisch.

on standby — in Bereitschaft

the star turn — die Hauptattraktion

s.th. stares s.o. in the face — etwas ist für jdn. nicht zu übersehen

stark mad — vollkommen verrückt

start:
~ a hare	ein Thema anreißen, eine Diskussion starten
~ to rot	anfangen zu verrotten
to ~ with	zunächst einmal
That gave him a ~.	Das ließ ihn zusammenzucken/zusammenfahren.

state:
a ~ of affairs	die Umstände
a ~ of grace	Zustand der Seligkeit
the ~ of play	der Spielstand, die Lage bis jetzt

stay:
a ~ of execution	ein Aufschub der Hinrichtung
~ the course	bis zum Ende weitermachen
~ put	1. sich nicht bewegen, 2. halten

1. Stay put while I look for John.
2. This car just won't stay put, it breaks down once a week.

Steady on! — Vorsichtig!, Langsam!
Steady on, the two of you, you are going to hurt yourselves!

steal:
~ away	sich davonstehlen
~ the show/scene	jdm. die Show stehlen
~ s.b.'s thunder	jdm. den Applaus, die Lorbeeren stehlen

steer:
~ clear of	vermeiden, umgehen
~ a middle course	eine gemäßigte Position einnehmen

stem:
~ the flow	die Flut eindämmen
~ the tide	eine Bedrohung abwenden, zurückdrängen

step:
~ in	einschreiten, unterbrechen

~ on it (Sl.)	einen Zahn zulegen, sich beeilen
~ on the gas	Gas geben, sich beeilen
~ out of line	aus der Reihe tanzen

stick:

~ around	herumlungern
~ to the point	bei der Sache bleiben
get hold of the wrong end of the ~	auf dem Holzweg sein
~ by s.o.	jdm. treu bleiben, unterstützen
~ one's neck out (Sl.)	seinen Kopf riskieren
~ s.th. out	etwas aushalten
~ up for s.o.	jdn. unterstützen

My brother always stuck up for me at school when we were young.

the ~ing point	die Grenze
be a stickler for s.th.	es mit etwas peinlich genau nehmen
Still waters run deep. (Sprichw.)	Stille Wasser sind tief.

stink:

~ like a polecat	stinken wie die Pest
~ing rich	stinken vor Geld

stint:

do a ~ on s.th.	zeitweise an etwas arbeiten
~ on s.th.	mit etwas geizen
stir one's blood	jdn. aufrütteln, jds. Herz höher schlagen lassen
A stitch in time saves nine. (Sprichw.)	Was du heute kannst besorgen, das verschiebe nicht auf morgen.

stock:

one's ~ is high/low	jds. Aktien steigen/fallen (fig.)
Stolen sweets are sweetest. (Sprichw.)	Je strenger das Verbot, je süßer schmecken die Äpfel.
a stone's throw of	nur einen Katzensprung/ Steinwurf entfernt

stop:
~ dead	plötzlich stehen bleiben
~ short	vor etwas anhalten
~ off	Zwischenstation einlegen

We are going to stop off in Salzburg on the way to Vienna.

~ behind	da bleiben
~ by (Am./Sl.)	vorbeischauen

store:
be in ~ for s.b.	jdm. bevorstehen
set great ~ by	Wert legen auf

a storm in a teacup — ein Sturm im Wasserglas

story:
the ~ goes	man erzählt sich
cut a long ~ short	kurz gesagt

Stout fellow! (Sl.) — Tapferer Kerl!

straight:
give it to s.o. ~	mit jdm. ohne Umschweife reden
keep a ~ face	ernst bleiben
~ ahead	geradeaus
~ answer	eine direkte Antwort
~ away/off	sofort
~ from the shoulder	direkt, geradeheraus
~ up (Sl.)	Ehrlich!
~-forward	schlicht, einfach, geradeheraus

strain:
~ at a gnat and swallow a camel. (Sprichw.)	Mücken seihen und Kamele verschlucken.
~ed relations	gespannte Beziehungen

a stranger in a strange land — nicht vertraut mit seiner Umgebung

straw:
a ~ in the wind	ein Vorzeichen
the ~ that breaks the camel's back	der Tropfen, der das Fass zum Überlaufen bringt

That's the last ~.	Das ist der Gipfel.
clutch catch/grasp at (a) ~(s)	sich an einen Strohhalm klammern
the stream of consciousness	Bewusstsein
street:	
~s ahead of s.b./s.th.	viel besser als
right up one's ~	genau nach jds. Geschmack
strengthen s.b.'s hand	jds. Position verbessern
stresses and strains	Belastungen
stretch:	
~ a point	großzügig verfahren
~ one's legs	sich die Beine vertreten
strictly speaking	genau genommen
strike:	
~ a bargain	sich geschäftlich einig werden
~ home	tief treffen
~ at the root of	an der Wurzel treffen
~ a happy medium	zu einem Kompromiss kommen
be struck all of a heap (Sl.)	da vergeht einem Hören und Sehen
~ s.o. as	jdm. als ... erscheinen
~ while the iron is hot	das Eisen schmieden, solange es heiß ist
~ up a conversation	ins Gespräch kommen
have s.o. on a string	jdn. am Gängelband haben
a stroke of good luck	Glücksfall
strong:	
~ language	Kraftausdrücke
~ meat	starker Tobak
a ~ point	eine Stärke
protest in ~ terms	energisch protestieren
stuck for s.th.	etwas fehlt jdm.

*I seem to be stuck for change,
can you lend me a pound?*

stuff:
made of the same ~	aus dem gleichen Holz geschnitzt sein
know one's ~	auf Draht sein
~ and nonsense!	Unsinn!
a ~ed shirt (Sl.)	ein aufgeblasener Kerl
a stumbling block	Stolperstein

subject:
~ to this	unter diesem Vorbehalt
~ to change	Änderungen vorbehalten
sore ~	wunder Punkt

such:
~ is life.	So ist das Leben.
no ~ thing	nichts dergleichen
a sucker for s.th.	man kann etwas nicht widerstehen

I know it's expensive, but I have always been a sucker for fast cars.

not to suffer fools gladly	keine Geduld mit dummen Leuten haben
suffice it to say	es genügt zu sagen, dass …

sufficient:
~ unto oneself	selbstständig
~ unto the day	man soll sich nicht vorab Sorgen machen
a sugar daddy (Sl.)	ein älterer Mann, der ein junges Mädchen aushält
Suit yourself.	Mach, wie du meinst.
the sum total	das Endergebnis

Sunday:
one's ~ best	die besten Kleider

a month of ~s	lange Zeit

sure:
~ enough	genau, wie erwartet
a ~-fire method	eine ganz sichere Sache
~ of oneself	sehr selbstbewusst
~ thing! (Sl.)	Natürlich! Sicher!

surprise:
~, ~	(iron.) Überraschung!
a ~ packet (Sl.)	Überraschung

swallow:
~ the dictionary	ungewöhnliche Worte benutzen
~ one's pride	seinen Stolz hinunterschlucken, über seinen Schatten springen

He had to swallow his pride and admit he was wrong.

~ the pill (Sl.)	in den sauren Apfel beißen
~ s.th. hook, line and sinker (Sl.)	etwas ohne weiteres glauben
~ an insult	eine Beleidigung hinnehmen

swear:
~ black is white	eine unhaltbare Position energisch verteidigen
~ blind that (Sl.)	bekräftigen
~ at s.b.	auf jdn. fluchen
~ by s.th.	auf etwas schwören
~ in	vereidigen

sweat:
~ blood (Sl.)	Blut schwitzen
be in a cold ~ (Sl.)	Blut und Wasser schwitzen

sweep:
~ the board	alle nur möglichen Preise gewinnen
make a clean ~	reinen Tisch machen
~ across one's mind	einem in den Sinn kommen
~ s.o. off his feet	jdn. umhauen (fig.)

sweet:
~ Fanny Adams	unwesentlich, wertlos

~ tooth	Naschkatze
keep s.o. ~	jdn. bei Laune halten
in full swing	voll im Gange
The party was in full swing by the time we got there.	
be switched on (Sl.)	auf Draht sein

T

T:
cross the ~'s	sehr genau/pedantisch sein
to a ~	aufs Haar, ganz genau

This description is correct to a T.

keep tabs on s.o. — jdn. kontrollieren

be on the wrong track — auf dem Holzweg sein

tail:
~ after s.b.	jdm. hinterherlaufen
~ between his legs	wie ein erschrockener Hund, mit eingezogenem Schwanz
~-end Charlie	langsam, zu spät
turn ~ on s.b.	vor jdm. davonlaufen
~ off	schwächer werden
~ wagging the dog	das Unwichtige maßgebend sein lassen
~s up	in guter Stimmung

take:
~ advantage of s.b./s.th.	jdn./etwas ausnutzen
~n with s.th.	von etwas eingenommen sein
~n aback	überrascht

I was quite taken aback when I opened the door and saw my long-lost uncle.

~ after s.o.	jdm. ähneln
~ the air	einen Spaziergang machen
~ a back seat (Sl.)	jdm. den Vortritt lassen, die Kontrolle aus der Hand geben
~ a beating	Prügel beziehen
~ the bull by the horns (Brit.)	den Stier bei den Hörnern packen
~ exception to s.th.	an einer Sache etwas auszusetzen haben
~ a fancy to s.b.	sich vernarren in, eine Vorliebe entwickeln für

~ in for a ride	betrogen, auf die Schippe genommen
~ for granted	als Tatsache hinnehmen, voraussetzen
~ s.o. for granted	jdn. nicht genügend beachten
~ in good/bad part	in guter/schlechter Laune etwas hinnehmen

He usually takes my advice in good part.

~ heart	sich ein Herz fassen
~ hold of s.th.	etwas ergreifen
~ in	irreführen, betrügen

We were completely taken in by his story.

~ it from me	Sie können mir glauben
~ a joke	Spaß verstehen
~ it or leave it	wie Sie wollen
~ liberties with	sich Freiheiten herausnehmen bei
~ a liking to s.o.	jdn. mögen
~ note of	notieren, festhalten
~ notice of	beachten
~ offence at	Anstoß nehmen an
~ one's hat off to s.b.	vor jdm. den Hut ziehen
~ one's leave	sich verabschieden
~ one's life in one's own hands	die Verantwortung für sich selbst übernehmen
~ one's life	Selbstmord begehen
~ s.b.'s life	jdn. töten
~ one's time	sich Zeit lassen
~ pity on	sich erbarmen, jdm. helfen
~ the plunge	den entscheidenden Schritt wagen
~ revenge	sich rächen
~ s.b. at his word	jdn. beim Wort nehmen

I hope you are serious about inviting me to stay for the weekend as I intend to take you at your word.

~ s.b's breath away	jdm. den Atem verschlagen

She was so beautiful it took my breath away.

~ s.o. down a peg or two	jdm. einen Dämpfer verpassen
~ s.o. for s.o.	jdn. mit jdm. verwechseln
~ s.th. amiss	etwas übel nehmen
~ s.th. at face value	etwas für bare Münze nehmen

~ s.th. in one's stride	etwas leicht schaffen
~ s.th. out on s.o.	etwas (Ärger etc.) an jdm. auslassen
~ s.b.'s mind off s.th.	jdn. von etwas ablenken
~ stock	Bilanz ziehen
~ the edge of	mildern, die Schärfe nehmen
~ things as they come	die Dinge auf sich zukommen lassen
~ to one's heels	die Beine in die Hand nehmen
~ s.b. to task for s.th.	jdn. zur Rede stellen
~ turns at	sich abwechseln mit
What do you ~ me for?	Wofür halten Sie mich denn?
That ~s the biscuit!	Jetzt schlägt's 13!

talk:

~ back	frech antworten

How many times have I told you that it is rude to talk back at your elders?

~ big (Sl.)	angeben
~ down to s.o.	herablassend zu jdm. sprechen, sich einfach ausdrücken

The Prime Minister was very conscious of his office and tended to talk down to journalists and members of parliament.

~ like a Dutch uncle	jdn. ermahnen, ernsthaft mit jdm. sprechen
~ shop	fachsimpeln
~ s.o. down	jdn. im Gespräch überzeugen, jdn. überreden
~ s.o. into doing s.th.	jdn. zu etwas überreden
~ s.o. out of s.th.	jdm. etwas ausreden
~ s.o.'s head off (Sl.)	zu viel reden
~ s.o. round	jdn. überreden
~ round s.th.	drumherum
~ until one is blue in the face (Sl.)	reden bis man schwarz wird/bis zur Erschöpfung reden

tall:

a ~ order	viel verlangt
a ~ story	ein Lügenmärchen

It takes two to tango.	Es gehören immer zwei dazu.
teach:	
~ s.b. to do s.th.	jdm. beibringen, etwas zu tun
You can't ~ an old dog new tricks.	Der Mensch ist ein Gewohnheitstier.
~ one's grandmother to suck eggs	jdm. mit mehr Erfahrung gute Ratschläge geben
team spirit	Teamgeist
tear:	
~ away from	sich losreißen
~ down	abreißen
~ into s.o/s.th.	jdn. auf das Schärfste kritisieren
~ one's hair	sich die Haare raufen, wütend sein
~ to pieces	in Stücke reißen, verreißen
The critics tore the performance of Hamlet to pieces.	
~ up by the roots	mit der Wurzel ausreißen, ausrotten
in the teeth of	entgegen, trotz
tell:	
~ a mile off	leicht erkennen können
~ all	ein umfassendes Geständnis ablegen
~ told	alles in allem
~ s.b. different	jdn. berichtigen
~ against s.th.	gegen etwas sprechen
~ apart	auseinander halten, unterscheiden
~ on s.o.	jdn. verraten/verpetzen
~ s.o. off	mit jdm. schimpfen
~ s.o. porkies (Sl.)	jdn. anschwindeln
~ s.o. where to get off (Sl.)	jdm. die Leviten lesen
~ tales	flunkern
temper:	
have a quick ~	heftig sein, schnell in Wut geraten
He has such a quick temper, every discussion ends in an argument.	

keep one's ~	sich nicht aus der Ruhe bringen lassen
lose one's ~	die Beherrschung verlieren
tempt fate	das Schicksal herausfordern

ten:
~ feet tall	sehr zufrieden mit sich selbst
~ to one	sehr wahrscheinlich

tend to — zu etwas neigen
These animals tend to get nervous during a thunderstorm.

tender loving care — liebevolle Pflege

terms:
be on bad ~ with	sich schlecht verstehen mit
come to ~ with	sich einigen mit, sich auf ... einstellen
in ~ of	hinsichtlich
not on speaking ~	zerstritten
on equal ~	zu gleichen Bedingungen, auf gleiche Weise

test:
put to the ~	auf die Probe stellen
stand the ~	bestehen, sich bewähren

The old car stood the test and finished the race without breaking down.

be at the end of one's tether — am Ende seiner Kräfte sein

He won't set the Thames on fire. — Der reißt keine Bäume aus.

thank:
~ goodness/heaven	Gott sei Dank
~s to	dank, wegen

that:
~ does it	das war es, mir reicht es, ich kann nicht mehr

~ is not to say	das soll nicht heißen
~ will be the day	das wird nie passieren
~ will do	das reicht
~'s all I can say	das ist alles

then:

~ and there	da und dort, auf der Stelle
~ again	andererseits

thick:

as ~ as two short planks (Brit./Sl.)	dumm wie Bohnenstroh
as ~ as thieves	wie Pech und Schwefel

They do simply everything together, they're as thick as thieves.

a bit ~ (Brit./Sl.)	leicht unverschämt

To expect me to pay all your bills is a bit thick.

come ~ and fast	vor ... hageln, auf jdn. einstürmen

After she had told her mother about her problems, the advice came thick and fast from all parts of the family.

in the ~ of	im dichtesten ..., mittendrin

We were suddenly caught up in the thick of the crowd.
Don't keep me talking, please, I'm in the thick of a job.

~-skinned	dickfellig

He's too thick-skinned to see what everybody thinks of him.

through ~ and thin	durch dick und dünn

thing:

a good ~	zum Glück, gute Sache

It is a good thing you are wearing your coat, as the weather is just turning nasty.

have a ~ about (Brit./Sl.)	besessen sein von
just one of those ~s	da kann man nichts machen, das ist nicht zu ändern
just the ~/the very ~	genau das Richtige
the ~ about s.th. is ...	die Sache ist die, dass ...

think:

~ better of s.th.	einen schon gefassten Entschluss ändern

He thought better of his plan to go away and stayed at home.

~ fit	beschließen, für angemessen erachten

The young man, having neither a job nor any money, thought fit to get married.

~ highly of	bewundern, viel von jdm. halten
~ the world of s.o.	jdn. vergöttern, jdn. bewundern
put on one's ~ing cap	scharf über etwas nachdenken

He's a thorn in my side/flesh. — Er ist mir ein Dorn im Auge.

thought:

A penny for your ~s!	Woran denkst du?
not to give s.th. another ~	keine Ursache

Thank you!
Don't give it another thought!

on second ~s	nach reiflicher Überlegung

On second thoughts, I think I'd prefer to fly.

thread:

lose the ~	den Faden verlieren

The professor lost the thread in the middle of his lecture.

pick up the ~	den Faden wieder aufnehmen

It is difficult to pick up the thread in a discussion after an interruption.

take s.o. through s.th. — jdm. etwas erklären

throw:

~ away	durch Nachlässigkeit verlieren/wegwerfen

He threw away his chances of getting the job.

~ in	hinzufügen, einwerfen
~ light on	Licht werfen auf
~ open	eröffnen, aufreißen (Tür)

~ one's money about	mit Geld um sich werfen
~ s.b. into work	sich in die Arbeit stürzen
~ o.s. at s.o.	sich jdm. an den Hals werfen
~ a spanner in the works	ein Hindernis in den Weg legen, eine Sache hintertreiben
~ s.o. off balance	jdn. aus dem Gleichgewicht bringen
~ s.o. over	jdm. den Laufpass geben
~ up	sich übergeben

under s.o.'s thumb — unter der Fuchtel von jdm.

thunderstruck — wie vom Blitz getroffen

a tissue of lies — von A bis Z erfunden

tick:
in a ~	gleich, sofort
make s.o. ~ (Sl.)	jdn. motivieren
~ s.o. off	mit jdm. schimpfen

tickle:
~ s.b.'s ribs	jdn. amüsieren
~d to death (Sl.)	äußerst amüsiert
~ s.o.'s fancy	jdn. interessieren, neugierig machen

the tide turns	die Dinge verändern sich
a tidy sum	eine ordentliche Menge Geld

tied up — ausgebucht, beschäftigt

tight:
a little ~	in finanziellen Schwierigkeiten
in a ~ corner	in der Klemme
~-fisted	geizig

tighten one's belt — den Gürtel enger schnallen

time:
ahead of ~ — früher als erwartet
The expedition reached its destination well ahead of time.

before one's ~	vor jds. Zeit, bevor man geboren wurde
for the ~ being	vorläufig
from ~ to ~	dann und wann
once upon a ~	Es war einmal ...
pressed for ~	sehr unter Zeitdruck
race against ~	Wettlauf gegen die Zeit
~ after ~	immer wieder
~ and ~ again	immer und immer wieder
~ of one's life	eine sehr schöne Zeit

It was a great holiday we had the time of our lives.

have ~ on one's hands	Zeit zur Verfügung haben
to make good ~ (Am.)	gut vorankommen
give tit for tat	Gleiches mit Gleichem vergelten
today of all days	ausgerechnet heute
toe:	
~ the line	sich den Regeln/dem Druck beugen

The Prime Minister expects her cabinet to toe the line.

keep s.o. on their toes	jdn. nicht zur Ruhe kommen lassen
tread on s.o.'s ~s	jdm. auf den Schlips treten
put heads together	gemeinsam überlegen
tongue:	
hold one's ~	den Mund halten, schweigen
get one's ~ around s.th.	etwas aussprechen
lose one's ~	kein Wort herausbringen
be on the tip of one's ~	auf der Zunge liegen
~ in cheek	ironisch
long in the tooth	alt
over the top	übertrieben
touch:	
get in ~ with	sich in Verbindung setzen mit
~ one's hat at s.o.	jdn. grüßen

~ and go	riskant
~ wood	auf Holz klopfen

track:
cover one's ~s	seine Spuren verwischen
off the ~	auf dem Holzweg
keep to the beaten ~	nichts Originelles wagen
make ~s	sich auf den Weg machen
off the beaten ~	abseits viel befahrener/ besuchter Routen

There weren't any tourists there at all, it was completely off the beaten track.

treat:
It is my ~.	Das geht auf meine Rechnung.
~ s.b. to s.th.	jdm. etwas spendieren, mit etwas verwöhnen

Grandma took the children to the park and treated them to an ice-cream.

trial and error	Versuch und Irrtum

trick:
be up to every ~	mit allen Wassern gewaschen sein
do the ~	den gewünschten Zweck erfüllen

not stick at trifles	sich nicht mit Kleinigkeiten abgeben

trouble:
ask/look for ~	Ärger suchen
take the ~	sich die Mühe machen

have no truck with s.th. (Sl.)	mit einer Sache nichts zu tun haben

true:
come ~	sich bewahrheiten
be ~ of	zutreffen auf
be ~ to s.b.	jdm. treu sein

show one's ~ colours	sein wahres Gesicht zeigen
come up trumps	eine Sache oder ein Problem zur allgemeinen Zufriedenheit lösen

try:

~ one's hand at	sich in etwas versuchen, seinen ersten Versuch machen

John tried his hand at cooking while Mary was away.

~ s.o.'s patience	die Geduld von jdm. auf die Probe stellen
sing another tune	einen anderen Ton anschlagen

turn:

~ a deaf ear to	sich taub stellen
~ against s.o.	sich gegen jdn. stellen
not to ~ a hair	unbewegt bleiben, nicht mit der Wimper zucken
~ down	ablehnen
~ in	ins Bett gehen
~ inside out	das Innere nach außen kehren
~ one's back on s.b.	jdm. den Rücken zuwenden, sich von jdm. abwenden

He turned his back on me to indicate his displeasure.

~ one's hand to s.th.	sich einer Sache zuwenden
~ out to be	sich herausstellen als/dass ...
~ over a new leaf	ein neues Leben beginnen, von vorn anfangen
~ s.b.'s brain/head	jdm. den Kopf verdrehen
~ s.o. in	jdn. bei der Polizei anzeigen/verraten
~ s.th. over in one's mind	sich etwas im Kopf herumgehen lassen
~ s.th. upside down	das Unterste zuoberst kehren
~ tail	weglaufen, davonlaufen
~ the tables	den Spieß umdrehen

The arrival of the police on the scene turned the tables.

~ to one's advantage	etwas zu seinem Vorteil wenden
~ up	aufkreuzen, erscheinen

~ tail	abhauen
~ upon s.b.	jdm. die Schuld geben, jdn. angreifen

The boy turned on his mother and said it was all her fault.

twiddle one's thumbs — Däumchen drehen, Zeit verschwenden

Don't just sit there twiddling your thumbs, get on with your work.

twig s.th. (Sl.) — etwas herausfinden, etwas merken

Jennifer finally twigged that Frank had been lying to her for absolute ages.

twist:
~ s.o.'s arms — jdn. unter Druck setzen

I had to twist his arm a little, but he finally came out with the full story.

~ s.o. round one's little finger — jdn. um den kleinen Finger wickeln

It takes two to tango. — Es gehören immer zwei dazu.

U/V

U speech	Sprechweise der Oberklasse

ugly:
an ~ duckling	ein hässliches Entlein
as ~ as sin	hässlich wie die Nacht

the unacceptable face of s.th.	Aspekt einer Sache, den man auf keinen Fall tolerieren kann

unaware:
be ~ of s.th.	sich einer Sache nicht bewusst sein, etwas nicht merken
catch s.o. ~	jdn. überraschen

under:
come ~	klassifiziert werden als
~ the aegis of	unterstützt durch
~ cover of	im Schutz von
~ foot	am Boden
~ the guise of s.th.	in Verkleidung
~ s.b.'s nose	offen, in Gegenwart von jdm.
~ his own name	unter seinem eigenen Namen
~ one's own steam	mit eigener Kraft
~ par	nicht gut, unwohl
~ protest	etwas tun, aber sich zugleich dagegen verwahren
~ construction	im Bau befindlich
~ the counter	illegal, unter der Hand
~ the weather (Sl.)	unpässlich, krank

John isn't coming to work today, he is feeling under the weather.

unfit for	ungeeignet zu, nicht fähig zu
Unity is strength.	Einigkeit macht stark.
United we stand (divided we fall). (Sprichw.)	Nur gemeinsam sind wir stark.

unwept, unhonoured and unsung — von niemandem beachtet oder vermisst

an unwritten law — ein ungeschriebenes Gesetz

up:
~ in arms — empört
She was up in arms about the way everybody had been treating her.
~ and coming — auf dem Weg zum Erfolg
~ and down the country — überall im Land
~s and downs — Höhen und Tiefen
~ and about — (wieder) gesund und munter
Mary was ill for a while, but now she is up and about again.
~ against s.th. — in Schwierigkeiten stecken, vor einem Problem stehen

be ~ to s.th. — einen Plan aushecken
~ to it — in der Lage sein, etwas zu tun
You can't expect him to do that, he is simply not up to it.
~ to no good (Sl.) — etwas im Schilde führen
~ hill and down dale — in allen Ecken des Landes
~ to scratch (Sl.) — den Erwartungen/Anforderungen gewachsen

John wants to compete in the tournament, but he is not really up to scratch.
~ a tree (Sl.) — verzweifelt
Poor Gillian is up a tree after she lost everything in that fire.
~ with s.th. — 1. los sein mit jdm.,
2. sich auskennen mit etwas

1. What's up with John? He certainly looks unhappy.
2. Is Henry up with the new technology they installed last week?
not ~ to much — nicht viel taugen
It's ~ to you. — Das liegt bei dir.
~ to par — durchschnittlich

upfront:
be ~ about s.th. — offen über eine Sache reden

want s.th. ~ (Sl.)	einen Vorschuss haben wollen
upon my soul	ich schwöre es
the upper crust	die Aristokratie
upset:	
~ over s.th.	ärgerlich über etwas sein
~ s.th. (Sl.)	eine Sache durcheinanderbringen
upset s.b.'s applecart	jdm. in die Quere kommen
quick on the uptake	schnell kapieren
use:	
make ~ of	verwenden, ausnutzen
~ one's head	den Verstand gebrauchen
~ s.th. up	etwas aufbrauchen
~d to s.th.	an etwas gewöhnt sein
It's no ~.	Es hat keinen Zweck.
about as useful as	(iron.) so nützlich wie
vain:	
in ~	vergeblich
take in ~	leichtfertig mit etwas umgehen
Did someone take my name in ~?	Habe ich eben meinen Namen gehört? Hat da jemand von mir gesprochen?
the valley of the shadow of death	im finstren Tal
vanish into thin air	sich in Luft auflösen
variations of the theme *His letters were generally variations of the theme of his earlier complaints.*	Abwandlungen eines Motivs
Variety is the spice of life. (Sprichw.)	Abwechslung macht das Leben erst interessant.
with velvet gloves	sanft, mit Samthandschuhen

verge:
be on the ~ of doing s.th. — im Begriff sein, etwas zu tun
be on the ~ of madness — am Rande des Wahnsinns stehen

this very — ganz genau, ausgerechnet
I shall complain to the police this very minute of you don't switch off the radio.

the vexed question — die viel diskutierte Frage

a vicious circle — ein Teufelskreis, Circulus vitiosus

view:
bird's-eye ~ — Vogelperspektive
in my ~ — meiner Meinung nach
in ~ of — angesichts
take a dim ~ of s.th. — etwas missbilligen
take a long ~ — langfristig planen

the villain of the piece — der Bösewicht

virtue:
~ is its own reward. (Sprichw.) — Die Tugend trägt ihren Lohn in sich selbst.
by ~ of — aufgrund, infolge
have the ~ of — den Vorteil besitzen, zu
The sofa has the virtue of being convertible into a bed.
make a ~ of necessity — aus der Not eine Tugend machen

one's vital statistics — jds. physische Werte wie Größe, Gewicht etc.

voice:
the ~ of conscience — die Stimme des Gewissens
at the top of one's ~ — so laut wie möglich
give ~ to — zum Ausdruck bringen
raise one's ~ — lauter werden, schreien
Don't raise your voice at me, I will not stand it!
the ~ of reason — die Stimme der Vernunft
with one ~ — einstimmig

W

the wages of sin	der Sünde Lohn, die gerechte Strafe
waifs and strays	obdachlose Kinder
go on the waggon (Sl.)	unter die Abstinenzler gehen

wait:
~ **for it**	abwarten
keep s.b. ~ing	jdn. warten lassen
lie in ~	auf der Lauer liegen
~ **and see**	abwarten
~ **on s.b.**	jdn. bedienen
~ **until the cows come home**	lange warten, warten bis man schwarz wird

If he expects me to give up, he can wait until the cows come home!

wake the dead	Tote wecken, Krach machen

walk:
~ **all over s.o.**	jdn. sehr schlecht behandeln
~ **off with**	sich davonmachen mit
~ **on air**	glücklich sein
~ **out on s.b.**	jdn. verlassen/im Stich lassen
~ **the plank**	umgebracht werden
~ **a tightrope**	einen Balanceakt vollführen
~ **of life**	Beruf, sozialer Hintergrund

One of the benefits of this job is the opportunity to meet people from all walks of life.

wall:
~s have ears	die Wände haben Ohren, jmd. hört zu
~-to-~	viel von etwas

The place was covered in wall-to-wall greenery, it looked like a jungle to me.

a Walter Mitty	ein Möchtegern-Held
a wandering Jew	eine rastlose Person

want:
for ~ of	mangels
~ s.th. badly	etwas unbedingt wollen
~ out of s.th.	von etwas zurücktreten

war:
a ~ of nerves	ein Nervenkrieg
~ to the knife	Kampf bis zum bitteren Ende
be at ~ with	auf Kriegsfuß stehen mit
be in the ~s	angeschlagen sein, mitgenommen aussehen

warm the chockles of s.b.'s heart	jdn. erfreuen und beruhigen
the warp and woof	Kette und Schuss
warts and all	mit allen seinen/ihren Fehlern

wash:
~ one's hands of s.th.	seine Hände in Unschuld waschen
~-out	komplettes Versagen, Desaster

I tried to make a living as an artist, but it was a wash-out.

waste:
~ not, want not. (Sprichw.)	Spare in der Zeit, dann hast du in der Not.
~ away	dahinsiechen
~ s.b.'s time	jds. Zeit verschwenden
~ one's breath	Zeit verschwenden, umsonst reden

watch:
~ every penny	sparsam sein
~ s.th. like a hawk	etwas genau beobachten
~ this space	pass genau auf (gleich passiert etwas)
~ it!	Aufpassen!

water:
be in low ~	auf dem Trockenen sitzen
fish in troubled ~s	im Trüben fischen
hold ~	schlüssig sein
His account of the robbery won't hold water.	
in hot ~	in Schwierigkeiten
make s.b.'s mouth ~	jdm. den Mund wässrig machen
Still ~s run deep. (Sprichw.)	Stille Wasser sind tief.

way:
by the ~	übrigens
get into the ~ of	sich angewöhnen zu
You will soon get into the way of using the computer.	
go out of one's ~ to do s.th.	sich große Mühe geben, etwas zu tun
have one's ~	seinen Willen durchsetzen
pave the ~ for	den Weg bereiten für

wear:
~ s.b. out	jdn. erschöpfen, auslaugen
~ s.th. down/out	abnutzen, verbrauchen
~ on	sich dahinschleppen
The evening wore on and the guests were getting restless.	
~ the trousers	in einer Beziehung die Hosen anhaben
~ and tear	Abnutzung

weather:
feel under the ~	sich gesundheitlich nicht wohl fühlen
the ~ breaks/holds	das Wetter schlägt um/hält sich
~ the storm	Schwierigkeiten überstehen
The financial crisis plunged the company into severe difficulties, but they were able to weather the storm.	

weave one's spell — jdn. verzaubern

weigh:
~ anchor	den Anker lichten

~ the consequences	die Folgen abschätzen
~ the evidence	die Beweise abwägen
~ s.o. down	jdn. belasten, bedrücken
~ a ton	sehr schwer sein
~ on one's mind	jdn. beschäftigen, belasten
~ one's words	seine Worte abwägen, bedenken
~ up	einschätzen, beurteilen

He is a difficult person to weigh up.

weight:
take the ~ off one's feet	sich setzen
throw one's ~ about (Sl.)	sich aufspielen

you are welcome	bitte sehr, gern geschehen

well:
~ I never!	Na so etwas!
~ met	was für ein glücklicher Zufall
~ and truly	gänzlich, gründlich

wet:
~ the baby's head	aus Anlass einer Geburt einen trinken gehen
a ~ blanket	ein Spielverderber, ein Miesmacher
~ behind the ears	grün hinter den Ohren, unerfahren, unreif
~ one's whistle (Sl.)	etwas trinken

have a whale of a time	eine tolle Zeit haben

what:
~ are we waiting for?	Worauf warten wir?
~'d you call him? (Sl.)	Wie heißt er doch gleich?
~ do you know!	Was für eine Überraschung!
and ~ have you	und so weiter
~ the eye doesn't see (the heart doesn't crave for). (Sprichw.)	Aus den Augen, aus dem Sinn.
I tell you ~.	Ich mach dir einen Vorschlag.

I tell you what: let's go to the cinema.

so ~	na und, was macht das schon
~ a hope!	Schön wärs!
~ have you (Brit./Sl.)	Ähnliches, der Rest

Just put the suitcases and what have you in the boot.

whatever:
~ happened to …?	Was ist aus … geworden?
~ is, is right	die Dinge sind in Ordnung, wie sie sind
~ you do	unter allen Umständen

wheeling and dealing — Verhandlungen und Intrigen

wheels:
the ~ of government	die Mühlen der Regierung
~ within ~	komplizierte Arrangements

where:
~ does one go from here?	Wie geht es jetzt weiter?
~ on earth	wo auch immer
~ there's a will, there's a way. (Sprichw.)	Wo ein Wille ist, ist auch ein Weg.

which is not saying much — was nicht viel heißt
He was by far the best player in his team, which is not saying much.

a whiff of grapeshot — der begrenzte Einsatz von Feuerwaffen

have the whip hand — die Oberhand haben

white:
a ~-collar job	eine Schreibtischtätigkeit
a ~ elephant	nutzloser Gegenstand, Fehlinvestition
show the ~ feather	den Schwanz einziehen
tell a ~ lie	nicht ganz die Wahrheit sagen
a ~ night	eine schlaflose Nacht

who am I to argue — was rechtfertigt meinen Widerspruch

wild:
~ goose chase	ein sinnloses Unterfangen

~ guess	blinde Vermutung
~ horses wouldn't make me do it.	Keine zehn Pferde bringen mich dazu.

will:
against s.o.'s ~	gegen den Willen von jdm.
Where there is a ~ there is a way.	Wo ein Wille ist, ist auch ein Weg.

win hands down	spielend gewinnen

wind:
get ~ of	spitz kriegen, in Erfahrung bringen, von etwas Wind bekommen
get the ~ up (Sl.)	Angst haben
like the ~	schnell wie der Wind
put the ~ up s.o. (Sl.)	jdm. Angst einjagen
see which way the ~ blows	sehen, wie der Hase läuft
~ s.o. up (Sl.)	jdn. veralbern
take the ~ out of s.o.'s sails	jdm. den Wind aus den Segeln nehmen

wipe out (Sl.)	auslöschen, ruinieren

Many companies were wiped out when the stock index crashed.

wise:
get ~ to s.th. (Sl.)	etwas merken
put s.o. ~ to s.th. (Sl.)	jdm. etwas erklären, jdn. einweihen

Max finally put Jeremy wise to the tricks of his business.

~ up to s.th. (Sl.)	den Tatsachen ins Gesicht sehen

wit:
be at one's wit's ends	mit seinem Latein am Ende sein
keep one's ~s about one	seine fünf Sinne beisammen halten
out of one's ~s	von Sinnen

within:
~ an ace of	beinahe

I was within an ace of being run down by the van.

~ easy reach	leicht erreichbar
throw a wobbly (Sl.)	eine Szene machen
keep the wolf from the door	sich (finanziell) über Wasser halten
put the wool over s.o.'s eyes	jdm. Sand in die Augen streuen

word:
have a quick ~ about s.th.	kurz über etwas reden
be as good as one's ~	sein Wort halten
be unable to get a ~ in edgewise	nicht zu Wort kommen
by ~ of mouth	mündlich
have the last ~	das letzte Wort haben
have ~s with s.o.	sich mit jdm. streiten
waste ~s	Worte verschwenden, vergeblich reden
~s fail me	ich bin sprachlos

work:
make short ~ of	kurzen Prozess mit etwas machen, schnell beenden
~ **upon**	einwirken auf
~ **one's way up**	sich hocharbeiten
~ **out**	1. ausrechnen, 2. planen, 3. sich belaufen auf, 4. Sport treiben

1. The architect worked out how many apartments could be built on the site.
2. We'll work out the details of our holiday trip later.
3. The cost works out at 5 pounds a head.
4. He used to be overweight, but since he has taken to working out regularly, he has lost twenty kilograms.

~ **wonders**	Wunder wirken
for all the world	in jeder Hinsicht
worse for wear	abgenutzt, abgetragen

for what it's worth — ohne Gewähr

wrap:
~ped up in — vollständig in Anspruch genommen von

He is wrapped up in his family.

write:
nothing to ~ home about — nichts besonderes
~ off — abschreiben, aufgeben
The goods are unsaleable, we had better write them off.

hold the wrong end of the stick — etwas vollkommen falsch verstehen

Y/Z

year:
~ in, ~ out	Jahr für Jahr; Jahr ein, Jahr aus
all the ~ round	das ganze Jahr über
not for donkey's ~s	seit Ewigkeiten

yearn for   sich sehnen nach
When I was a kid I yearned for a little dog, but my parents would not allow it.

yell out   hinausschreien
He yelled out when the horse trod on his foot.

not yet   noch nicht

yield:
~ place to	Platz machen für
~ the right-of-way	jdm. die Vorfahrt lassen
~ to despair	sich der Verzweiflung hingeben
~ up s.th.	etwas aufgeben

zap (Sl.)   schnell irgendwohin flitzen
I'll just zap down to the supermarket and get some snacks.

zero in on s.th.   etwas anpeilen, zielen auf

zip:
~ along	schnell fahren
~ up	den Reißverschluss hochziehen

Register

A und O 20
ab und zu 8
Aber 121
abfinden 36
abgenutzt 238
abhauen 21
abkühlen 51
Abkürzung 56
abmachen 60
Abneigung 143
Abrakadabra 114
Abschied 138
Abschluss 54
absichtlich 36
abspülen 65
Abstinenzler 232
Abwesenheit 50
Ach und Krach 37
Achsel 200
Adamskostüm 25
adlig 27
Affäre 110
Ahnung 47, 69
Aktie 210
Akzent (haben) 6
Alarm 55, 119
Alkohol 69
allen Leuten recht machen wollen 11
alles in allem 10, 19
allgemein 33
Allgemeinwissen 50
allmählich 36
Allüren 9
Alter 9, 61, 123
Amen 73
Anblick 110
andererseits 8
Anfang 16, 92
anfangen 75
Anfängerglück 22

angeben 28
Angeklagter 23
Angelegenheit 35
angeln 86
angeschrieben 26
Angesicht 78
Angst 89, 237
Anker 234
anrufen 38
anschließen 126
anschnauzen 28
anschwärzen 26
Ansehen 146
Ansicht 42, 120
anstellen 16
Anstoß 217
anstrengen 23
Antrieb 6
Anzahlung 40, 67
Apfel 44, 104, 210, 214
Applaus 33, 34, 96, 209
Arbeit 126, 150, 151, 189, 223
Ärger 41, 53, 225
Arm 35, 71
Arm in Arm 13
Ärmel 188
Armut 92
arrogant 114
Art 11
Ass 115
Ast 25, 131
Atem 217
Atemzug 32, 67, 135
attraktiv 80
auf allen vieren 10
auf Grund 6
aufatmen 5
aufbürden 18, 192
aufdonnern 99
aufdrängen 121
auffrischen 33
aufgeben 239
aufgehoben 81
aufgetakelt 88
Aufhebens 79, 93, 150, 198, 204

Aufmerksamkeit 41, 67
aufpassen 233
aufpeppen 125
aufregen 61
Aufruhr 171
Aufsehen 41
aufstöbern 63
Auge 12, 21, 27, 46, 55, 76, 77, 78, 122, 129, 130, 146, 150, 161, 166, 194, 198, 200, 202, 222, 235, 238
Augenweide 82
Augenwinkel 168
ausbaden 18
Ausbund 170
Ausdruck 231
Auseinandersetzung 20
ausführlich 16
aushalten 5, 39
auskommen 65
Ausnahme 76
ausnehmen 26
ausplaudern 21
Ausschau 146
Aussteuer 31
auswalzen 87
Ausweg 14

B 122
babyleicht 14
bagatellisieren 141
Bahn 202
Balanceakt 232
bald 22
Band 206
Bange 159
Bank 92
Bär 179
bar 40
Bau 228
Baum 161, 220
bedeuten 7
bedeutungslos 6
Bedingung 23, 50
Bedrohung 209
beeilen 110, 119
beeindruckend 114

beenden 33
befördern 131
Begeisterung 210
beglückwünschen 119
Begriff 118, 203
beharren 129
beherrschen 50
Beherrschung 28, 39, 88, 220
Bein 5, 67, 89, 104, 111, 113, 154, 167, 180, 196, 206, 207, 212, 218
Beispiel 196, 198
Belieben 17
bekannt 36
Belangloses 75
beliebt machen 13
Bemerkung 25, 139
Benehmen 5
benehmen 9
bereit 7, 11
Bereitschaft 208
bereuen 189
Berg 157
Bericht 6
berücksichtigen 21
berufen 151
Berufung 84
beruhigen 51
Berührung 110
Bescheidenheit 80
Bescherung 130
beschimpfen 38
Besen 110, 120, 159
Besitz 116
Besitzer 42, 107
Besserwisser 18
bestätigen 18
Beste(s) 20, 23
bestenfalls 23
besuchen 38
Betracht 11
betrifft 13, 14, 30
betrunken 106
Bett 115, 226
Beute 72
bewusst 10

Bewusstsein 26, 212
Beziehungen 50
Biegen 117
Biegen und Brechen 36
Bienchen 25
bienenfleißig 14
Bier 126
Bilanz 19, 218
Bild 169, 173
billig 193
Bindfaden 184
Binsen 67
bis jetzt 14
blank 109
Blatt 58, 153
blaublütig 27
Blaue 199
Blick 26, 57, 76, 78, 85, 99, 153, 195, 199, 201
blind 161
Blinder 27
Blitz 15, 20, 28, 29, 142, 223
blitzschnell 22, 27
Blödsinn 114, 118
Blumenkind 87
Blut 18, 27, 87, 198, 214
Boden 33, 94, 104, 111, 228
Bohnenstroh 15, 221
Bombe 19
Boot 29
bösartig 19
Bösewicht 231
Braten 185
brav 14
Brechen 117
Brei 21
Brennpunkt 118
Brieftasche 72
Brille 189
Brücke 34
Brunnen 200
brüten 162
Büchse 167
Bündel 169
Bürde 60
Busenfreund 30

Chance 42, 63, 97, 208
Chaos 50, 110

Dach 19, 107, 197
dahinschleppen 67
Damm 187
Dampf 28, 96, 139
Dämpfer 172, 217
Dank 168, 220
Däumchen 227
Daumen 54, 129
davonkommen 111
Decke 99, 101, 115, 149, 153
Deckel 120
Deckung 31
Definition 36
demütigen 73
denken 14
deprimiert 28
Detail 84, 127
Dichter 151
dichthalten 28
dick 82, 101, 221
Dienst 7, 196
Dinge 14
diskutieren 43
Distanz 13, 64
Doppelleben 137
Dorf 103
Dorn 222
Draht 19, 213, 215
drauf und dran sein 5
Dreck 64, 156
dreizehn 19, 218
Droge 117
Druck 180, 227
Drum und Dran 144
dulden 208
dumm 60, 75, 109, 112
Dummheit 114, 180
Dummkopf 104
Dunkeln 16
durchblättern 137
durchboxen 74
durchdrehen 101, 112
durchhalten 21, 52

Durchschnitt 6
Durst 74
Dutzend 37

Ecke 34, 68, 161
egal 39
Ehe 33, 152
Ehre 82, 98, 115
Ehrensache 117
Ehrenschulden 117
ehrgeizig 115
ehrlich 5, 117
Ehrlichkeit 117
Ei 89, 142, 172, 204
Eifer 113
Eile 119, 152
Eilschritt 17
Eimer 40, 67
Eindruck 53
einfach 14
einfallen 41
einhämmern 69
einholen 41, 94
Einkaufsbummel 199
einmischen 116
einnicken 69
einordnen 78
einstimmig 6, 36
einverstanden 79
Einwand 11
Einzelheiten 123, 168
Eis 32, 120
Eisen 112, 124, 212
Elefant 22, 34, 142, 150
Element 69
Elfenbeinturm 124
Eminenz 104, 177
Ende 11, 49, 67, 74, 111, 131, 181, 193
endlich 16
entlassen werden 85
Entlein 228
Entrüstung 119
Entscheidung 127
erblicken 41
Erfahrung 51, 137

Erfolg 24, 119, 127, 174, 229
erfolgreich 22, 39
Erinnerung 67
erkälten 41
erklären 6
Erleuchtung 141
ermutigen 74
erröten 42
erschöpft 20
Erstarrung 54
Erwartung 8, 10
erwischen 41
Esel 177
Espenlaub 137, 197
essen 73
Eule 39
Exempel 149
Exzentriker 182

Fach 197
fachsimpeln 199, 218
Faden 108, 146, 154, 179, 222
Fährte 165
Fall 16, 36, 37, 40, 55
Falle 136
fallen 115
Fantasie 204
Farbe 48
Fass 135, 211
Fassung 180
Fauna 87
Faust 20, 117
Fäustchen 135
Feder 172
federleicht 15
Fee 79
Fehler 29, 80, 202, 208
Feierabend 38, 47
Feigling 200
Feindschaft 18
Feld 103
fertig 10
festnageln 158
Fettnäpfchen 69, 89
Feuer 85, 164, 165, 175
Feuerprobe 6

finden 84
Finger 29, 84, 85, 97, 108, 130, 141, 155, 202, 227
Firlefanz 91
Fisch 86
fischen 234
fix und fertig 17
fixe Idee 22
Flamme 35, 164, 173
Flasche 53, 60
Flausen 120, 180
Fleisch 55, 207
Fliege 25, 131
Flora 87
fluchen 73
Flucht 190
Flügel 47
flunkern 219
Flur 175
Flut 209
Folgen 36
Fortschritt 199
Frage 22, 138, 182, 201, 231
frech 12
Frechheit 43, 159, 163
Fregatte 68, 131
Freiheit 25, 217
fressen 120
Freude 20
Freund 79, 85, 91, 113
Freundlichkeit 131, 205
Frieden 143, 150
Frucht 90, 92
Früchte 20
Fuchs 123
Fuchtel 223
Führung 112, 186
fünf vor zwölf 17
Fuß 97, 134, 144, 169, 180, 187, 197, 198
Fußstapfen 88

Gang 122, 215
Gängelband 212
Ganovenehre 117
Gänsehaut 87, 97

ganz und gar 29
Gardinenpredigt 55
Gas 210
Gasse 125
Gaul 85, 97
Gedächtnis 38
Gedanke 47, 61, 147, 155
Geduld 17, 213, 226
Gefahr 90, 109, 188
Gefallen 82
gefasst sein/machen 6, 31
Gefecht 113, 180
gefeuert 44
Gefühl 30, 82, 119, 186
Gegenseitigkeit 183
geheim 18, 58
Geheimnis 99, 111, 139, 206
gehupft wie gesprungen 33
Geist 97, 99, 138, 198, 207
geistesabwesend 81, 111, 122
Geistlicher 151
gelassen 51
gelb 104
Geld 47, 72, 76, 131, 143, 156, 172, 173, 193, 206, 210, 223
Geldgier 147
Gelegenheit 8
gemeinsam 228
Gemeinwohl 50
Generalprobe 68
Gerede 204
gerissen 51
Geschäft 35, 46, 198
Geschichte 207
Geschmack 113, 212
geschniegelt 206
Geschwätz 45
geschwätzig 43
Gesellschaft 11, 130
Gesicht 21, 45, 78, 83, 92, 166, 179, 193, 207, 226, 237
Gespräch 35, 212
Geständnis 219
gestern 30, 161
gesund 106, 229
Getümmel 75

gewagt 79
Gewähr 238
Gewalt 7, 24, 34
Gewerbe 165
Gewinn 166
gewinnen 107
gewisses Etwas 112
Gewissen 45, 231
Gewohnheit 90, 106, 150
Gewohnheitstier 219
Gipfel 212
Glanzleistung 54
Glanzstück 170
Glas 182
glasklar 55
Glaube 125
gleich 11, 142
Gleichgewicht 223
gleichgültig 39
Gleis 191
Glotze 31
Glück 10, 23, 42, 62, 90, 115, 124, 148, 202, 221
glücklich 59
Glücksfall 212
Glücksklee 91
Glückstopf 148
Gold 137
golden 102, 207
Goldmine 102
Gott 47, 102, 151, 172, 175, 192, 204, 220
Gottesgeschenk 97
Grab 89
Gras 25, 34, 70, 132
Grenze 67, 202, 210
Griff 94
griffbereit 16
Grimasse 78, 149
Großen und Ganzen 36
Größenwahn 62
größenwahnsinnig 24
Grube 63
grün 26, 38, 106, 147, 235
Gründervater 91
Grundzüge 19

Gunst 82, 198
Gürtel 223
Gürtellinie 115
gut stehen 22
Gute 76

Haar 16, 73, 74, 81, 106, 216, 219
Haarspaltereien 106
Hacken 46
Hahn 117
Hals 74, 112, 165, 200, 223
Halt 108
Hamsterkäufe 136
Hand 39, 40, 48, 73, 74, 84, 85, 98, 104, 107, 110, 113, 118, 136, 138, 151, 158, 166, 183, 187, 197, 201, 206, 216, 218, 228, 233
handeln 7
Handumdrehen 123
Hansdampf 125
Hase 40, 123, 203, 237
Haus 36, 58, 149
Häuschen 18, 20
Haut 19, 72, 88, 121, 193, 199, 202
Hehl 29
Heidenangst 193
Heim 113
Heimweg 151
heimzahlen 75
heiraten 152
heiter 12
helfen 166
Hemd 146
herabsehen 145
herausrücken 49, 52
Herd 113
Hering 169
Herr 102, 125
herumlungern 108
herumnörgeln 129
Herumtoben 118
herunterspielen 150
Herz 19, 30, 66, 105, 111, 113, 144, 181, 196, 217

Heuhaufen 159
Hilfe 79
Himmel 132, 142, 157, 165, 178, 197
Himmelstür 172
hineingeraten 29
hin und her 18
hinauslaufen 29
hinauswerfen 130
Hindernis 223
hineinziehen 67
hinschmeißen 44
Hintergrund 18, 22
Hinterhand 202
hinterherjagen 8
Hintern 130
Hinweis 115
Hinz und Kunz 11
hinzuziehen 33
Hirngespinst 83
hochnäsig 111
Hochtouren 26
Hochzeit 109
Hof machen 57
Hoffnung 34, 58, 125, 164
Hoffnungsschimmer 99, 185
Höhe 229
hohes Tier 24
Hölle 24, 62, 157
Holz 213, 225
Holzweg 20, 210, 216, 225
Honig 35, 134
Honigkuchenpferd 104
Honigschlecken 173
hören 12
Hören 212
Horn 205, 216
Hose 127, 201, 234
Huhn 66, 76
Hühnchen 29, 110
Hund 20, 66, 102, 133, 139, 147, 187, 196, 216
hundeelend 15
Hundeleben 66, 136
Hunger 119
Hut 105, 164, 184, 217

Idee 173
im Allgemeinen 36 181, 196, 217
im Geheimen 22
im Nu 17, 122
im übrigen 14
immer 8, 16
in flagranti 41
Innera 226
irren 75, 117
Irrenanstalt 135
Irrtum 225
interessieren 31

Jacke 201
Jahr 11, 81, 240
Jubeljahre 29, 165
jucken 121
Jugendjahre 192
Junggeselle 50
Junggesellenabschied 207

Kaff 166
Kaiser 69
kalt 15
kaltblütig 27, 48, 122
Kamel 211
Kante 180, 184, 192
Kapital 40
Karriere 9, 95
Karte 136, 200
Kartenhaus 118
Kartenverkauf 31
Kartoffeln 44
Kasse 40, 199
Kater 106
Katerstimmung 156
katzbuckeln 31
Katze 36, 40, 67, 80, 139, 142, 173
Katzensprung 210
käuflich 76
Kauz 164
kehren 118, 226
Kehrseite 167
Keil 68
Keim 160
keineswegs 6

Keller 201
Kerl 61
Kern 180
kerngesund 14
kerzengerade 211
Kelle 41, 233
Kettenreaktion 132
Kieker 67
Kind 19, 26, 165 176, 200, 206
Kinderkram 131
kinderleicht 14
Kinderspiel 44
Kindheit 151
Kino 201
Klappe 36, 125, 131
klar 68
klären 9
klar Schiff 45
Klartext 143, 175
Klasse 25
Klatsch 146, 170
Kleider 84
Kleidung 23
Kleingedruckte 203
Kleinigkeit 182, 225
Kleinkram 26, 163
kleinkriegen 65
Kleinvieh 151
Klemme 24, 62, 116, 117, 223
Klotz 154
klug 110, 112
Klugscheißer 46, 203
knallhart 15
Kneifzange 120
Kneipentour 179
Knie 191
Knochen 202
Knüppel 180, 206, 207
Koch 119
Kohle 109, 184
kommen 49
Kompetenz 100
Kompliment 50, 138
Kompromiss 20, 107, 212
konfrontiert 78

konfus 122
König 55
Kontakt 130
Kontrolle 95, 107
Kopf 19, 22, 34, 43, 108, 110, 112, 115, 120, 126, 130, 140, 158, 159, 165, 169, 173, 174, 180, 184, 188, 194, 196, 210, 226
Korn 103
Krach 232
Kraft 206, 220, 228
Kraftausdruck 212
Kragen 37, 159, 188
krähen 117
Kram 30
krank machen 9
kränken 119
Krankheit 55
Krieg 116
Kriegsbeil 35, 110
Kriegsfuß 57, 163, 233
Krokodilstränen 54
Krone 181, 198
Kropf 159
Kübel 184
Küche 118
Kuchen 7
Kuckucksei 55
Kuh 192
Kumpel 30
Kurs 42
kurzfristig 16

lächeln 193
lachen 135
Lachen 35, 116, 135, 200
Lackaffe 86
Laden 200
Ladenschluss 8
Lage 19
Landei 52
lang 16
Länge 67, 207
Langohr 177
langweilen 61
Last 21, 121

Register

Laster 62
lästern 25
Latein 237
Lauer 232
Lauf 52
Laufbahn 43
Laufende 147
Lauffeuer 207
Laufpass 97, 223
Laune 21, 26, 119, 215, 217
laut 6
Leben 53, 114, 137, 144, 196, 226
lebendig 9, 35
Lebensabend 74
Lebensunterhalt 31, 72
Lebenswandel 42
Leder 137
Lehre 66, 177
Leib 129
Leiche 61, 139, 168, 201
Leid 66
leise 32
Leviten 219
Licht 99, 141, 179, 198, 222
Liebe 147, 148
Liebesmüh' 27
Lippen 108, 140
Liste 152
Loch 68, 135
Löffel 30, 131, 159
Lohn 232
Lorbeeren 136, 187, 209
Los 125
Löwenanteil 143
Luft 46, 115, 230
Luftschlösser 34
Lüge 140, 169
Lügengeschichte 47, 79
Lumpenhändler 184
Lunte 203
Lust 111
Luxusleben 103

Macht 154
Mächtige 24
mahlen 85

Mahlzeit 207
Mammon 84
Mann 151
Märchen 165
Märchenprinz 157
Mark 196
Markt 51
Maßen 24
Maus 174
Medaille 47, 167
meiden 17
meinetwegen 10
Meinung 9, 18, 22, 30, 42, 52, 65, 206, 231
Meister 153, 177
Melodie 172
Menschenverstand 50, 118
Miene 150
Milch 134
Mimose 200
Missverständnisse 45
Mist 151, 154
Mitleid 174
mitleidig 12
mitmachen 12
mitmischen 44, 111
mittendrin 19, 23
Möglichkeiten 6, 17
Moment 13, 20, 107
Mond 152
Mördergrube 113
Mordsspaß 111
Morgenstund' 25
Mücke 150, 211
Mühe 18, 29, 36, 131, 137, 156, 169, 225, 234
Mumm 111
Mund 48, 116, 127, 153, 157, 193, 199, 200, 207, 224, 234
mündlich 37
Münze 47, 78, 98, 192, 218
Murmeltier 202
Musik 172
Muskel 87
Mut 29, 70, 113, 146, 194, 200

Muttersöhnchen 156
mysteriös 46

nachdenken 39
Nachsicht 11
Nächste 43
Nacht 34, 41, 156, 160, 202, 228, 236
Nachteil 17
Nacken 32
nackt 25
Nadel 159
Nagel 115, 158, 180
nagen 73
Naivling 18
Name 38, 150, 176, 206, 228
Narr 88, 89
Naschkatze 215
Nase 27, 79, 88, 161, 176, 189
natürlich 52
Nebel 156
Neid 104
Neige 199
Nerv 97, 159, 169
nerven 112
Nervenbündel 19
nervös 54, 73
Nest 90, 121
neu 32
Neuanfang 35
Neugier 55
Nickerchen 40, 90
Niederlage 78
Niere 181
Niete 67, 134
Not 114, 158, 193, 196, 202, 231, 233
Notgroschen 136
notieren 127
Nu 17
Nummer 17, 192
Nuss 109, 162
Nutzen 156

Oberfläche 184
Oberhand 236
Ochse 69

offensichtlich 13, 15
ohnmächtig 50
Ohr 10, 20, 47, 71, 73, 77, 101, 106, 112, 115, 138, 174, 178, 188, 195, 232, 235
Öl 164
Ölgötzen 69
Opium 167
Ordnung 10, 45, 80, 187, 196, 198, 205
Ort 91, 113, 114

Paar 109
Pack 194
Palme 68
Pandora 167
Panik 20, 207
Papiertiger 169
Papst 156
Paradies 109, 197
Partei 170, 200
Party 31
Patsche 173, 205
Peanuts 43
Pech 15, 67, 147, 148, 221
Pechsträhne 171
Pechtag 184
pedantisch 216
Pest 210
Peter 171
Pfeffer 203
pfeifen 135
Pferd 40, 118, 181, 237
Pflicht 12, 31, 62, 65
Pflichtbesuch 70
Pille 26, 98
Pionierarbeit 26
Plage 162
Plan 110, 229
Platz 174
pleite sein 20, 33
Pornofilm 28
Porzellanladen 142
präzise 15
Preis 16, 43, 51
Pro 178

Probe 69, 220, 226
probieren 178
Problem 54, 124
Prophet 157, 178
Prozess 238
Prüfung 181
Prügel 216
Punkt 176, 205
Pyrrhussieg 181

Quatsch 10
Quelle 92, 118
Quere 54, 230
quietschfidel 14

Rache 187
rächen 17
Rad 163
Rädchen 47
Radieschen 180
rastlos 16
Ratte 185
Räuber 51, 62
Räuberhöhle 21
Rechnung 70, 118, 182, 194, 225
Recht 128, 154, 187
rechtfertigen 12
Rede 111, 218
reden 116
Regel 14, 30, 53, 150
Regen 76, 92, 127, 168
Regenwetter 160
regnen 113, 184
reichlich 19
Reichweite 13
Reihe 210
Reim 181
Reinfall 57, 152
reinknien 18
reinlegen 64
reizen 18
Renner 24
Reserve 124
Reue 22
Richtung 42
Riemen 97

Risiko 42
Rockzipfel 156
Rolle 163
Rosenpfad 178
Ross 118
rot 48
Ruck 104
Rücken 18, 22, 199, 226
Rückschlag 29, 60, 196
Rückzieher 44
Rückzug 21
Ruf 27, 45, 47, 96, 163
Rufweite 106
Ruhe 14, 18, 72, 117, 136, 138, 220, 224
Ruhm 80
Ruhmeshalle 107
ruinieren 237

Sache 175
Sack 143, 173
Sackgasse 26
Saft 127
Samthandschuh 99, 108, 230
Sand 70, 110, 194, 238
Sarg 158
Säugling 18
Säule 174
schäbig 66
Schachtel 164
Schaf 26
Schafspelz 198
Schälchen 52, 82
schämen 197
Schärfe 218
Schatten 175, 180, 197, 198, 214
Schatzkammer 9
Scheck 40
Schein 13
Scheunendrescher 73
Schicksal 81, 194, 220
schief gehen 10
Schiff 185
Schilde 229
Schippe 187, 217
Schlaf 55, 81, 201

schlafen 60
Schlag 16, 163, 166, 201, 208
schlagen 49
schlagfertig 182
Schlamassel 84, 85
schlau 15
schlicht 179
schließlich 8
Schlips 224
Schlot 203
Schmeichelei 204
Schmetterlinge 35
schmieden 124
schmieren 103
Schmiergeld 164
Schmutz 64
Schnäppchen 20
Schnecke 32, 110, 127
schneeweiß 15
Schnitzer 32
schnorren 34
Schnorrer 91
schnüffeln 161
Schnürchen 46, 101
Schock 86, 199
schön 42
Schönheit 22, 185
Schoß 201
Schrank 111
Schranken 129
Schraube 111, 146
Schrei 11, 184
Schritt 130, 217
Schuh 181, 199
Schuld 38, 136, 181, 189, 227
Schulter 48, 97, 48
Schürzenzipfel 156
Schuss 233
Schuster 47
Schutz 228
schützen 53
Schutzengel 105
schwach 18
Schwäche 207
Schwachpunkt 27
schwachsinnig 157

Schwachstelle 44
Schwalbe 166
Schwamm 139
Schwanz 216, 236
schwänzen 117
schwärmen 129
schwarz 26, 29, 122, 218, 232
Schwarze 117
schwarzes Schaf 26
Schwätzchen 43
Schweigen 177
Schwein 143
Schweiß 37
schwer nehmen 39
schwerhörig 109
Schwert 155, 172
Schwierigkeit 13, 15, 51, 54, 109, 122, 194, 223, 229, 234
schwimmen 62
Schwindel 50
Seele 43, 96, 131
Seemannsgarn 86, 207
Segel 206, 237
Sehen 212
Sekunde 22, 66
selbstverständlich 14
Seligkeit 209
Semmel 38, 118
Sensationspresse 105
Seufzer 32
Show 209
sich drücken 31, 64
sicher 10, 23, 41, 192
Sicherheit 15
sicherlich 15
Sieg 39, 48
Siegel 46
Silber 137
Sinn 48, 75, 111, 161, 214, 235, 237
Sinneswandel 42
Sippe 15
sofort 17
Sohn 142, 178
Sommer 166
Sonne 41
sonnenklar 15

Sonntagsstaat 123
Sorge 136, 213
Spanner 172
sparen 56
Spaß 5, 57, 90, 111, 131, 135, 217
Spatz 25, 73, 107
Spiel 31, 33, 94, 110, 150, 175, 208
spielen 175
Spielregel 94
Spielverderber 26, 235
Spieß 226
spindeldürr 19
Sprache 40, 146, 206
Sprung 126, 176
Spur 53, 130, 159, 225
spüren 82
Stadt 169
Standpauke 68
Standpunkt 108, 198
Staub 131, 193
Steckenpferd 187
Stegreif 107
Stein 13, 19
Steinwurf 210
Stempel 208
sterben 54
Stern 15, 55, 185
Stich 18, 138, 139, 232
Stiefel 140
Stier 216
stillschweigend 186
Stimme 184, 231
Stimmung 216
stinkfaul 29
stinksauer 117
Stirn 92, 77, 78, 132
stockbesoffen 69
stockblind 14
stocktaub 60
Stolperstein 213
Stolz 35, 214
Strafe 232
Stränge 130
Straße 151
Streber 71
Strecke 33, 119

Streich 177
Streik 123
Streit 111
streiten 182, 238
Streitfrage 13
Strich 8, 11, 100, 154, 182, 192
Strick 121
Strippe 28
Strohfeuer 86
Strohhalm 41, 212
Stubenarrest 104
Stubenhocker 116
Stück 25, 58, 196, 219
Stuhl 201
Sturm 211
Sande 232
Sündenbock 79
Sündenpfuhl 62
Suppe 88
Süßes 111
Szene 238

Tacheles 96
Tag 25, 26, 44, 46, 52, 59, 67, 34, 41, 122, 166
Tagedieb 178
Tagesanbruch 16
Tageslicht 33, 141
Taktik 43
Tal 230
tanzen 210
Tasche 23, 64, 132, 175, 207
Tasse 23, 111
Tat 7, 102, 156, 177
Tatendrang 21
Tatsachen 204
tatsächlich 7
taub 60, 80, 226
Taube 107
Teamgeist 219
Telefonhörer 109
Tellerrand 39
Tellerwäscher 91
teuer 51
Teufel 22, 57, 69, 81, 114, 118, 159, 206

Teufelskreis 122, 231
Theater 7, 150
Tiefe 229
Tiefgang 44
Tiefpunkt 115
Tiefschlaf 134
Tinte 154
tipptopp 206
Tisch 45, 136, 214
Toast 114
Tobak 212
Tod 16, 41, 127, 193
Todeskuss 132
Todesstoß 205
todmüde 60
Todsünde 197
Ton 38, 42, 161, 226
Torheit 89
tot 59
töten 65
Toter 184, 232
Träne 35, 188, 198
Tratsch 146
Traufe 127, 168
Traum 57
traurig 73
Treiben 119
Treue 175
Tricks 19
Tritt 180
Trockene 234
trödeln 134
Tropfen 135, 211
tropfen 69
Trost 11, 48, 126, 159
Trottel 7
trotzdem 10, 11
Trübe 234
Trumpfkarte 20
Tuch 186
Tugend 170, 171, 184, 231
Tunichtgut 103
Tür 34, 46, 118, 167
turteln 25
typisch 10, 11

übel 12
Übel 62, 139, 186
überall 11
überarbeiten 39
übereinstimmen 12
überlegen 23
Überlegung 195, 222
überraschen 21
Überraschung 30, 214, 235
überschätzen 5
überschlagen 80
übertreffen 23
übertreiben 136
übertrieben 81
überzeugen 39, 40
Uhr 46, 184, 202
Uhrwerk 15
Umschweife 211
Umweg 189
unerfahren 44
unerträglich 24
Unfug 144
ungewiss 9
Ungewissen 130
unglaublich 38
Unglück 124, 177, 184
unhöflich 18
Unkenntnis 129
Unkraut 121
unordentlich 13
Unruhe 40
Unschuld 45, 233
Unsinn 120, 213
unter „ferner liefen" 12
unterbrechen 56
Unterstützung 36, 83
Untersuchung 21
unterwürfig 39
unvernünftig 25
unverschämt 14
unverständlich 14
unvorstellbar 24
Urteil 171

Vater 113, 142
verabscheuen 110

verabschieden 24
Verantwortung 12, 18, 26, 38, 198, 217
verantwortungsbewusst 7
Verbindung 224
Verbot 210
verbünden 121
Verdacht 5
Verderben 51
verdrängen 74
Verfassung 15, 50, 122
verflixt 58
Verfügung 13
vergeben 90
vergewissern 41
Vergleich 8
vergöttern 222
Verhältnis 24, 144
verkommen 184
verlassen 114
Verlegenheit 147, 181
verletzen 56
verlieben 79
verloren gehen 7
Verlust 166
vernachlässigbar 43
vernachlässigen 139
Vernunft 33, 231
verpetzen 219
verraten 21, 28, 204
verrotten 209
verrückt 15, 68, 112, 148, 149, 162
Verrücktheit 118
verschonen 139
Versenkung 201
Verstand 230
Versuch 226
Versuchskaninchen 105
Vertrauen 113, 122
Vertrautheit 80
verunglücken 6
verursachen 33
verzählen 52
verzaubern 234
Verzweiflung 68
Vogel 20, 25, 88, 142, 201

Volldampf 10
vollfressen 28
volljährig 9
volltrunken 27
vorbeikommen 68
vorbeischauen 38, 68
vorbeugen 178
Vorbild 105
vorlesen 185
Vorliebe 143
Vorschein 33
Vorsicht 64
Vorstellung 120
Vorteil 8, 121, 226, 231

Wagen 163
Wahl 44
Wahnsinn 231
wahnsinnig 68
Wahrheit 49, 71, 141, 155
Wald 161
Wand 18, 46, 232
Wandervogel 25
Wange 188
wappnen 13
wann 115
warnen 39
warten 51
waschen 173
Wasser 39, 58, 61, 80, 104, 112, 130, 147, 157, 164, 210, 214, 225, 234, 238
Wässerchen 35
Wasserglas 211
Wechselgeld 42
Wechseljahre 42
Weg 26, 136, 137, 150, 153, 172, 203, 223, 225, 234, 237
wegkommen 23
Wehwehchen 6
weinen 55, 135
weise 15
Weisheit 16
weiterwursteln 126
Wellen 41
Welt 20, 51, 124, 135, 141, 164

Wenn und Aber 35
wenig 8
Werbebranche 114
Wert 176, 211
Wespennest 117
Wetter 234
Wettkampf 190
Wettlauf 8, 224
wichtig 40
Widerspruch 11
Widerstand 8, 208
wiederkäuen 43
Wiege 91
Wildnis 119
Wille 124, 234, 236, 237
willkommen 30
wimmeln 10
Wimper 20, 226
Wind 28, 47, 96, 206. 237
Wink 115
Winkel 161
Wirt 118
Wissen 8, 9, 23
Witz 53
Witzfigur 83
Woche 59
Wogen 177
Wolf 123, 144, 198
Wolke 47
Wort 18, 32, 84, 96, 120, 135, 156, 157, 180, 217, 224, 235, 238, 239
Wörtchen 111
Wunde 140
Wunder 238
wunderbar 84
Würgen 202
Wurzel 188, 212, 219
Wut 27, 28, 87, 219
Wutanfall 110
wütend 15

zäh 15
Zahl 185
zählen 52
Zahn 13, 19, 46, 104, 210
Zähneknirschen 100
Zankapfel 13, 30
zanken 80
Zauber 32
Zaunpfahl 115
Zeche 197
Zeile 23, 185
Zeit 5, 9, 10, 52, 59, 66, 85, 114, 115, 122, 131, 139, 154, 171, 189, 224, 233
Zeitdruck 224
Zeitvertreib 187
zerronnen 72
Zeter 28
Zeug 59
Ziel 168, 185, 201
ziellos 115
zieren 9
zischen 33
Zivilcourage 111
Zorn 78
zu Hause 72
Zuckerbrot 39
Zufall 138
zufällig 6, 36, 42
Zufallsbekanntschaft 42
Zufriedenheit 226
Zug 2, 155
Zügel 186
Zugeständnis 176
Zukunft 101, 145
zum Besten halten 94
zumuten 25
Zunge 32, 46, 111, 146, 224
Zünglein 19
zusammenreißen 7
zu sprechen 30
Zustimmung 36
zwanglos 72
Zwangsvorstellung 86
Zweck 12, 62, 196, 230,
zwei 219, 227
Zweifel 23, 160
Zwietracht 205
zwölf 74
zynisch 125

False Friends

aktuell

false friend → *actual* **true friend** → *1. current*
 2. up to date

Beispiele:
1. Gesundheit und Ernährung sind fast überall von großem **aktuellen** Interesse.
   *Health and nutrition are of great **current** interest almost everywhere.*
2. Die Liste, die du mir gestern gegeben hast, ist nicht **aktuell**.
   *The list you gave me yesterday is not **up to date**.*

Der richtige Gebrauch des englischen Begriffs:
actual   eigentlich

*Thomas runs the business, but the **actual** owner of the shop is his wife.*
Thomas führt das Geschäft, aber der **eigentliche** Besitzer des Ladens ist seine Frau.

Art

false friend → *art*
true friend → *1. kind, sort, type*
 2. (Art und Weise) way
 3. (Wesen) nature
 4. (Verhalten) behaviour

Beispiele:
1. Diese **Art** von Büchern finde ich überhaupt nicht interessant.
   *I do not find this **kind** of book interesting at all.*
2. Ich mag die **Art**, wie er mit Kindern umgeht.
   *I like the **way** how he interacts with children.*
3. Es ist nicht meine **Art** andere anzulügen.
   *It is not of my **nature** to lie to others.*
4. Seine **Art** ist zwar seltsam, aber eigentlich ist er ein netter Mensch.
   *His **behaviour** is rather strange, but actually he is a nice person.*

Der richtige Gebrauch des englischen Begriffs:
art Kunst

*While living in Paris, he used his time intensively and visited a different **art** gallery every day.*
Während er in Paris lebte, nutzte er die Zeit intensiv und besuchte fast jeden Tag eine andere **Kunst**galerie.

bekommen

false friend → *become*
true friend → *1. (erhalten) receive, get*
2. (gut tun) do someone good
3. (Essen usw.) not agree with someone
4. (ein Baby ~) have

Beispiele:
1. Heute morgen habe ich einen Brief von meiner Mutter **bekommen**.
   *This morning I **received** a letter from my mother.*
2. Ich weiß, dass der Urlaub ihm sehr gut **bekommen** wird.
   *I know that the holiday will **do** him good.*
3. Frau Brown macht sich Sorgen, weil Milch ihrem Baby nicht **bekommt**.
   *Mrs Brown is worried because milk doesn't **agree** with her baby.*
4. Es wundert mich, dass sie plötzlich unbedingt ein Baby **bekommen** möchte.
   *I am surprised that suddenly she badly wants to **have** a baby.*

Der richtige Gebrauch des englischen Begriffs:
become 1. werden, sich entwickeln
2. (emotional, physisch) werden
3. (~ of) werden

1. *I want to **become** a doctor.*
   Ich möchte Arzt **werden**.
2. *When I mentioned my Swiss bank account, the waiter suddenly **became** very friendly.*
   Als ich mein Schweizer Bankkonto erwähnte, **wurde** der Kellner plötzlich sehr freundlich.
3. *"What will **become** of me?" wondered the old man when he had to move out of his flat.*
   „Was wird aus mir **werden**?", fragte sich der alte Mann, als er aus seiner Wohnung ausziehen musste.

Biene

false friend → *bean* **true friend** → *bee*

Beispiel:
Die Frühlingswiese war voller Blumen und **Bienen**.
*The spring meadow was full of flowers and **bees**.*

Der richtige Gebrauch des englischen Begriffs:
bean Bohne

*Most British people enjoy eating **beans** on toast.*
Die meisten Briten essen gern **Bohnen** auf Toast.

brav

false friend → *brave* **true friend** → 1. *well-behaved*
2. *good*

Beispiele:
1. Leider sind Kinder nicht immer **brav**.
   *Unfortunately, children are not always **well-behaved**.*
2. „Du bist so ein **braver** Hund, Snoopy", sagte das Herrchen zu seinem Beagle.
   *"You're such a **good** dog, Snoopy" the master said to his beagle.*

Der richtige Gebrauch des englischen Begriffs:
brave mutig, tapfer

*It was very **brave** of her to have a tooth removed without anaesthetia.*
Es war sehr **tapfer** von ihr, sich ohne Betäubung einen Zahn ziehen zu lassen.

Chef

false friend → *chef* **true friend** → *boss*

Beispiel:
Der **Chef** war gut gelaunt und die Stimmung im ganzen Büro war heiter.
*The **boss** was in a cheerful mood and the atmosphere in the whole office was good.*

Der richtige Gebrauch des englischen Begriffs:
chef   Küchenchef, Koch

*The **chefs** at the Savoy Hotel in London are probably among the best in the world.*
Die **Küchenchefs** des Savoy-Hotels in London gehören wahrscheinlich zu den besten der Welt.

dick

false friend → *thick*   **true friend** → *fat*
Beispiel:
Für sein Alter ist mein Neffe ziemlich **dick**.
*My nephew is rather **fat** for his age.*

Der richtige Gebrauch des englischen Begriffs:
thick   1. dicht
              2. (umgangssprachlich) blöd

1. *We had to drive very slowly because of the **thick** fog.*
   Wir mussten wegen des **dichten** Nebels sehr langsam fahren.
2. *Peter is always so **thick**!*   Peter ist immer so **blöd**!

eventuell

false friend → *eventually*   **true friend** → *1. possible*
                                                  2. perhaps, maybe
Beispiele:
1. Du musst dir einen Plan machen, um **eventuelle** Schwierigkeiten zu umgehen.
   *You have to make a plan in order to avoid **possible** difficulties.*
2. Wir können **eventuell** um 7 Uhr bei euch vorbeikommen.
   ***Perhaps** we will be able to come around at 7 o'clock.*

Der richtige Gebrauch des englischen Begriffs:
eventually   schließlich, endlich

*He **eventually** found his way home after he had been missing for several days.*
Nachdem er mehrere Tage vermisst gewesen war, fand er **schließlich** den Weg nach Hause.

familiär

false friend → *familiar* **true friend** → *1. personal*
  2. relaxed, informal
  3. intimate

Beispiele:
1. Aus **familiären** Gründen musste er früher abreisen.
   *He had to return earlier for **personal** reasons.*
2. Mir gefällt die **familiäre** Atmosphäre an meinem neuen Arbeitsplatz.
   *I like the **relaxed** atmosphere in my new office.*
3. Offensichtlich gefiel ihr die **familiäre** Art ihres Chefs nicht.
   *Apparently she didn't like the **intimate** manner of her boss.*

Der richtige Gebrauch des englischen Begriffs:
familiar 1. (wohl)bekannt
  2. (wohl)vertraut
  3. vertraut, freundschaftlich
  4. vertraulich

1. *Kate und Elizabeth were almost as **familiar** as old friends.*
   Kate und Elizabeth waren miteinander fast so **bekannt** wie alte Freunde.
2. *She was very **familiar** with computers, which immensely increased her chances to get the job.*
   Mit Computern war sie sehr **vertraut**, was ihre Chancen, den Job zu bekommen, stark verbesserte.
3. *I'm on **familiar** terms with most people on my street.*
   Zu fast allen Menschen in meiner Straße habe ich eine **freundschaftliche** Beziehung.
4. *After only a few days, my colleague became very **familiar**.*
   Schon nach wenigen Tagen wurde meine Arbeitskollegin allzu **vertraulich**.

famos

false friend → *famous* **true friend** → *excellent*

Beispiele:
„Vielen Dank für den schönen Abend und das **famose** Essen", bedankte sich Cedric bei seinen Gastgebern.
*"Thank you for the wonderful evening and the **excellent** meal" Cedric thanked his hosts.*

Der richtige Gebrauch des englischen Begriffs:
famous berühmt

> *Edinburgh is **famous** for its beautiful old castle and the festival, which takes place every August.*
> Edinburgh ist **berühmt** für sein schönes altes Schloss sowie die Festspiele, die jeden August stattfinden.

Flug

false friend → *fly*
true friend → *flight*
Beispiel:
Der **Flug** nach Australien dauert manchmal bis zu 35 Stunden.
*The **flight** to Australia sometimes lasts up to 35 hours.*

Der richtige Gebrauch des englischen Begriffs:
fly Fliege

> *When Brian was dozing in the sun, and a **fly** suddenly landed directly on his nose, he immediately jumped onto his feet.*
> Als eine **Fliege** plötzlich auf Brians Nase landete, während er in der Sonne döste, sprang er sofort auf.

Gymnasium

false friend → *gymnasium*
true friend → *grammar school*
Beispiel:
Robert besuchte das **Gymnasium**, weil seine Eltern wollten, dass er an der Universität Jura studierte.
*Robert attended **grammar school** because his parents wanted him to study law at university.*

Der richtige Gebrauch des englischen Begriffs:
gymnasium (gym) Turnhalle

> *My sister wants to become a gymnast and practises in the **gym** every evening.*
> Meine Schwester möchte Kunstturnerin werden und übt jeden Abend in der **Turnhalle**.

Hausaufgaben

false friend → *housework* **true friend** → *homework*
Beispiel:
Wir können heute Abend nicht weggehen, weil wir so viele **Hausaufgaben** zu machen haben.
*We can't go out tonight because we have so much **homework** to do.*

Der richtige Gebrauch des englischen Begriffs:
*Hinweis: "Homework" verwendet man im Englischen nur in der Einzahl. "Homeworks" gibt es nicht.
housework   Hausarbeit

*She hates **housework** and lets her husband do everything, except for the ironing, which she enjoys.*
Sie hasst **Hausarbeit** und lässt alles ihren Mann machen, außer dem Bügeln, das sie gern macht.

Hose

false friend → *hose*
true friend → *trousers (UK), pants (US)*
Beispiel:
„Was steht mir besser – die grüne oder die lila **Hose**?"
*"Which suit me better – the green or the purple **trousers**?"*

Der richtige Gebrauch des englischen Begriffs:
hose   Schlauch

*It's better to water the garden with a **hose** than with a watering can.*
Es ist besser, den Garten mit einem **Schlauch** als mit einer Gießkanne zu bewässern.

Igel

false friend → *eagle* **true friend** → *hedgehog*
Beispiel:
Die Kinder entdeckten einen **Igel**, dessen Winterschlaf gestört worden war und der im Garten umherirrte.
*The children discovered a **hedgehog** which was running confusedly around the garden because its hibernation had been disturbed.*

Der richtige Gebrauch des englischen Begriffs:
eagle   Adler

*The **eagle** flew majestically over the mountains and then suddenly dropped from the sky to catch a mouse with his claws.*
Der **Adler** flog majestätisch über die Berge und stürzte plötzlich vom Himmel, um eine Maus mit seinen Krallen zu fangen.

Kost

false friend → *cost*   **true friend** → *1. food*
                                                                  2. diet

Beispiele:
1. Sie bevorzugte vegetarische **Kost** gegenüber Fleisch.
    *She preferred vegetarian **food** to meat.*
2. Mr Smith wurde von seinem Arzt geraten, fettfreie **Kost** zu essen.
    *Mr Smith was advised by his doctor to maintain a fat-free **diet**.*

Der richtige Gebrauch des englischen Begriffs:
cost   Kosten, Preis

*Unfortunately the **cost** of petrol has risen dramatically in the last few years.*
Die Benzin**preise** sind in den letzten Jahren leider dramatisch gestiegen.

Kritik

false friend → *critic*   **true friend** → *criticism*

Beispiel:
Meine Chefin lobt uns oft und übt nur konstruktive **Kritik**.
*My boss praises us often and offers only constructive **criticism**.*

Der richtige Gebrauch des englischen Begriffs:
critic   Kritiker

*After the musician had read the very unflattering review of his concert, he called the **critic**.*
Nachdem der Musiker die sehr unschmeichelhafte Kritik seines Konzertes gelesen hatte, rief er den **Kritiker** an.

Lager

false friend → *lager* **true friend** → *storeroom*
Beispiel:
Die Hafenarbeiter brachten die Waren gleich in das **Lager**.
*The wharfies brought the goods directly to the **store-room**.*

Der richtige Gebrauch des englischen Begriffs:
lager   Bier

*A cold **lager** on a hot day is always a great pleasure.*
Ein kaltes Lager-**Bier** an einem heißen Tag ist immer ein großer Genuss.

Mappe

false friend → *map* **true friend** → *folder, file*
Beispiel:
Nach dem Unterricht packte der Junge all seine **Mappen** in die Tasche und lief gleich von der Schule aus zum Strand.
*After the lesson, the boy put his **folders** into his bag and ran to the beach straight from school.*

Der richtige Gebrauch des englischen Begriffs:
map   (Land)Karte, Stadtplan

*It's impossible to find your way around London without a **map**.*
Es ist unmöglich, sich in London ohne **Stadtplan** zurechtzufinden.

Mist

false friend → *mist* **true friend** → *dung*
Beispiel:
Der Bauer düngte sein Feld mit **Mist** und hoffte auf eine gelungene Ernte im Herbst.
*The farmer fertilised his field with **dung** and hoped for a successful harvest in the autumn.*

Der richtige Gebrauch des englischen Begriffs:
mist   1. Nebel
             2. Dunst

1. *The young couple kissed passionately as they watched the **mist** rise on the mountains together.*
   Das junge Paar küsste sich leidenschaftlich, während es zusah, wie der **Nebel** auf den Bergen aufstieg.
2. *In the early hours of the morning, they walked through the meadows and finally returned only when the **mist** had dispersed.*
   In den frühen Morgenstunden gingen sie durch die Wiesen und kehrten erst dann wieder zurück, als sich der **Dunst** aufgelöst hatte.

Note

false friend → *note*　　　　　**true friend →** *mark, result*
Beispiel:
Tom war über seine schlechten **Noten** enttäuscht.
*Tom was disappointed about his poor **results**.*

Der richtige Gebrauch des englischen Begriffs:
note　　　　1. Zettel, Notiz
　　　　　　　　2. Note (musikalisch)

1. *My husband had left a **note** to let me know that he would come home later.*
   Mein Mann hatte eine **Notiz** hinterlassen, um mir mitzuteilen, dass er später nach Hause kommen würde.
2. *C was the first musical **note** that he learnt.*
   Das C war die erste **Note**, die er lernte.

Notiz

false friend → *notice*　　　　　**true friend →** *note*
Beispiel:
Bei Vorträgen mache ich mir immer **Notizen**.
*I usually take **notes** during a lecture.*

Der richtige Gebrauch des englischen Begriffs:
notice　　　　Kündigung, Kündigungsfrist

*When my brother wanted to quit his job at the factory, he had to give six weeks **notice**.*
Als mein Bruder seine Arbeit in der Fabrik aufgeben wollte, hatte er eine **Kündigungsfrist** von sechs Wochen.

Oldtimer

false friend → *oldtimer*
true friend → *vintage car*
Beispiel:
Er nimmt jedes Jahr am **Oldtimer**rennen zwischen London und Edinburgh teil.
*He takes part in a **vintage car** race between London and Edinburgh every year.*

Der richtige Gebrauch des englischen Begriffs:
oldtimer „alter Hase"; jemand der bei etwas schon lange dabei ist

*If you need help, just ask one of the **oldtimers** who have been working here for years.*
Solltest du Hilfe brauchen, frage einfach einen der **alten Hasen**, die hier seit Jahren arbeiten.

ordinär

false friend → *ordinary*   **true friend** → *vulgar*
Beispiel:
Die ältere Dame war von der **ordinären** Sprache der jungen Leute schockiert.
*The elderly lady was shocked by the **vulgar** speech of the young people.*

Der richtige Gebrauch des englischen Begriffs:
ordinary   1. normal
2. alltäglich

1. *She had always had a crush on Jose Carreras, but now that she had met him, she was disappointed by his ordinary appearance.*
   Sie hatte immer für Jose Carreras geschwärmt, aber nachdem sie ihn kennengelernt hatte, war sie von seinem **normalen** Aussehen enttäuscht.
2. *As manageress of an advertising agency, a good meal in an expensive restaurant is an **ordinary** happening for her.*
   Als Leiterin einer Werbeagentur ist ein gutes Abendessen in einem teuren Restaurant ein **alltägliches** Ereignis für sie.

Pest

false friend → *pest*
true friend → *plague*

Beispiel:
Im Mittelalter starben viele Menschen an der **Pest**.
*In the Middle Ages, many people died of **plague**.*

Der richtige Gebrauch des englischen Begriffs:
pest 1. Ekel, lästiger Mensch
2. Schädling

1. *"I like most of my colleagues, but Diana is a real **pest**", Karen complained.*
   „Ich mag die meisten meiner Kollegen, aber Diana ist ein ganz schönes **Ekel**", klagte Karen.
2. *The **pests** in the garden are destroying the plants.*
   Die **Schädlinge** im Garten zerstören die Pflanzen.

Rate

false friend →, *rate*
true friend → 1. *installment*
2. *hire purchase*

Beispiele:
1. Wir haben von den zwölf Monats**raten** schon sechs abbezahlt.
   *We have already paid six of the twelve monthly **installments**.*
2. „Ich würde das Auto gerne auf **Raten** kaufen", sagte die Kundin.
   *"I'd like to buy the car on **hire purchase**", said the customer.*

Der richtige Gebrauch des englischen Begriffs:
rate 1. Quote
2. Tempo
3. Zinssatz
4. Gemeindesteuern

1. *The **rate** of success at this school is very high.*
   Die Erfolgs**quote** in dieser Schule ist sehr hoch.
2. *The world changes at a very fast **rate** these days.*
   Die Welt ändert sich heutzutage in einem sehr schnellen **Tempo**.

3. *She received only a very low **rate** of interest on her savings.*
   Sie bekam nur einen sehr niedrigen **Zinssatz** auf ihre Ersparnisse.
4. *Because the residents were so angry when the council decided to raise the **rates** again, they organised a protest.*
   Die Bürger waren so verärgert, als der Stadtrat sich entschloss, die **Gemeindesteuern** noch einmal zu erhöhen, dass sie dagegen einen Protest organisierten.

Rente

false friend → *rent*   **true friend →** *pension*

Beispiel:
Heutzutage kann der Durchschnittsbürger normalerweise ganz gut von seiner Alters**rente** leben.
*Nowadays the average person can normally live quite well on his old-age **pension**.*

Der richtige Gebrauch des englischen Begriffs:
rent   Miete, Mietzins

*Last year, our **rent** has been increased once again by 50 pounds.*
Unsere **Miete** wurde im letzten Jahr nochmals um 50 Pfund erhöht.

See

false friend → *sea*   **true friend →** *lake*

Beispiel:
Der **See** in der Nähe meines Heimatortes ist von mehreren beliebten Campingplätzen umgeben.
*The **lake** near my hometown is surrounded by several popular camp sites.*

Der richtige Gebrauch des englischen Begriffs:
sea   Meer

*He doesn't allow his children to go swimming when the **sea** is as rough as today.*
Er erlaubt seinen Kindern nicht, schwimmen zu gehen, wenn das **Meer** so unruhig ist wie heute.

Smoking

false friend → *smoking*
true friend → *dinner jacket, tuxedo (US)*
Beispiel:
Paulas Mann trug gewöhnlich eine alte Jeans und ein T-Shirt und sie verliebte sich erneut in ihn, als er für die Hochzeit ihrer Schwester einen **Smoking** anzog.
*Paula's husband usually wore old jeans and a t-shirt, and she fell in love with him again when he wore a **dinner jacket** to her sister's wedding.*

Der richtige Gebrauch des englischen Begriffs:
smoking Rauchen

*She gave up **smoking** when she was pregnant with her first child.*
Sie gewöhnte sich das **Rauchen** ab, als sie mit ihrem ersten Kind schwanger war.

sympathisch

false friend → *sympathetic* **true friend →** *nice, likable*
Beispiel:
Die meisten Leute mochten Tom Ripley nicht, aber ich fand ihn sehr **sympathisch**.
*Most people didn't like Tom Ripley, but I found him very **nice**.*

Der richtige Gebrauch des englischen Begriffs:
sympathetic mitfühlend

*All his friends were very **sympathetic** when his girlfriend left him.*
Alle seine Freunde waren sehr **mitfühlend**, als seine Freundin ihn verließ.

Tablett

false friend → *tablet*   **true friend →** *tray*
Beispiel:
Nach einem anstrengenden Arbeitstag isst sie ihr Abendbrot am liebsten auf einem **Tablett** im Wohnzimmer vor dem Fernseher.
*After a hard day at work, she prefers eating her evening meal on a **tray** in the sitting room in front of the television.*

Der richtige Gebrauch des englischen Begriffs:
tablet   Tablette

*Do I get these **tablets** for free or do I have to pay for them?*
Bekomme ich diese **Tabletten** umsonst oder muss ich etwas dafür zahlen?

Unternehmer

false friend → *undertaker*   **true friend →** *entrepreneur*

Beispiel:
Letztes Wochenende schlossen sich mehrere **Unternehmer** zu einer Holding-Gruppe zusammen.
*Last weekend, several **entrepreneurs** joined together and created a holding company.*

Der richtige Gebrauch des englischen Begriffs:
undertaker   Leichenbestatter

*The **undertaker** came on the very same day to take the body to the funeral parlour.*
Der **Leichenbestatter** kam noch am selben Tag, um den Toten ins Bestattungsinstitut zu bringen.

virtuos

false friend → *virtuous*   **true friend →** *virtuose, virtuosic*

Beispiel:
Die Aufführung von Beethovens Klaviersonaten war **virtuos** und hinreißend.
*The performance of Beethoven's piano sonatas was **virtuosic** and thrilling.*

Der richtige Gebrauch des englischen Begriffs:
virtuous   tugendhaft

*The knights and ladies in the old sagas were nearly always beautiful and **virtuous**.*
Die Ritter und Damen in den alten Sagen waren fast immer schön und **tugendhaft**.

Wunder

false friend → *wonder* **true friend** → *1. miracle*
  2. surprise

Beispiele:
1. „Es ist ein **Wunder** für mich, wie du die Prüfung schaffen konntest", sagte Chris zu seinem Bruder.
   *"It is a **miracle** to me how you managed to pass your exam" Chris said to his brother.*
2. Es war kein **Wunder**, dass er den Brief nicht finden konnte: Seine Frau hatte ihn weggeworfen.
   *It was no **surprise** that he couldn't find the letter: his wife had thrown it away.*

Der richtige Gebrauch des englischen Begriffs:
wonder sich fragen

*I **wonder** why he didn't arrive here on time.*
Ich **frage mich**, warum er nicht pünktlich kam.

Ziel

false friend → *zeal* **true friend** → *1. goal*
  2. destination

Beispiele:
1. Ihr **Ziel** im Leben war es, viel Geld zu verdienen.
   *Her **goal** in life was to earn a lot of money.*
2. Er hatte Freudentränen in den Augen, als sich sein Traum erfüllte und der Zug sein **Ziel** erreichte.
   *There were tears of joy in his eyes as his dream came true and the train reached its **destination**.*

Der richtige Gebrauch des englischen Begriffs:
zeal Eifer

*She started her new job with great **zeal**.*
Sie ging ihre neue Stelle mit großem **Eifer** an.